The Knights Templar
at War
1120–1312

The Knights Templar at War

1120–1312

PAUL HILL

Pen & Sword
MILITARY

First published in Great Britain in 2018
reprinted in 2018 and reissued in 2023 in this format by
Pen & Sword MILITARY
An imprint of Pen & Sword Books Ltd
Yorkshire – Philadelphia

A CIP catalogue record for this book is available from the British Library

Typeset in Times New Roman by Chic Graphics
Printed and bound by CPI Group (UK) Ltd, Croydon, CR0 4YY

Pen & Sword Books Limited incorporates the imprints of Atlas, Archaeology,
Aviation, Discovery, Family History, Fiction, History, Maritime, Military, Military
Classics, Politics, Select, Transport, True Crime, Air World, Frontline Publishing, Leo
Cooper, Remember When, Seaforth Publishing, The Praetorian Press, Wharncliffe
Local History, Wharncliffe Transport, Wharncliffe True Crime and White Owl.

For a complete list of Pen & Sword titles please contact
PEN & SWORD BOOKS LIMITED
47 Church Street, Barnsley, South Yorkshire, S70 2AS, England
E-mail: enquiries@pen-and-sword.co.uk • Website: www.pen-and-sword.co.uk
Or
PEN AND SWORD BOOKS
1950 Lawrence Rd, Havertown, PA 19083, USA
E-mail: Uspen-and-sword@casematepublishers.com
Website: www.penandswordbooks.com

Contents

List of Photographs, Illustrations, Maps and Tables

Illustrations

Maps

List of Grand Masters
of the Temple

Hugh of Payns, c.1119–c.1136
Robert of Craon, c.1136–49
Everard des Barres, 1149–52
Bernard of Tremelay, 1153
Andrew of Montbard, 1154–6
Bertrand of Blancfort, 1156–69
Philip of Nablus, 1169–71
Odo of Saint-Amand, c.1171–9
Arnold of Torroja, 1181–4
Gerard of Ridefort, 1185–9
Robert of Sablé, 1191–2/3
Gilbert Erail, 1194–1200
Philip of Plessis, 1201–9
William of Chartres, 1210–c.1219
Peter of Montaigu, c.1219–c.1231
Armand of Périgord, c.1231–c.1244/6
William of Sonnac, c.1247–50
Reginald of Vichiers, 1250–6
Thomas Bérard, 1256–73
William of Beaujeu, 1273–91
Theobald Gaudin, 1291–2/3
James of Molay, c.1293–1314

List of Military Campaigns and Milestones

1120–9	Pilgrim Protection and escort duties. Probable presence in the King of Jerusalem's armies
1128	Establishment at Soure castle in Portugal
1129	The Damascus Campaigns
1130	Grant of Granyena castle to Templars by Raymond Berenguer III, Count of Barcelona
1136–7	Establishment of fortifications in the Amanus Mountains
1137	Action around Montferrand and the Nosairi foothills
	Templars and Hospitallers form part of Raymond of Poitiers' army during Byzantine Siege of Antioch
1139	Defeat of Frankish force at Hebron
1143	Six major castles in north-east Spain given to Templars by Raymond Berenguer IV
1147–8	The Second Crusade
	Templar reorganisation of French forces after Mount Cadmus disaster
	Failure at Damascus
1147	Siege of Santarém, Portugal
1148	Christian attack on Tortosa, Iberia
1149	Campaign around Antioch in response to Frankish defeat at Battle of Inab
1149–50	Acquisition of Gaza fortification
1153	The Siege of Ascalon
1153	Granting of Miravet castle to Templars, Tarragona
1154	Capture and ransom by Templars of Nasr al-Din
1157	Capture of Bertrand of Blancfort and Odo of Saint-Amand in wake of siege of Banyas
	Templars abandon Calatrava in Spain
1158	Possible Templar contingent at Baldwin III's victory at Butaiha in 1158
1160	Founding of Tomar, Portugal
1163	Nur ed-Din's forces defeated by Gilbert de Lacy's Templars escorting noble pilgrims
1164	Battle of Artah, Siege of Banyas

1154–68	Egyptian Campaigns
1170	Action at Daron against Egyptian army
1171	Templars obtain Almourol castle on the Tagus, Portugal
1173	Templar attack on Assassin envoy
1177	Campaigns in Antioch and at Hama and Harim
	Victory over Saladin at the Battle of Montgisard
1179	Battle of Marj Ayyun and the Siege of Chastellet (Jacob's Ford)
1187	Battles of the Springs of Cresson and the Horns of Hattin. Saladin triumphant
	Tyre narrowly survives with naval Templar help and new crusader arrivals
	Fall of Acre, Sidon, Beirut and Jerusalem
1188	Fall of Baghras and Darbsak castles in the Amanus March
	Defence of Tortosa
1189–92	The Third Crusade and the Battles of Acre and Arsuf
	Establishment of Acre as new Christian capital including Templar Headquarters
	Purchase of Cyprus from King Richard I by the Templars
1190	Almohad invasion of Iberia. Defence of Tomar
1201–2	Large-scale Muslim raids around County of Tripoli
1210	Siege of Al-Damus (Ademuz), Spain
1211	Armenian ambush of Templars in northern marches and reprisal attacks
1212	The Battle of Las Navas de Tolosa, Spain
1216	Baghras regained
1217	Battle of Alcácer do Sal, Portugal
1217–21	The Fifth Crusade
	The building of 'Atlit (Château Pèlerin)
	Siege of Damietta
	Flooding of the Nile
1223	Templars acquire Montémor-o-Velho and Alenquer, Portugal
1229	Quarrels and stand-offs with Frederick II in Outremer and Italy
1229–30	Conquest of the Balearic Islands
1230	Combined campaign with Hospitallers to Hama
1231	Combined campaign with Hospitallers on Jabala
1233	Combined campaign of reduction with Hospitallers and secular forces around Hama
1237	Templars defeated by Muslim foraging force between 'Atlit (Château Pèlerin) and Acre losing over 100 knights
	Templars of Baghras raid Turcomen tribesman east of Antioch. Subsequently defeated trying to retake Darbsak
1238	Conquest of Valencia, Spain

1239–41	Theobald, King of Navarre and Count of Champagne's Crusade. Richard of Cornwall's crusade Defeat around Gaza
1241–4	Sporadic fighting amongst Templars and Hospitallers
1241	Central Europe – Battle of Liegnitz Central Europe – Battle of Mohi
1242	Templar raid on Hebron (spring) Templar sacking of Nablus (autumn) Probable actions around Gaza
1244	Khwarismian Turks overrun Jerusalem Battle of La Forbie
1248–54	The Seventh Crusade – Siege of Damietta and actions in the Nile Delta Battle of Mansourah (1250)
1256–8	The Wars of Saint Sabas. Minor actions in Acre
1261	Stephen of Saissy, Templar Marshal leads failed expedition against Turcomen tribesmen near to Sea of Galilee
1264	Combined raid with Hospitallers to capture Lizon. Raids around Ascalon
1265	Caesarea, Arsuf and Haifa fall
1266	Fall of Safad
1267	Baibars fails to take Acre
1268	Antioch and Baghras fall. Jaffa and Castle Beaufort also lost
1269	Abortive crusade of James I of Aragon
1271	Chastel Blanc falls
1277–82	Civil war in Tripoli. Templars ally with Guy of Embriaco, Lord of Jubail
1289	Fall of Tripoli
1291	Siege of Acre and fall of Outremer states
1299	Battle of Homs
1291–1302	Templar naval raids
1302	Templar last stand on the island of Arwad (Ru'ad)
1307	Templars in France arrested on orders of King Philip IV
1311–12	Council of Vienne. Pope Clement abolishes Templars – Hospitallers receive their assets
1319	Order of Montessa in Valencia and Order of Christ established in Portugal – inherit Templar property

Introduction

The Knights Templar have attracted a vast amount of interest over the centuries and many books have been written on this subject. Some of this material supports remarkable notions of the Templars' continuing clandestine existence and of the religious and esoteric secrets the Templars may have kept. The order, which officially 'existed' for two action-packed centuries is still to be found in the popular culture of the Western world today. A Templar knight may appear on a computer screen in anyone's living room, if a certain game is in play. In books, television and on the silver screen the Templars still wage their wars in the Holy Land, or wield a dark power over those less illuminated.

This book will examine something which has not immediately attracted attention in the past. The mythology surrounding the order has grown so strong that seldom has their *raison d'être* been examined. The Templars were two things: a religious order and a military organisation. Originating in around 1119 out of a need to protect Christian pilgrims in the East, some two decades after the end of the First Crusade, they fought their wars as committed Christian warriors. As such, they came to the Holy Land and to the Iberian Peninsula and Eastern Europe imbued with the tactics and strategies known to many warlike cultures of the West. But the specific nature of their task and their subsequent increasing involvement in the wide-scale defence of the Holy Land meant that the order approached things differently than secular forces.

We will find evidence of spectacular victories and heavy defeats, of heroic self-sacrifice and seemingly irresponsible recklessness. The military endeavours of the order are not to be judged by these individual encounters alone, however. The organisational response to the requirements of fighting on the frontiers of Christendom included methods of recruitment, logistics and finance, raiding, training, castle building, battlefield tactics and an inevitable involvement in Grand Strategy which was not always to the liking of others. Sometimes things did not go according to plan and we will look at the reasons why.

At the Templars' peak it is probable that there were up to 20,000 members of the order with only about a tenth of these being brother knights, the rest providing invaluable supporting roles including those in the commanderies (a French term) or preceptories (a Latin term) of the West. These Templar houses were the geographical building blocks of the order with each commander acting like a lord of the manor who collected the rents and sent money on to the regional headquarters. The colossal logistical enterprise of the order is therefore of great importance. Despite their numbers many people will have viewed the Templars as distant or secretive. But their approach to managing their affairs was more cautious than overly secretive.

However, the conspiracy theories abounded. The Templars' lengthy experience of the myriad of cultures in the Middle East led to a business-like diplomacy and pragmatism in their dealings with the Muslims which may have seemed to some people in the West as extraordinary and even suspicious.

The crusader states became increasingly dependent on immediately available military muscle to survive. The military orders in the form of the Templars and the Hospitallers (and later, the Teutonic Knights) provided a growing military presence in the landscape. The orders were granted important strategic castles as early as the 1130s. However, the geographical and logistical difficulties presented by having to defend a narrow strip of coastal territory would ultimately prove too difficult for the leaders of the crusader states and in 1291 the last Christian warriors were defeated and expelled from the city of Acre which they had called their capital since the fall of Jerusalem in 1187. For the Hospitallers, whose role had arisen from a core function of caring for sick pilgrims, there was much to fall back on. They survived the loss of Acre. For the Templars, whose role had been inextricably linked to the political and military fate of the Holy Land, the loss of Acre – although not immediately apparent – would spell the beginning of the end.

In 1312 Pope Clement V (1305–14) disbanded the Templars. Most of their possessions were given to the Knights Hospitaller. This came after a sustained onslaught against the Templars from King Philip IV of France (1285–1314), allegedly deeply indebted to the order on account of his costly wars with the Kingdom of England. On Friday, 13 October 1307, a date imbued with superstition, the king ordered wide-scale and simultaneous arrests across his kingdom and concocted a number of allegations against the Templars which led to a notorious trial. The accusations were remarkable. The men who had fought for Christ and would lay down their lives for the cause were now accused of denying Christ, of spitting on the cross, of undertaking bizarre initiation practices such as indecent kissing, of homosexuality and of worshiping idols, one of which was said to have been a mysterious entity known as Baphomet which to some was a corrupted form of the word 'Mohamed'. As King Philip piled the pressure onto the Pope, confessions were extracted, many under torture. James of Molay, the last Grand Master of the Templars (c.1293–1314), and Geoffrey of Charney, the Templar Preceptor of Normandy, having retracted their confessions, were nevertheless burned in Paris on 18 March 1314. It was an abrupt end to a staggering rise to power and importance of what had begun as an austere and poor brotherhood. The order, whose brothers had become advisors to kings in both East and West, who had begun what was to become the profession of modern banking, who had charged across the battlefields of Palestine, was gone in an instant. This is notwithstanding the recent discovery (in 2001) of the Chinon parchment uncovered in the Vatican archives showing that Pope Clement had in fact had absolved the Templars of all heresies in 1308.

The Templars have been associated with esoteric knowledge. Here, they are linked to the Rosicrucians, the Priory of Sion, Rex Deus, the Cathars, the Hermetics, the Gnostics, the Essenes and to the lost teachings of Jesus. All of this theorising occupies the shadowy world between mystery and real history which seems to thrive upon the fact that it is never fully resolved. Whatever the mystical legacy of the Templars, it is with their approach to warfare that we are chiefly concerned. Understanding the strength of the faith which drove men to fight in religious wars goes a long way to explaining the Templars' commitment. This was a time of intense spiritual devotion. But the last Grand Master James of Molay never really lost sight of the military role of his order. Towards the end of his life, he was planning another crusade to the East, even after the loss of Acre.

This volume is not a history of the crusades. There is a vast array of material available for anyone wishing to understand the wider history of the crusading movement. However, the story of the crusades collides with that of the Templars so often that it is necessary to give some background or explanation. Therefore, certain characters will enter the stage and come and go as the story of the Templars is told.

Crusading fervour had its roots in eleventh-century Europe. The campaigns of the Norman Robert Guiscard, Duke of Apulia and his brother Roger against the Muslims of Sicily in the 1060s had received papal backing in what must have seemed to contemporary observers as a 'crusade' as later writers would come to understand the term. However, when Pope Urban II (1088–99) made a speech at the Council of Clermont in November 1095 he called for Western Christendom to take arms and assist the Christian brothers in the Holy Land who were suffering under Muslim overlordship. Urban's speech was made against a backdrop of perceived Muslim persecution of the Christians in the East and of the Byzantine Emperor's loss of Asia Minor to the ferocious and numerous Seljuk Turks after the disastrous Battle of Manzikert in 1071. But when the Western crusaders set out for the East nobody could have known how electrifying the results would be. In July 1099, the streets of Jerusalem ran red with blood. The crusaders' carnage and slaughter of the inhabitants of the city set two great faiths against each other. But it also marked the beginning of something which was cherished in the West: the new Kingdom of Jerusalem and its accompanying crusader states, called by the French 'Outremer', or 'Overseas', states. Here, in these lands beyond the sea, the Knights Templar first made their entrance onto the stage of the greatest drama in medieval history.

Map 1 – The Outremer states on the eve of the fall of Edessa, 1144.

Part 1

Origins

Chapter 1

The Danger to Pilgrims

One of the greatest problems for the Franks during the early years of the Kingdom of Jerusalem was one of manpower. In fact, this was true for all the Frankish states in Outremer. Persuading fighting men to travel to the East was a hard enough task but asking them to remain there was more so. The priest Fulcher of Chartres, who was a first generation settler, recorded that only 300 knights and 300 foot soldiers remained in the Jerusalem area in 1100. Although this number would have been augmented by each knight's entourage, it was still precious little for the defence of the crusader states. Outremer's territories were therefore scattered and sparsely populated by Frankish folk. This left their settlements and more importantly the roads along the popular pilgrim routes vulnerable to attack. The flow of pilgrims was an important part of the young kingdom's economic life. These routes were numerous and were particularly concentrated in an area of land stretching from the Sea of Galilee in the north through Samaria and Judaea to Hebron in the south (see Map 2).

The road between Ramla and Jerusalem was particularly treacherous with bandits hiding in caves ready to pounce on pilgrims coming up from Jaffa. Turks, Egyptians, roving Bedouin and even Ethiopians posed a threat to the Christian pilgrim, with the problem of security extending into the open country. Just a few years into the kingdom's existence an Anglo-Saxon traveller named Saewulf visited Jerusalem in 1102–3. He not only left us one of the earliest surviving accounts of a pilgrimage in the newly founded kingdom, but also compiled a guidebook to the most important sites, not forgetting to remind his readers of the dreadful dangers faced by travellers. He travelled from Joppa to Jerusalem, a two-day journey along mountainous and rocky roads. The Saracens, he said – in this case Bedouins – lay hidden in the hollow places of the mountains and in caves ready to lay traps for the Christians, who carried much personal portable wealth. They waited through both day and night seeking to attack parties who were few in number or had become weak and weary. The resulting effects of these attacks were all too apparent:

> Oh, what a number of human bodies, both in the road and by the side of it, lie all torn by wild beasts! . . . On that road not only the poor and the weak, but even the rich and the strong, are in danger. Many are cut off by the Saracens, but more by heat and thirst; many through scarcity of drink, but many more perish through drinking too much.

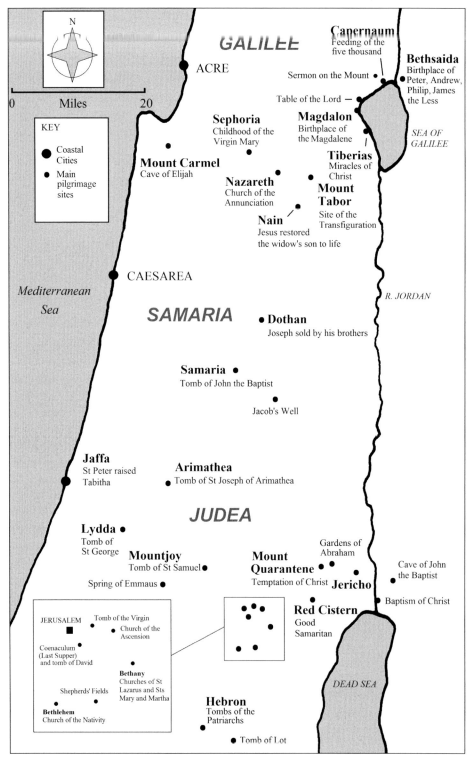

Map 2 – The main pilgrim sites during the era of the Crusades (after Barber)

Anyone who survived these attacks did not dare to split from their own party, not even to bury their dead. The road from Jerusalem to Jericho, taken by those wanting to visit the Jordan, was little different. A Russian abbot, Daniel of Kiev, visited the Holy Land between 1106 and 1107. He told his readers that here too the road was very troublesome and lacked water. Brigandage was rife in those high rocky mountains and 'fearful gorges'. Daniel was widely travelled within the Holy Land. He told of the Muslims of Ascalon – in this case under the control of Fatimid Egyptians – killing travellers at the springs near Lydda not far from Jaffa. He further warned of the dangers for pilgrims travelling between Hebron in the south and Jerusalem. Between these two places were rocky mountains and deep forests from which the Muslims launched attacks.

When Abbot Daniel journeyed north to Galilee he passed near the town of Baisan, west of the Jordan. Seven rivers flowed from this town and it was 'very difficult of access'. But the greatest danger came to anyone attempting to cross the fords he said, 'for here live fierce pagan Saracens who attack travellers at the fords on these rivers'. Daniel was no less concerned about the many lions which inhabited the area too, mentioning them twice in the same passage. But to all of the Christian pilgrims the dangers of visiting the holy sites were largely of human origin.

William, Archbishop of Tyre (d. c.1186), whose great work *A History of Deeds Done Beyond the Sea* provides so much evidence for the twelfth-century events in the Holy Land, gives us a telling picture of the precarious world outside the main Frankish cities:

> The cities which had come under our power were but few, and these were so situated in the midst of the enemy that the Christians could not pass from one to another, when necessity required, without great danger. The entire country surrounding their possessions was inhabited by infidel Saracens, who were most cruel enemies of our people. These were all the more dangerous because they were close at hand, for no pest can more effectively do harm than an enemy at one's very doors.
>
> Any Christian who walked along the highway without taking due precaution was liable to be killed by the Saracens, or seized and handed over as a slave to the enemy.

William goes on to tell us that the situation was not much better for those Franks inside the cities. Even here, there were too few defenders to prevent thieves and robbers climbing the walls and attacking the new settlers in their homes.

Then, at Easter 1119 occurred perhaps the most shocking of all the atrocities, an act which sent reverberations around Europe. A party of several hundred unarmed pilgrims were cut to pieces on their way from Jerusalem to the Jordan by a Muslim force from Ascalon, the sixty or so survivors being sold into slavery. They had been on a journey to the traditional baptism site of Jesus, along a road fraught with danger. King Baldwin II of Jerusalem (1118–31), when he heard of the slaughter, had sent out some armed knights, but their enemy had long departed. The pilgrims' fate was recorded by Albert of Aachen, who says they had set out from the Holy Sepulchre 'in joy and with a cheerful heart' only to meet a tragic end. Although he never visited the Holy Land himself, he received his information from returning crusaders and his subsequent dissemination of the news captured the mood in both Outremer and in the West.

The atmosphere within the leadership of the crusader states at this time can only be imagined. Undermanned and always at peril in the open landscape, it must have been clearer than ever at Easter 1119 that something had to be done not only to protect the Christians of the Kingdom of Jerusalem, but to ensure the Frankish hold on the Outremer states was robust. Just a few months after the Easter massacre, in June of the same year the urgency was compounded by the annihilation at Sarmada of Roger of Salerno's Antiochene army at the battle known as Ager Sanguinis (The Field of Blood). Ilghazi of Mardin, the Artuqid ruler of Aleppo, had out-generalled Roger (the regent of the crusader principality of Antioch) in a landscape he knew more about than Roger. Roger's camp was surrounded at night and he was out-flanked on the battlefield the next day amidst a storm of dust and confusion. The Patriarch of Antioch had advised Roger to call for the help of Baldwin II and Pons (the Count of Tripoli) in the lead-up to the battle, but Roger had decided – perhaps with good reason – that he did not have the time. Although Ilghazi was defeated by Baldwin II at the Battle of Hab in August that year, the totality of the defeat at Ager Sanguinis had shown the vulnerability of the undermanned Franks.

Chapter 2

The Poor Knights of Christ

The concept of protecting pilgrims was not entirely new. From the late tenth century in the West, pilgrims and other travellers were included in lists of groups who should not be attacked according to the Church. Moreover, in 1059 Pope Nicholas II (1059–61) had taken up the idea of protecting travellers' persons and properties as an obligation of the papacy. Bands of fighting Christian knights were not a new concept, either. Confraternities of such men were known in the West. Wazo, the Bishop of Liège in the 1040s, had obtained oaths from a small group of warriors who pledged their support to him. Also, at the monastery of Grande-Sauve near Bordeaux ten noblemen had their swords consecrated in the monastery church, their role being to defend the monks and the property of the church as well as to protect the pilgrims who visited. It might be argued that the first Templars who were attached to the Holy Sepulchre were similar in nature. It may have been a confraternity which Hugh, Count of Champagne had joined in 1114 when Bishop Ivo of Chartres wrote to him chastising him for abandoning his wife and giving himself to the militiae Christi, or Knighthood of Christ, in order to partake of 'that gospel knighthood' (*evangelicam militiam*). Some have sought to see this event as an early foundation date for the Templars but Ivo does not mention them by name. It is perhaps more likely that the terminology of Ivo's letter reflects the Count's taking of crusader vows and crusader zeal in general, although in spirit at least, the move might reflect a growing religious feeling amongst many Frankish nobles of a desire to fight for the continuing defence of the holy places.

It is generally accepted that the Templars came into being as a reaction to the attacks against pilgrims on the roads to the holy places. The physical protection of such pilgrims might be seen as a complement to the care already afforded to them by the Hospitallers, who had been in a form of existence since 1080. The Hospitallers had been attached to the monastery of Santa Maria Latina in Jerusalem. The medical care and shelter they provided for pilgrims had already gained them royal favour and in 1113 they received papal recognition. In fact, what little is known of the early Templars would suggest a close relationship between the two orders in Jerusalem, with some Templars witnessing charters mainly concerning the Hospital. If the Templars had relied on this early association with the Hospital for their survival it would also be the case that as the Templars flourished, their militarism would in turn influence the Knights of the Hospital. The Frankish leadership in Outremer was keenly aware of the need for the pilgrims to be both accompanied and protected on their journeys but they clearly lacked the human resources to do it.

The sources which survive concerning the foundation of the Templars are not exactly contemporary with this early period. Nor do they say the same thing, with some seeking to emphasise one aspect of the foundation story over another. William of Tyre, Michael the Syrian, the Jacobite Patriarch of Antioch (d. 1199) and Walter Map, the Archdeacon of Oxford, each contributed to the foundation story, as did a history of the Kingdom of Jerusalem in Old French usually attributed to Ernoul, a squire of Balian II of Ibelin (d. c. 1194). So too, more obliquely, does Simon the monk from the abbey of Saint-Bertin (who wrote between 1135 and 1137) and Orderic Vitalis, the Anglo-Norman monk of Saint-Évroul who wrote in the 1120s or 1130s.

William of Tyre presents an account which is perhaps the most widely quoted source for the foundation of the Templars, although his chronology is sometimes questioned. He criticised the Templars for taking advantage of the privileges they had subsequently been given and he seems to take a negative view of the order as it was at the time he wrote. In *A History of Deeds Done Beyond the Sea*, under an entry for the year 1118, William recounts the circumstances of the foundation of the Order of the Temple. It was the very same year that both the new King of Jerusalem Baldwin II was consecrated and a new Patriarch of Jerusalem Warmund of Picquigny was appointed after the death of Arnulf of Chocques. Here is what he says:

> In this same year, certain pious and God-fearing nobles of knightly rank, devoted to the Lord, professed the wish to live perpetually in poverty, chastity and obedience. In the hands of the patriarch they vowed themselves to the service of God as regular canons. Foremost and most distinguished among these men were Hugh de Payens [Hugh of Payns] and Godfrey de St. Omer. Since they had neither a church nor a fixed place of abode, the king granted them a temporary dwelling place in his own palace, on the north side by the Temple of the Lord [the name the Franks gave to the Dome of the Rock, which is to the north of al-Aqsa mosque]. Under certain definite conditions, the canons of the Temple of the Lord also gave them a square belonging to the canons near the same palace where the new order might exercise the duties of its religion.
>
> The king and his nobles, as well as the Patriarch and the prelates of the churches, also provided from their own holdings certain benefices, the income of which was to provide these knights with food and clothing. Some of these gifts were for a limited time. Others in perpetuity. The main duty of this order – that which was enjoined upon them by the Patriarch and the other bishops for the remission of sins was 'that as far as their strength permitted, they should keep the roads and highways safe from the menace of robbers and highwaymen, with especial regard for the protection of pilgrims'.

Baldwin II had given these knights residence in his own palace. This palace was at al-Aqsa mosque which the crusaders believed was on the site of the ancient and revered Solomon's Temple. Moreover, the canons of the Temple of the Lord had given the knights an area around the palace. William of Tyre goes on to say that for the first nine years they wore secular garb and were only nine in number. Their given task – to protect pilgrims – may seem to be a particular challenge in respect of their apparently small numbers. This seeming lack of military resources has led people to speculate that the first Templars were in fact more interested in something other than merely protecting pilgrims. Templar excavations beneath the southern end of the Haram al-Sharif or Temple Mount in Jerusalem are postulated by many. Secretive searches for the Ark of the Covenant, or the Holy Grail are sometimes purported to be the goals of Hugh of Payns and his companions. The paucity of historical evidence exposes this period of time to extravagant theories designed to fill the gaps. It is certainly the case that the choice of the site as the first home of the order was no accident. They would take their very name from it. As to what the true motives were for these first few, we cannot really say. It may also be important that nine knights is not the sum total of the force in question. The knights had their entourages, other attendants and possibly were assisted when the time came by a number of stipendary turcopoles, native auxiliary troops who were nominally Christian. The numbers Hugh of Payns could bring to answer the Patriarch's call will almost certainly have been more than nine, but the figure remained stubbornly attached to Templar mythology.

Hugh of Payns, First Templar Grand Master (c.1119–c.1136)
About 8 miles north of Troyes in France lies the village of Payens, or Payns, Hugh's seat from at least 1113 or before. Hugh was closely associated with his overlord, Hugh the Count of Champagne whose charters he witnessed. The two men may have gone on crusade together in 1104 and returned again to the East in 1114. However, Hugh of Payns did not assume his role as Master of the Temple until around 1125, at about the same time as the Count of Champagne joined the order himself in a move which placed the Count under the leadership of his own vassal. The first Grand Master's role in the early years between c.1119 and c.1125 remains unclear. He is recorded as 'Master of the Temple' in 1125 at Acre in a royal confirmation of a grant of privileges to the Venetians at Tyre. Hugh tirelessly travelled across Europe seeking support for his fledgling brotherhood. He came to England in 1128 to the court of Henry I (1100–35). This resulted in the Templars receiving much-needed wealth. Hugh was able to argue his case for his order's acceptance at the Council of Troyes in January 1129 from a position of growing strength.

Michael the Syrian provides some further information which is thought to be less reliable than William of Tyre, but which raises the numbers of those early Templars by at least a factor of three. Michael, although ambiguous in his account of the founding of the order, says it was King Baldwin II who persuaded Hugh and thirty of his men to serve as guardians against robbers. Hugh had come to the East and served in the king's army for three years, intending to become a monk afterwards. The brothers lived without spouses, possessions or bathing. Those who died and were found to have kept back possessions from the order were denied burial. Michael the Syrian's Templars were kind to Christians, charitable to pilgrims, buried any who died and gave a tenth of the order's goods to the poor. Moreover, as the order grew, it became more involved in fighting battles against the Turks and building castles, becoming rich whilst individual brothers remained poor.

Walter Map (who died around 1210) recounts a tale of a knight from Burgundy named Paganus. This knight, perhaps Hugh of Payns, heard of pilgrims being attacked at a horse pool near Jerusalem and decided to protect them. He could not do it alone so he was given lodgings by the canons of the Temple of the Lord and recruited from there amongst the pilgrim knights who visited the city. In an interesting observation as to an early modus operandi for the fledgling Templars Map says 'he frequently sprang to their [the pilgrims'] aid from well-chosen hiding places and slew many of the enemy'. The knights led chaste and sober lives together. Map also states that some 'warlike pilgrims' in this early period joined the Templars 'for only a time', allowing room for an argument that in these early days numbers may have been in flux.

Ernoul's *History of the Kingdom of Jerusalem*, written in the 1190s, gives us an account which links the early Templars with the prior of the Sepulchre. After the first crusaders had taken Jerusalem, a large number of knights went to the Holy Sepulchre and were joined by more from many countries. They gave their obedience to the prior but were frustrated that their martial skills were not being put to use. They chose themselves a master and approached King Baldwin II, who received them willingly. Summoning the Patriarch, senior clerics and barons, the king made a decision to support these knights with gifts of lands, castles and villages. Pressure was thus put on the prior of the Sepulchre to release the knights from obligations to him. The freed knights took with them only a part of the emblem of the habit of the Sepulchre, this being a one-barred cross instead of the Sepulchre's two bars. Of the king's three rich manors in Jerusalem, the knights lobbied for the one 'in front of the Temple where Christ was offered, called Solomon's Temple . . . As it is called the Temple of Solomon, and they lived there, they are called Templars'. It was here the Templars provided a banquet for the king on his coronation day (Easter, 14 April 1118). They went on to construct a splendid manor next to the Temple, but this, our chronicler states, was destroyed when the Saracens conquered Jerusalem.

Simon of Saint-Bertin, writing closer to the times he was mentioning, hints in his *Deeds of the Abbots of Saint Bertin* that it was the secular nobility who urged the militarisation of the early Templars and he does not mention the Patriarch. He stresses the devout nature of the early order. Some crusaders had decided not to return home to the West, but to remain in the Holy Land after the First Crusade and

1. and 2. The Church of the Holy Sepulchre, Jerusalem. One of the key attractions for Christian pilgrims.

devote themselves to the Temple. 'On the advice of the princes of God's army' they swore themselves to 'God's Temple under this rule' says Simon. He goes on to say 'they would renounce the world, give up personal goods, free themselves to pursue chastity, and lead a communal life wearing a poor habit, only using weapons to defend the land against the attacks of the insurgent pagans when necessity demanded'.

Orderic Vitalis (1075–1141), in his *Ecclesiastical History*, mentions that Count Fulk of Anjou (d.1143) had for a short time joined the 'Knights of the Temple' during a pilgrimage to Jerusalem in 1120. He returned to the West but continued to pay the order 'thirty pounds of Anjou' to support them. Fulk would go on to play a leading role in the kingdom as king alongside Baldwin's daughter Melisende after Baldwin's death in 1131. Orderic Vitalis was praiseworthy of the knights of the Temple in that he styled them *venerandi milites*, or soldiers who should be honoured. They were pious and devoted themselves to God, although Orderic's take on the early Templars was more that they were God-fearing warriors who faced martyrdom on a regular basis, as opposed to Simon of Saint-Bertin's monks who fought when the need required it.

A charter granted to the Templars by William, Castellan of Saint-Omer, who may well have been a relative of Godfrey of Saint-Omer (Hugh's companion amongst the early Templars), reveals perhaps the most succinct summary of all the 'foundation' sources. Dated to 1137, it states 'to the knights of the Temple, whom divine providence deputed to the defence of the land of Jerusalem and the protection of pilgrims with the counsel of the Patriarch Warmund and the barons'.

On Christmas Day 1119 Hugh of Payns and his knightly companions took their vows before the Patriarch in the Church of the Holy Sepulchre. According to the prologue of their own Rule which was put together from around 1129, the Templars in these early days had gone by the name of 'The Poor Knights of Christ of the Temple which is in Jerusalem'. But these were austere and tough years which affected the early Templars greatly. Their poverty was exemplified by the brothers' borrowing of clothes and also by the fact that the Franks could not even afford to maintain their building which became run-down, according to Fulcher of Chartres. These austere beginnings are also reflected in the design of the Templars' seal which depicts two knights mounted on one horse taken by some to represent frugality and humility.

The Seal of the Templars

The Grand Master's seal was double-sided. It showed on the reverse the dome of the Church of the Holy Sepulchre and on the obverse was the symbol of two knights on one horse. Another Templar seal simply displayed the one side with the dome of the church. The earliest seal showing the two riders motif is that of Grand Master Bertrand of Blancfort (1156–69). The meaning of the device is obscure. It perhaps suggests the order's humble beginnings and humility with the early brothers only able to afford one horse between two knights, but the Templar Rule forbade the sharing of a horse for obvious practical reasons. Around the edge of the motif was written '*Sigillum Militum*', a phrase indicating a military seal. The seal went through minor variations throughout the history of the Templars with the later seal of Reginald of Vichiers (Grand Master between 1250 and 1256) bearing the legend '*Sigillum militum xpisti*', adding the name of Christ which at its beginning incorporates a chi-rho symbol. The two riders device was not used by the provincial masters of the order. Those in England, for example, preferred the use of the Agnus Dei (Lamb of God) motif, as did the Master of Provence.

Although it would be another nine years before the Templars would become a fully-fledged military order, it is possible they had begun to gain acceptance within the Kingdom of Jerusalem by 1120 after the Council of Nablus. Convened in the wake of the disaster at Ager Sanguinis and a number of other military set-backs in the East, this council consisted of prelates and secular rulers, its purpose to find a solution to the problems faced in the young kingdom. The atmosphere was one of desperation. A high mortality rate amongst the Franks in Outremer had left widows and minors in the charge of fiefs and consequently they were vulnerable. At around this time a letter was written by Warmund the Patriarch to Diego Gelmirez, the Archbishop of Compostella, pleading for help. Jerusalem was surrounded on all sides

Fig. 1. The obverse of the Templar seal from the time of Grand Master Reginald of Vichiers (1250–6)]

by Saracens from Baghdad, Ascalon, Tyre and Damascus. Moreover, there had been crop failures to exacerbate the problem. The twenty-five canons, or laws which were written up as a result of the Council of Nablus (which focused on the relations between Franks and Muslims), even began with the mention of a plague of mice and locusts which had beset the kingdom for four years. It was God's punishment for the sins of the people, or so it seemed. Clause 20, however, might seem to have opened the door for a new way of thinking: 'if a cleric takes up arms in the cause of defence, he is not to be held guilty', it said. A greater theological shift was needed however, if such violence was to switch to the offensive.

Chapter 3

The Council of Troyes, 1129

The years after the Council of Nablus had not been easy for King Baldwin. Count Joscelin I of Edessa had been captured in September 1122 and Baldwin himself had even been held captive by the Emir of Aleppo between 1123 and 1124. But Baldwin, who had been Count of Edessa until he took the crown, was nothing if not resilient. A Venetian fleet played a significant part in the crusaders' capture of Tyre in July 1124. This event typified what was to become a long association of the Italian seafaring states with the coastal cities of Outremer. Baldwin, released in August 1124, went on the offensive. A four-month siege of Aleppo ended in a withdrawal but in June 1125 the king won a fierce encounter at the Battle of A'zaz against the Seljuk atabeg of Mosul Aq-Sunquril-Bursuqi. Later, Baldwin commenced raiding around Damascus and ordered a full assembly of 'all the Knighthood' of his realm according to William of Tyre. Although Baldwin won an encounter around Ascalon his main aim was clearly Damascus, and so in January 1126 a wide-ranging call-out was ordered by the king and a huge army was assembled which marched to Tiberias. There followed another thumping encounter at Marj al-Saffar, which the crusaders won against Tughtigin, Atabeg of Damascus. Only a strong attack late on in the battle had won the day for Baldwin in what was otherwise a withering experience for his men and the ultimate prize of Damascus would remain unclaimed unless more resources could be thrown into the enterprise.

It was around this time of the Damascus thrust that the fledgling Templars had received Hugh, Count of Champagne into their ranks. Baldwin II clearly saw the value of the Templars at a time when manpower was short and military needs great. We know little about the Templars' military role in these actions around A'zaz and Marj al-Saffar, but it is clear that the king was receptive towards the order. Although there are some doubts as to its authenticity, Baldwin is thought to have sent a letter to Bernard of Clairvaux, the leading Cistercian abbot (who died in 1153 and was canonised in 1174). St Bernard was probably a relative of Hugh of Payns and an acquaintance of Hugh of Champagne. The letter outlined the Templars' desire to obtain 'apostolic confirmation' and to have a 'certain rule in life'. Two knights, Andrew and Gondemar, were sent westwards so that they could obtain approval of their order from the Pope himself, so the letter says. The period from 1126 to 1129 has a distinct air of a king seeking to entice Western military aid into the Kingdom of Jerusalem.

Baldwin II had four daughters and no male heir. It was decided, probably in 1127 that his eldest daughter Melisende would be offered in marriage to Count Fulk of Anjou. Baldwin sent to the West William of Bures, Prince of Galilee and Guy of Brisbarre, Lord of Beirut, their purpose to meet with Fulk. But also amongst this party, which probably sailed in the autumn of 1127, was Hugh of Payns who would go to the West with two goals in mind. The first was to establish a landed and financial backing for his order and the second, no less important, was to recruit for a renewed campaign against Damascus. It was during this trip that Hugh began to build the connections which would prove so valuable to the order in the future. Theobald, Count of Blois who succeeded the absent Hugh in Champagne, gave land to the Templars and also allowed his own vassals to perform similar donations, provided he lost no service in the process. William Clito (son of the crusading Norman Duke Robert Curthose), now ruling as Count of Flanders, gave the Templars the right to feudal reliefs on his lands. Similar success occurred in Poitou in terms of silver, horses and armour for Hugh and his companions. The destinies of Anjou and the Kingdom of England were to be closely linked in the near future as the marriage of Fulk's son Geoffrey of Anjou to Matilda, the heiress of King Henry I's Norman kingdom of England took place at Le Mans in 1127. Hugh of Payns was present at the wedding and it is no surprise to find him recruiting in England, and indeed in Scotland in 1128. Hugh had met with King Henry I in Normandy where he spoke of a great impending battle between the Christian and Heathen. He was given riches of gold and silver and sent on to England and Scotland where further riches were given to him 'by all good men', says the Anglo-Saxon Chronicle. But, as the Chronicle explains, Hugh did not leave with just treasure, he also left with large numbers of people the like of which had not been seen since the days of the First Crusade.

With men, money and a gradually increasing landed base from which to draw an income, Hugh and his companions travelled to Cassel in Flanders, where more gifts were received. A hugely successful tour of Western Christendom had ignited passion in warriors and generosity in kings and counts. And so, able to argue from a position of strength, Hugh headed for the Council of Troyes, arriving in January 1129.

Presided over by the Cardinal-Bishop Matthew of Albano on behalf of Pope Honorius II (1124–30), the Council of Troyes was attended by some important individuals, including the archbishops of Reims and Sens and their own bishops in addition to seven abbots including the Abbot of Citeaux, Stephen Harding. The Latin Rule of the Templars states that it was Bernard of Clairvaux 'at whose instigation the Council was convened' and he too was present. There were also secular figures there, amongst whom was Theobald of Blois who was sympathetic towards both the Templars and Hugh of Champagne. The Council's purpose was mainly to settle some of the affairs of the Bishop of Paris and regulate other matters concerning the Church. But it was here, on the Feast of Saint Hilary on 13 January 1129, that Hugh of Payns gave a speech which paved the way for the acceptance of his order.

Speaking in front of the Council and also before his own attendant brothers Godfrey of Saint-Omer, Brother Roland, Brother Geoffrey Bisot, Brother Payen of

Montdidier (who in 1130 was given responsibility for the 'French' Templar Lands north of the Loire) and Brother Archambaud of Saint-Amand, Hugh explained before the Council the practices of his militia. How they joined with the regular canons in the offices of the choir, how they dressed austerely, sat at communal meals and avoided contact with women. He told them that his knights had been allowed one horse each, later increased to three, plus a small number of servants. He told them how his men owed obedience to himself, the Master, but how the wider order came under the authority of the Patriarch of Jerusalem.

Hugh's words were picked over by those present. They went over every detail rejecting what they thought was poor practice and praising the good. If the Templars were to be accepted into the Church as a religious order there would have to be a written Rule for them to follow and as it transpired, it would be Bernard of Clairvaux's influence which was most evident in the formulation of what has come to be known as the Latin Rule, incorporated in later versions as the 'Primitive Rule' of Templars.

Chapter 4

The Latin Rule

Before the Templars' Rule was written the brothers followed the Rule of Saint Augustine, but under the reforming Cistercian influence of Bernard of Clairvaux, the Rule took on a Benedictine flavour. The concern was of course for the correct type of observances to be followed. The daily life of a Templar was to be an austere one. On military matters however, this early Rule was somewhat sparse with only the later Hierarchical Statutes (written between 1165 and 1187) outlining tactics and other campaign expectations (see pp. 147–60). However, in the prologue there was an emphasis on the giving of one's life, where such an offering to God was deemed as a welcomed sacrifice. Also, within the wording of the various clauses are hints at the order's main purpose. The opening clause of the Rule reminds the brothers how they should hear the divine office, but acknowledges that for the salvation of their souls the brothers were serving a higher king with their horses and their arms. Another section outlines the clothing of the brothers. It is here that the Knight Templar acquired his famous white habit, but not yet his equally famous red cross (see p. 30). Habits, it was written, should always be of one colour, 'that is white or black or brown'. The Knights themselves were to wear white all year around as a symbol that they had put the dark life behind them. It also represented purity and chastity.

Clothing and shoes were to be simple so that they could be put on and taken off easily. Also, the wearing of pointed shoes and laces was banned, as these are the garments of the Saracen, and are therefore considered an abomination. No white clothes or cloaks were to be assigned to servants, as had been the case with sergeants and squires before now. This had led to even permanent sergeants becoming arrogant inasmuch as their appearence was so similar to that of the knighthood itself. Such men should always wear black, and if appropriate clothing could not be found, they were to wear what was available where they lived or else wear 'donkey brown'. Unless he has received the name 'Knight of Christ' says the Rule, none are allowed to wear the white habit. The Templars' appearance was also a frequent theme. Excessive hair was forbidden and the emphasis was on short hair and trimmed beards and whiskers.

Although later versions of the Rule would greatly expand upon military matters, giving the impression of a medieval military manual (pp. 171–80), there are some basic provisions in the Latin Rule which show that practical military concerns had not entirely escaped the attention of St Bernard. We might permit ourselves to believe that for all the earnest discussion at the Council of Troyes on the formation of the religious guidelines for the new order, there was an equal amount of discussion amongst Hugh and his men as to how to provide for the basic military requirements. The emphasis here was to be on simple functionality with no unnecessary extras. For example, there is a specific requirement that shields and lances should not have any covers or scabbards. These coverings, used by contemporary warriors to keep lance heads protected were considered by the Templars to be of no real use. In fact, they were a hindrance. The emphasis here is presumably on the efficiency of use. Valuable time would be lost removing such weapons and armour from their claddings before action.

Each knight was allowed three horses and a squire but his equipment should be plain and not decorated with gold or silver, these being 'private riches'. Bridles, breastplates, spurs and stirrups were often attractively decorated possessions within the secular knighthood, so for this reason no Templar was permitted to purchase any of them. Charitable donations of older equipment decorated in this way would have to be painted over before use. For newer decorated trappings, the decision as to how to dispose of these would be the Master's alone.

The limit on horses at this stage was put down to the early Templars' poverty. The number could not be increased except at the Master's discretion. It fell to the Master to provide replacement horses lost in service by knights who had joined the order for a fixed period. Such knights were required to buy their own horses and arms which were then to be valued 'by each side'. When it was time for the temporary knight to return to his country the knight in question should, 'out of divine love', leave to the house half of the horse's price. He could if, he wished, receive the other half from the house. One imagines that the original valuation was a matter of careful negotiation.

Strict discipline and an adherence to the Master's word were clearly important from the start. The Master's word was to be heeded as if it were God's word. The theme of discipline frequently reappears in the Latin Rule and in the later French translation and additions. It was forbidden for a Templar to ask for a replacement horse or armour. He should simply explain his predicament to the Master or the person designated for the appropriate office and patiently wait for a decision to be made. In fact, the power of the Master was everywhere in evidence in the Latin Rule. He was permitted to give anyone horses and arms and if he took these from a brother knight, there was to be no complaint. The Master also had an intrusive but necessary control on any letters which the brothers wished to send or receive. His, or the local commander's permission, was required in these circumstances and if the Master wished, the letters received were to be read in his presence. This would have been a particularly important information management policy. For the same reason, lockable purses or bags were discouraged.

The majority of the clauses in the Latin Rule were however, focussed on the behaviour of the Templars and their adherence to the religious life. Also, knights should be allowed land and men and there was a further allowance for tithes. But elsewhere, the emphasis is on other matters. Not boasting about one's faults, not going hawking, caring always for the sick, not consorting with the excommunicated, praying in silence, equal distribution of food and avoiding the kisses of women all feature in separate clauses. And so the Rule set the boundaries for the behaviour of the Templars. It would soon be translated into French to reach a wider audience within the order. Over time, more operational detail and guidance would feature as the Templars would be able to provide examples from their campaigns of good and bad practice and the punishments to be expected for wrongdoing.

Chapter 5

In Praise of the New Knighthood

A new sort of knighthood, I say, unknown to the world, is fighting indefatigably a double fight against flesh and blood as well as against the immaterial forces of evil in the skies . . .

. . . when both sorts of men [physical and spiritual fighters] gird their swords of power and don their belts of nobility, who will not consider this to be most worthy of total admiration inasmuch as it is clearly unusual? Truly the knight is without fear and totally without worries when he has clothed his body with the breastplate of iron and his mind with the breastplate of faith. Indeed, endowed with both sorts of arms he fears neither demon nor man. Nor does he fear death, for he wishes to die. Why should he fear, whether living or dying, since for him life is Christ and death is reward?

St Bernard of Clairvaux, *In Praise of the New Knighthood.*
Sermon of Exhortation to the Knights of the Temple

The Templars were representative of some relatively new developments in Christian thinking. The fighting man and the monk had historically been separate concepts so the combination of the two into one man seemed to many to be an uncomfortable novelty. However, it was certainly the case that throughout the eleventh century and during the First Crusade the concept was gaining acceptance, as the Catholic Church sought to curb lawlessness in a violent society and provide a new knightly ideal in which the concept of the Crusade played no small part. Bernard of Clairvaux would write a hugely influential document called *De Laude novae militiae* (*In Praise of the New Knighthood*). It is not clear when this work was produced (perhaps in the middle of the 1130s) in an effort to promote what had now become an officially recognised order in the wake of the Council of Troyes in 1129. It is addressed to Hugh of Payns, whom it says asked Bernard to write it three times before he finally agreed to put quill to parchment. Hugh is addressed as 'knight of Christ and Master of the Knights of Christ'. The letter contains a lengthy exhortation of the idea of the warrior-monk, similar in feeling to a letter written by one Hugo Peccator (the sinner) at around the same period. Some attribute Hugo Peccator's letter to none other than Hugh of Payns himself, but whoever it was writing in support of the fledgling Templars, it was clear that he, and Bernard too, were writing to counter criticisms. There were misgivings about the dual role of the Knights Templar.

De Laude was written in Latin and was intended probably to be read in translation to the brothers whose main language would have been French. As well as exhorting the new order, the work outlined the religious significance of the holy places as if it was intended to be a helpful educational document. But the focus was on the nature of the order. It was a new type of knighthood. There was no vanity amongst these men, unlike in their secular counterparts who paid attention to their outward appearance. There was instead, an austere dress sense, with dirty skin darkened by mailshirts and the sun, and short hair. Their motives were praiseworthy. They did not fight for personal greed, pride, anger or power, but for the defence of Christianity and the destruction of evil.

But it was not just the joint role of the warrior-monk which caused consternation, it was its wider implications. Hugo Peccator wrote 'We say this because we have heard that certain of your number have been troubled by some people of no wisdom'. He then goes on to warn the Templars of the Devil and his works, reminding them to understand their inner state and to accept their lot, being sure that personal salvation has to be worked for. Hugo says that the Templars hated the sin and not the man in their enemies and that saved them from the Devil's temptation. So too with the despoiling of the enemy, which was also justified on account of their sin. But for Hugo Peccator the killing side had to be justified. The Devil, he says 'tempts you with anger and hatred when you kill, with greed when you strip your victims. Everywhere you repel his snares because you do not show hatred in the act of killing and you do not covet dishonestly in the act of despoiling.' Also, in a letter to Hugh of Payns from Prior Guigo of the Carthusian order, dated to c.1129, the prior warns that the main focus must be to follow Christian virtue before engaging worldly enemies. For Guigo there was a danger that the old knighthood would inevitably win through and humility and piety would be subverted. Pride, it seemed, was a characteristic which stubbornly reappeared.

But it was the subject of fighting and killing which needed the most eminent man of his day to write the final word. Bernard of Clairvaux is less ambiguous on the subject of killing for Christ. He says 'However, the knights of Christ fight the battles of their Lord in all peace of mind, in no way fearing to sin in killing the enemy or to die at his hands, since indeed death, whether inflicted or suffered, is not tainted by crime but is marked by a large degree of Glory.' Moreover, Bernard says that the member of the new knighthood preserves himself when he is killed and preserves Christ (as Christendom) when he kills. The argument was complete. The old secular knighthood, a 'malicia' (evil), had given way to a new knighthood, a 'militia'. Bernard went on to hint that he knew that the early Templars were already industriously applying themselves to the fight. He wrote that it was rare for them not to be on military duty. He also said that they chose their horses for their strength and speed and that it was the Templars' aim to instil fear in their enemies. He knew also that like the ancient Maccabees (a celebrated Jewish rebel army) their numbers were never great on the field, but this was not a problem, 'for victory in war is not in the multitude of the army, but strength cometh from Heaven'.

And so Hugh of Payns, at the head of this new knighthood, having witnessed Count Fulk's marriage to the heiress Melisende, and with papal backing for his new order and a written Rule, headed back to the East confident that a remarkable tour of the West had achieved much of what he had hoped. The recruitment of men and the establishment of an economic and landed base in the West, important though it was, provided only the basic support and backing for the real work ahead. There was to be real fighting in the East. Hugh had not forgotten the other reason Baldwin II had sent him away. The King of Jerusalem had his eyes fixed on Damascus.

Part 2
Battles and Campaigns

Chapter 6

Damascus and the Early Campaigns, 1129–47

The strategic importance of Damascus cannot be overstated. Nestled in the foothills of the Anti-Lebanon Mountains in south-western Syria, this famous ancient fortified city found itself in the crusader period hovering menacingly over the narrowest part of the Outremer states (see Map 1, p. xvii). Based just 50 miles from the Mediterranean Sea, a well-organised Damascene army could conceivably cut supply and communication links between the Kingdom of Jerusalem to the south and the County of Tripoli to the north. Baldwin II and the Templars must have been aware of the threat.

Fulk and his party of crusaders arrived in Acre in May 1129. The Muslim commentator Ibn al-Qalanisi noted that the Franks at this time had been 'reinforced also from the sea by the King Count . . . having with him a vast host'. Fulk's arrival coincided with two recent strokes of fortune. In February 1128 Tughtigin, Atabeg of Damascus had passed away and was replaced by his less competent son Buri. Buri had decided to rid himself of a thorn in his side, the Assassins. The Assassins were an Ismaili sect whose arrival some years earlier in Damascus did not sit well with the Sunni Muslim population of the town. In 1126 Tughtigin had handed the Assassin leader Bahram of Asterabad control of Banyas, the frontier fortress from where the Assassins intimidated the people of the region. Bahram was succeeded by a Persian named Ismail. Buri, following up on Tughtigin's growing impatience with the Assassins orchestrated a purge of the Assassins in September 1129 starting in Damascus with the murder of the Assassins' nominal protector and supporter, the vizier al Mazdaghani. Riots ensued around the city and Ismail, nervously observing events from Banyas, went straight to the Franks with an offer. They could have Banyas if they would provide Ismail with protection.

Baldwin arrived with his reinforced army at Banyas in November 1129. The site provided the perfect springboard for the planned campaign against Damascus. He marched to a place called the Wooden Bridge just 6 miles to the south-west of

Damascus. With him were the Count of Tripoli, the Count of Edessa, the Prince of Antioch and almost certainly a contingent of Templars. Buri placed his army between the crusaders and the city and waited. The standoff lasted several days until on the crusader side, William of Bures's forces were caught whilst foraging. They had gone 20 miles south of the Frankish camp to a place called Mergisafar. They were initially large in number but split their forces into smaller and smaller detachments. Command and control seems to have been lost as William of Tyre recounts how the Franks of lesser ranks simply pleased themselves in an ill-disciplined search for booty. They were overwhelmed by Turcomen cavalry, who took advantage of a superior knowledge of the landscape. With no chance of regaining cohesion, even the well-disciplined knights who had been sent out with the foragers to guard them were slain. The defeat was ignominious. William and forty-five of his comrades survived to bring the unfortunate news to the king. The king however, wanted quick revenge and wished to catch Buri whilst his forces were preoccupied celebrating. The order was given to advance against the Muslims. Ibn al-Qalanisi says that there was terror in the hearts of the Muslim forces at this development which was followed by feelings of great relief when a huge rain storm began to turn the plain into a sea of mud with huge rivers cutting through the trackways. 'Against the will of divine power, the purposes of man can make no progress', commented William of Tyre. With a heavy heart the crusaders turned back to Banyas and from there to Palestine before dispersing. Opportunities to move against Damascus were rare. In 1126 even after his victory at A'zaz the king had only managed to raid the vicinity of the city. Now, in 1129 with a large force, the elements had conspired against him. In the long term, this failure of the crusaders to take Damascus would have dramatic consequences.

We cannot be sure if Hugh of Payns' men were amongst those appointed to guard the foragers at Mergisafar, but given Hugh's purpose and mission at this time and his close links to the king, it seems likely that his forces were involved in the Damascus campaign. It is perhaps worth noting an English source, the Anglo-Saxon Chronicle, in the entry for 1129, which has something more to say after it records Hugh's visit to Britain that year. 'Little came of it' says the chronicler, referring to Hugh's enticement of western warriors from Britain: 'He [Hugh of Payns] said that a great battle was set between the Christians and the heathen; then when they came there, it was nothing but lies; thus all the people became wretchedly afflicted.' If the Templars' role in the Damascus campaign is enigmatic, then the lack of a mention of the Templars for the next six or seven years is more so. We are on surer ground, however, with evidence of papal support for the order at the Council of Pisa in 1135. This council was called by Pope Innocent II in the face of a challenge against his authority from Anacletus II of Rome. The result of Innocent's gratitude for the support of Bernard of Clairvaux (and by association that of the Templars) during this schism was clear. Although not able to return to Rome until 1138 on his rival's death, Innocent, with the wide support of the Frankish clergy, was able to reward the Templars with a mark of gold each year. His chancellor Aimeric provided 2 ounces of gold and each of the archbishops, bishops and 'other good men' a mark of silver.

Hugh died in around 1136, presumably content that his order was in the ascendancy. His successor as Grand Master was Robert of Craon, a courageous military man and great organiser. Whether the recent financial injection had anything to do with an increasing military profile for the order is not clear. However, the Templars are to be found performing a new strategic role in the Amanus Mountains between 1136 and 1137. The armies of the First Crusade had marched into Syria from south-eastern Cilicia via the Belen Pass about 16 miles north of Antioch. This was a well-trodden path used for centuries by many great commanders. At some stage in the middle of the 1130s the defence of the pass, also known as the 'Syrian Gates', was entrusted to the Templars in the form of the fortified site at Gaston (also known as Baghras – see p. 205). But this was not the only pass into Syria. Also entrusted to the Templars was the defence of the Hajar Shuglan Pass situated north of Alexandretta (Iskenderun). The key castles in this more northerly Hajar Shuglan Pass were La Roche Roussel (Chilvan), which dominated its surroundings from an impressive height of 1,200m above sea level, and the unlocated La Roche Guillaume (which may be identical with the site postulated as that of Roche Roussel, see p. 211 below). Situated between the eastern approaches of both passes sat another Templar castle at Darbsak. Also, in around 1137 the Templars took possession of Port Bonnel on the Gulf of Ayas. The practical consequence of controlling these fortified sites must have been a further boost in the income of the order, for a castle economically as well as militarily dominates its landscape and the advantages of controlling a sea port are obvious to all.

Hundreds of miles to the south at the other end of Outremer, in the Kingdom of Jerusalem, the recently militarised Hospitallers were the first order to be granted an important strategic castle at Bethgibelin. Here, the intention of the new King Fulk (who had succeeded Baldwin II and ruled along with his new wife Melisende from 1131) was to threaten Fatimid Egyptian Ascalon. Bethgibelin would soon work alongside the castles of Blanchegarde and Ibelin in the 1140s to both protect the kingdom from Fatimid raids from Ascalon and to provide springboards for offensive operations. The Templars would later be awarded the castle at Gaza as part of the same strategic plan between 1149 and 1150. However, before this they had been awarded the castle of Latrun, otherwise known as Toron des Chevaliers, guarding the road to Jerusalem from Jaffa between 1137 and 1141. This huge castle had been expanded into a larger keep and outer works from an earlier small tower by Count Rodrigo Gonzalez of Toledo whilst he was in the Holy Land on crusade according to the *Chronica Aldefonsi imperatoris*, a Castilian chronicle. When he had completed it Gonzalez garrisoned and equipped it and gave it to the Templars. It was again expanded later in its history. As for the reasons behind its early establishment we might surmise that the protection of pilgrims had a part to play, but the threat from Ascalon would appear to have dominated the thinking of Rodrigo Gonzalez and his successors.

As the Templars began to occupy these strategic strongholds and continued to perform their role of escorting and protecting pilgrims, there is further evidence of military activity. This time, the action centres on the County of Tripoli and the Templars' earliest recorded contact with Zengi, Atabeg of Mosul (to which he ascended in 1127) and of Aleppo. Zengi was a much celebrated leader in the Muslim accounts. He represented a new breed of Muslim ruler whose military and political expertise would overcome the disunity of the first few decades of the twelfth century and provide a formidable foe for the leaders of the Outremer states. Early in 1137 Count Pons of Tripoli was killed after being betrayed by Christian villagers to the forces of an aggressive new ruler called Basawash at Damascus. Zengi distrusted the new regime in Damascus and set about besieging Homs which was under Damascene control. For two weeks he camped before the fortification, but on hearing that Pons's son, the new Count Raymond II of Tripoli, was heading towards him, Zengi raised the siege of Homs and turned his attention to the newly arrived Franks. The result was that Raymond retired in the face of the threat and Zengi headed to the castle at Montferrand (Bar'in) on the eastern side of the Nosairi hills. Originally captured by the Franks in 1115, lost and again retaken in 1126, this castle had great strategic value. Zengi knew that if he could take it he could prevent the Franks of Tripoli from penetrating up the Orontes Valley and thereby allow for Zengi to increase his hold upon Homs and Hama.

Raymond II appealed to King Fulk for help. Fulk headed north with all he could gather which was less than he might have wanted, but which included a force of Templars. Their march was troubled. Many were in a poor state as they weaved their way through the Nosairi foothills. Zengi, who had distanced himself from the king's forces, on hearing the news about their condition, closed in on them. The Christians were heavily defeated. The Anglo-Norman historian Orderic Vitalis was moved to record it like this:

> Countless thousands of the Pagans fell, but by the will of God, whose judgments are just and right, almost the whole Christian force crumbled and all except thirty knights were slain. Only the king himself escaped with ten of his household knights and eighteen knights of the Temple, and fled to a castle . . . called Montferrand where they stoutly resisted, although besieged for some time . . . Zengi, although he had lost thousands of his men by the swords of the Christians, was nevertheless elated at winning the victory he had hoped for.

The Count of Tripoli had been taken prisoner according to William of Tyre. The king, holed up in Montferrand with the Templars, sent out for help from the Patriarch, the Count of Edessa and the Prince of Antioch. They each began to prepare to relieve the siege of Montferrand. By July 1137 these forces were in the region, but the king, acting out of desperation and on the advice of unknown persons, sent out a messenger to Zengi to ask for terms. To his surprise Zengi just wanted Montferrand. The king could have back his prisoners including Count Raymond. In a great ceremony the exchange took place and Zengi took his prize whilst the king's men marched away and came across the relieving Frankish forces in the fertile Buqaia (the Beqaa Valley) much closer than any of them had expected. It may have seemed to some that a rash deal had been made with Zengi given the proximity of the relieving force, but to others and just possibly to the Templars, the negotiations had meant the king had got off lightly and lived to fight another day.

By 1139 the Templars must have gained for themselves some sort of renown, for William of Tyre's record of a military defeat near Hebron includes the recording of the death in battle of an individual he describes as a well-known Templar. In these days he says, a certain Burgundian had come to Jerusalem. This was the new Templar Grand Master Robert of Craon. He had brought some of his brothers from Antioch. However, whilst the king's forces were away besieging a fortress beyond the Jordan 'certain Turks' seized the opportunity to cross the Jordan and take possession of Tekoah, south of Jerusalem. Robert, his brothers and a member of the king's household Bernard Vacher, who bore the royal standard of the Kingdom of Jerusalem, set out from Jerusalem for Tekoah. On hearing of the Christians' approach the enemy turned towards Hebron further south, with the intention of continuing to friendly Ascalon. In what would appear to be a repeat of the debacle at Mergisafar ten years before, the Frankish forces scattered in different directions to obtain plunder and were overconfident that their enemy had fled before them. But the Turks turned and rallied. They fell upon the unsuspecting Franks. A core of Christian warriors managed to form a defensive line amidst a cacophony of trumpet blasts and a cloud of dust created by their horses' hooves. But it was not enough. The Turks came on in their swirling masses before the foraging Franks could answer their comrades' trumpets. Valiant and defiant though the defence was, the Western knights in the remaining line were caught and defeated by their enemies. The casualty count greatly increased in the subsequent rout. There was nowhere for the fleeing Franks to go. A lack of pathways and steep rocky slopes meant that some men were hurled from precipices in the chase. For many miles around the Turks massacred their enemy. In what has sometimes been passed over as a minor skirmish by later observers, 'many noble and famous men' fell. These included Odo of Mountfaucon whose death caused 'universal sorrow and mourning'. William of Tyre tells us that the king's assault on the fortress beyond the Jordan was a success and that the forces of the king returned home in triumph, but nothing is said of what Robert of Craon may have learned from this dangerous practice of scattering one's forces in search of plunder, or whether Robert had any decision-making role in such a disaster.

In the same year of the Hebron incident the Templars received their first papal bull of privileges. Pope Innocent II, who had already provided his support at the Council of Pisa found himself in a position to return to Rome after the death of a rival Pope. On 29 March 1139 the bull *Omne datum optimum* was promulgated. Its title was taken from the Epistle of James which begins 'Every best gift and every perfect gift descends from above . . .'. It gave the Templars official papal backing in their role as defenders of the Church and attackers of the enemies of Christ. The bull mentioned that the Templars were already wearing a cross on their chest at this time, but does not specify its colour. It also quotes the Gospel of John (15:13):

just as true Israelites and warriors most skilled in holy war, are indeed fired up by the flame of charity and fulfil by your deeds the words of the Gospel that says: 'Greater love hath no man than this, that a man lay down his life for his souls [friends]', whence, in accordance with the words of the great Shepard, you are not afraid to lay down your souls for your brothers and defend them from attacks of the pagans.

Omne datum optimum conferred significant privileges upon the order. One of these will have had an impact on the approach to warfare. The Templars were permitted to keep the spoils of war. It said 'you can confidently put them [the spoils] to your own use, and we prohibit that you be coerced against your will to give anyone a portion of these'. The appetite for plunder, already in evidence, would now have official backing. All donations were to be placed under the protection of the Holy See. The order as a whole was answerable to the Pope alone, marking a significant (although not total) shift away from the Patriarch of Jerusalem. The Grand Master could be chosen from the ranks of the Templar knights without outside interference. The order was also given its own priesthood for the first time and these priests answered to the Grand Master despite the fact that he himself was not ordained. The Chaplains were full members of the order and could hear confessions and absolve the brothers. All this made the order independent of the diocesan bishops of Outremer. The Templars were also granted their own oratories where divine offices could be heard and were also granted exemption from tithes but were in turn free to collect tithes on their own properties.

Unsurprisingly, the Templars' privileges did not meet with universal approval. Criticism of the order was still very strong as late as the Third Lateran Council of 1179. There were some, such as John of Salisbury, writing in the 1150s who saw the privileges as at best confusing. He could not understand why those whose job it was to 'shed human blood in a certain way presume to administer the blood of Christ'. This sense of distance created by *Omne datum optimum* was soon compounded by two other papal bulls promulgated in relatively quick succession. On 9 January 1144 a new Pope, Celestine II (1143–4), issued *Milites Templi*, a bull which was addressed to the prelates of Christendom. It carried a strong message. The Knights of the Temple at Jerusalem were the new Maccabees. Here, the comparison was with the Jewish warriors who had risen in revolt against the Syrian King Antiochus Epiphanes (175–164 BC) after Antiochus had brought in a pagan cult at the Temple in order to eradicate Judaism. Through the Templars the bull said, God had 'freed the Eastern Church from the filth of the pagans and defeated the enemies of the Christian faith'. The Templars' successes to date were thus lauded by the Pope. As the Templars laid down their lives for their brothers and for the protection of pilgrims, the Pope called for the order to be given practical help from the prelates of Christendom. A carrot was waved in front of the readership:

Indeed, whoever helps them out from his own resources, accumulated through God, and becomes a member of this most holy brotherhood, granting it benefices annually . . . we will grant him an indulgence of the seventh part of any penance imposed upon him. If he dies and has not been excommunicated, ecclesiastical burial with other Christians will not be denied him.

The bull went on to say that when Templars went to any city, castle or village on the business of collection, and if that place had been placed under interdict (a papal prohibition on Christians practising certain rites within a specified region), then churches should be opened once a year to receive the knights. Divine offices could be heard in such churches, provided no excommunicates were present. Furthermore, the Templars' persons and goods were to be protected with no damage or injury to be inflicted on them.

Pope Celestine's short pontificate ended in March 1144. He was succeeded by Pope Lucius II who died in February 1145 and was himself succeeded as Pope by Eugenius III (1145–53). On 7 April 1145 another papal bull entitled *Militia Dei* further strengthened the Templars' position. The order was given the right to take tithes and burial fees and to bury their own brothers or sergeants in places where they had their own oratories. The prelates to whom the bull was addressed must consecrate these oratories and bless the cemeteries.

It may seem that the continuing granting of privileges to the Templars was being met with some consternation in certain clerical circles. It is unlikely however, that successive popes through three different papal bulls were trying to prop up a failing organisation. They were building on success. From the military point of view, we cannot know how many skirmishes or minor battles have gone without mention, but by 1145 when Pope Eugenius's *Militia Dei* was promulgated, the order had already seen numerous military actions fighting alongside the secular nobility of the Kingdom of Jerusalem. The three papal bulls reflect a continuing and growing need to promote and fund the Templars. Eugenius knew that the need was most pressing indeed, for in December 1144 a disaster had befallen Outremer.

Zengi, Atabeg of Mosul and Aleppo, had surrounded and besieged Edessa, the capital of the important crusader buffer state in the north-east. For a month from the end of November his siege engines and engineers battered and undermined the walls of the city with no apparent counter-mining repost. On 24 December 1144 part of the walls near the Gate of Hours collapsed and Zengi's men rushed through the breach. Many citizens were caught in the stampede and trampled underfoot or slaughtered where they stood, with some managing to retreat to the citadel, but there was no hope of defence. One of Zengi's commanders, Zayn ad-Din Ali Kutchuk, was appointed governor of Edessa, and whilst its remaining Christian population were spared, the news of the disaster began to travel back to the West. Outremer had been founded on the crusading zeal of dukes, princes and other European nobility during the First Crusade. Now, with the earliest established of those crusader states being the first to fall, Pope Eugenius would soon call upon none less than kings to help. The Templars would play no small part in what happened next.

Chapter 7

The Second Crusade, 1147–8

The survival of the Crusader states in the first few decades of their existence owed much to the disunity of the Muslim powers set against them. The Fatimid Egyptians, whose once wide-ranging power in the Levant was by the 1140s on the wane, were one such group, and there were also numerous Syrian and Iraqi urban based powers, mainly controlled by Turks. Sometimes to defend themselves against more aggressive Muslim powers, these city rulers would even seek out Frankish allies, such was the colourful world of Crusader politics. Zengi had changed the political landscape in this respect. Brought up by Kerbogha, the governor of Mosul, Zengi was a Seljuk Turk, a member of the fierce warrior peoples who had nearly destroyed Byzantine Asia Minor and whose distinctive mounted fighting style was and would continue to be a bane to the Christians.

The news of the fall of Edessa reverberated around the Muslim world with speed. Although Count Joscelin II of Edessa vainly held out west of the Euphrates at Turbessel, the alarms began to ring around Christendom. Not even the death of Zengi in September 1146 would negate what may have seemed an obvious need for a new crusade. A new champion of Islam, Nur ed-Din, second son of Zengi, was pressing down on Antioch and also brutally quelling any Edessan support for their erstwhile ruler Joscelin.

Bernard of Clairvaux spearheaded the preaching for a new crusade. Both the Pope and King Louis VII had appealed for help. Initially lukewarm to the idea, the barons of France came to hear Bernard preach at Vezelay in Burgundy on 31 March 1146. Bernard's energy led him to make a direct appeal to the people of England to take the cross which in turn led to an unexpected expedition of Anglo-Normans, Flemings and Frisians in Portugal en route to the Holy Land. At length, Bernard also persuaded King Conrad III of Germany to take the cross at Christmas 1146.

For the Templars, the Second Crusade was a watershed moment. On 27 April 1147 King Louis VII and Pope Eugenius III came to the Paris Temple. The purpose was to discuss the practical aspects of the proposed crusade. There were 4 archbishops and 130 Templars present. The plan was that the Templars would accompany the army to the East. William of Tyre recalls that it was in Pope Eugenius's time (1145–53) that the Templars won the right to sew their iconic red crosses onto their mantles so 'that they might be distinguished from others' and it would seem that the Paris meeting may have been the public forum for such an announcement. The red cross on its pure white background was imbued with symbolism. It was a sign of the Templars' willingness to become martyrs according to the thirteenth-century Bishop of Acre James of Vitry. The Pope also appointed the Templar treasurer to receive the taxes which had been imposed on all Church goods to finance the crusade thus beginning the role of the Paris Temple as a treasure house of France. Amongst the Templars at the Paris meeting was Everard des Barres, Master in France. He forged a close relationship with Louis VII and seems to have been his advisor in the months which followed. In fact, it was Everard who was sent ahead to Constantinople to play a key diplomatic role along with Bartholomew the Chancellor and Archibald of Bourbon.

King Louis and the bulk of the French army arrived at Constantinople on 4 October 1147. Conrad had already left with his own army shepherded by the emperor's Varangian guardsmen and took the route across Asia Minor to Nicaea and thence out into dangerous Seljuk territory. On 25 October near Dorylaeum, Conrad's forces were massacred where they rested, desperate for water and food. Conrad, with only a tenth of his force, made it back to Nicaea whilst the triumphant Turks plucked the booty from the corpses of the slain Germans and sold it in markets as far wide as Persia for months to come.

In early November the French arrived in Nicaea. News of the German disaster was conveyed to Louis by Frederick of Swabia (the future Holy Roman Emperor Frederick I) who was anxious for Louis to meet with Conrad. Between them the kings came up with a new route which did not lead directly into the heart of the Seljuk lands. It was a coastal route theoretically benefitting from Byzantine naval support. But when they got to Ephesus, Conrad fell ill and returned to Constantinople where he remained until he was personally conveyed into Palestine in March 1148. Meanwhile, the Byzantine Emperor had written to Louis telling him to proceed with caution and to avoid conflict with the Turks and stay within touch of Byzantine fortresses. Louis VII did not reply to the emperor. He carried onwards, and rested his army at Decervium in the Meander Valley. Here, Odo of Deuil tells us that the French were attacked by a Muslim Turkish force but were able to repel it. He also implies that the driving force behind the Turkish attack was in fact the Byzantines. As if this hint of Byzantine treachery was not enough to lower morale in the French army the craggy terrain of the Meander Valley concealed companies of Turks who were able to harass the army up to a point where it arrived at a bridge across the river near to Pisidian Antioch (not to be confused with the Principality of Antioch). Here, on 1 January 1148 the French were challenged at the crossing, but were able to force the crossing and even succeeded in capturing a number of the enemy. The subsequent retreat of the Turks to Pisidian Antioch (at this time a Byzantine fortress) only served to heighten the suspicion of Greek treachery amongst the crusaders.

By 4 January 1148 the French had arrived at a deserted Laodicea. The army wished to march to the port of Attalia (modern Antalya) but the route would now be treacherous. Moreover, Turkish attritional raids on the French marching column continued to have their effect. As they moved along the road to Attalia, they saw the bodies of German pilgrims who had split from Conrad's crusading force and taken this fateful route through the region a month or so before. Even Louis VII's wife, the redoubtable Queen Eleanor of Aquitaine, who had taken the cross at Vezelay, was having second thoughts about her decision.

At Mount Cadmus between Laodicea and Attalia in January 1148 supplies were running low and horses were scarce. Geoffrey of Rancon's advanced guard had separated itself too far from Louis's main force and had not camped on the summit of a pass, ignoring Louis's orders. Instead, they had wandered down into the plain. It was a gift for the Turks, whose whole approach to the campaign was designed to destroy the cohesion of the crusader army. The Turks began another withering attack. With crevices and steep drops to their sides, the French suffered terribly. Counterattacks were ineffective. The king himself fought alone with his back against a tree and barely managed to escape.

Louis's response to the Mount Cadmus disaster was to entrust the responsibility for the defence of the French crusading force to Everard des Barres and the Knights Templar. The results of this trust in the Templars were clear to see. Louis VII would later write a letter of high praise to Abbot Suger of Saint-Denis, to whom he had assigned the care of his kingdom: 'I cannot imagine how we would have subsisted for even the smallest space of time in these parts; had it not been for the Templars' support and assistance.'

Under Templar stewardship the army was reorganised. There were strict orders against untimely sorties and enemy provocation was to be suffered. Relieving charges were to return when recalled and flank and rear guards to be appointed. Keeping position in column was deemed paramount. The Templars had looked after their own supplies during the campaign, including a careful preservation of their horses. They were in a position to grasp the military leadership. According to Odo of Deuil, Everard organised the army into units of fifty, each unit given a Templar at its head. Each of these Templars were to look to their own commander, a man called Gilbert. It was an unusual moment in medieval military history. A military order had assumed – with the king's blessing – control over a royally led army in difficult circumstances. Oaths were sworn that the Templars were to be obeyed. But the crucial achievement was in the maintenance of cohesion when on the march (see pp. 166–70). When a medieval army begins to disintegrate due to a combination of enemy action (in this case, deliberate harassment by Turkish mounted archers) and depleting morale, there is a 'crowd' waiting to get out. From Odo of Deuil's account, it is clear that the Templars prevented this natural tendency through strict discipline.

The French army in some degree of order finally arrived in February at Attalia battered but not destroyed. From here, a small flotilla of Byzantine ships would assist some of the French in their journey to the Holy Land. Leaving many behind in

Attalia, together with a lump sum of 500 marks, Louis boarded the ships and set sail, arriving at Saint-Symeon on 19 March 1148. Sometime later there followed another modest fleet of French noblemen from Attalia and later still the bedraggled infantry who had decided out of desperation to take the landward route through Cilicia and who arrived eventually in Antioch in the spring of 1148.

The actions in Asia Minor were not the last of the Templar involvements in the Second Crusade. On 10 May 1148 Everard des Barres travelled to Acre from Antioch to raise money for the French king who was nearing a penniless state with only half his job done. The Templars were able to raise huge amounts of money either from their own resources or by securing loans against their assets. Louis was acutely aware of the debt and in his letter to Abbot Suger he asked for a quick repayment to be made of 2,000 marks of silver. But the cost had been huge. Louis also demanded that Raoul of Vermandois, Count of Péronne, find a repayment to the Temple of 30,000 livres Parisis, a sum which constituted at the time around half of the annual tax revenue of the French kingdom. Crusading was clearly an expensive business.

The troubles encountered in Asia Minor might have been half forgotten if the Second Crusade had ultimately been successful, but it faltered once again in a most ignominious way. Conrad had landed in Acre in April and had stayed with the Templars in Jerusalem over Easter. It was here where some discussion took place, according to the German Bishop Otto of Freising (who was present on the campaign), between the Templars, the Patriarch and the crusaders. The target would once again be Damascus. Near Acre, at Palmae on 24 June 1148 a great assembly was held of the crusader leaders and local Frankish leadership. It included Louis VII, Conrad III, the young Baldwin III of Jerusalem (whose redoubtable mother Melisende was also present according to William of Tyre), the Patriarch of Jerusalem, the archbishops of Caesarea and of Nazareth, Robert of Craon the Grand Master of the Temple and his counterpart from the Hospital Raymond du Puy. The detail of the discussion is lost, and there are hints of only a little opposition to the plan to attack Damascus. The obsession with this ancient city may have been in part to do with its strategic value, or partly to do with a desire to drive a wedge between Sunni and Shia Muslims (the Damascenes being largely affiliated with the latter), or in part due to the longing of the Franks to gain the fertile areas surrounding the city. But the complex political situation in the East made the adventure a risky one. Nur ed-Din was by now firmly established from Edessa to Hama. His threat to Outremer was obvious and no one had known this better than Prince Raymond of Antioch who had tried in vain to get Louis VII to attack Aleppo, the heart of Nur ed-Din's power base. To attack the Burid kingdom of Damascus, whose emir Unur saw Nur ed-Din as his natural enemy, would be to potentially drive the citizens of Damascus into an alliance with Aleppo. Somewhere in the to-ing and fro-ing at Palmae this argument was either lost or never made at all.

The crusaders set out from Tiberias, along the Sea of Galilee through Banyas arriving on Saturday 24 July in the orchards to the south of Damascus. The army leaders had made the decision to camp here after consulting with 'persons well acquainted with the situation of Damascus and the adjacent country' says William of Tyre. These orchards, it was said, afforded the city much protection and the city would fall quicker if they were seized. Moreover, the fruit and the water here could be used by the crusaders themselves. At Daria, 4 miles from the city and with its walls in plain sight, the signal was given to form an order of battle. At its head would be the King of Jerusalem, followed in turn by the King of France and then of the Holy Roman Empire. The military orders were there too. The forests around Damascus stretched for 4 or 5 miles. They were enclosed by walls of mud which outlined individual holdings and punctuated by paths and public ways for access. Unur's forces had already suffered a setback as they retreated, but as the French king led his column through the orchards it was clear that they were infested by the enemy who made good use of skirmishing and harassing tactics. From the various small buildings dotted around the orchards Ahdath (city militia) bowmen fired into the flanks of the proceeding crusaders. From behind the mud walls Muslim spearmen thrust their spears into the sides of the Christians passing through the paths. They even cut holes in the walls to achieve a better result. But the crusaders persevered, managing to hold the orchards, and were intent on getting to the River Barada beyond. They began to convert the wood from the orchards into palisades. As many citizens fled back to Damascus, an action took place on the riverbank. Unur had indeed called for help, not only from his surrounding dependencies but from Saif ed-Din Ghazi I of Mosul and Nur ed-Din as well. Reinforcements began to pour into the city. A Muslim cavalry force lined the riverbank denying the crusaders access to the water. Only the strenuous actions of Conrad, coming forward and dismounting to fight on foot, managed to push the enemy backward and ultimately force them to flee to the city.

The situation in Damascus was desperate now. As the crusaders began to besiege the city at the Bab al-Jabiya gate barricades were erected by the Muslims to delay the progress of the crusaders once they entered. The Muslim reinforcements had become large enough for Unur to organise a counter-attack and when this took place it caught the crusaders by surprise and hurled them back into the orchards where once again they fell prey to the skirmishing militia. A war of attrition followed during which Unur lost a number of men and on 26 July, two days into the siege, a militia force managed to decapitate some Frankish sentries much to the delight of the townsfolk.

On 27 July a peculiar decision was made which caused the writers who heard about it to seek out some sort of explanation. The crusader camp was shifted from the orchards to the plain on the east side of the city where supplies and water were scarce on the pretext that the walls could be attacked without hindrance. The result was catastrophic. The Ahdath militia moved back into the vacant orchards making it impossible for the crusaders to retrieve their position, creating barricades and posting units of bowmen. Then the food and water ran out in the crusader camp. Now facing continuing counter-attacks and still being unable to mount a realistic assault, the leaders of the Second Crusade decided to call it all off. Somewhere in the distance the forces of Nur ed-Din were at large, whilst other Muslim troops continued to pour into the city. On 28 July just five days into the siege the crusaders, starting with a disaffected Conrad III, struck camp and headed back to Galilee. They were harassed every inch of the way by Turcomen horse archers and the journey was nothing less than a shameful embarrassment.

For some, it smacked of treachery. The local Frankish barons who had been close allies of Unur in the past were thought once again to have intrigued with him and forced this disastrous move away from a position of strength. By the time William of Tyre was writing some fifty years later the culprits' identities had become somewhat mysterious, despite the fact that he had personally interviewed wise old men about their memories of it. There had been arguments in the crusader camp about who should have Damascus once it had fallen. Some had said that Count Thierry of Flanders had won the support of Conrad, Louis and Baldwin and this incensed the local Frankish leaders, who had stooped to this treacherous act in the hope that Damascus would remain in Unur's hands. Others had told William that Prince Raymond of Antioch had somehow scuppered the siege from afar, having already fallen out with Louis over his failure to support him. William of Tyre does not mention the rumours that Raymond had also rather publically had an affair with Eleanor of Aquitaine. William concluded that the stench of bribery hung heavy in the air but he could not identify its source. The crusaders turned for home and began thinking of other military plans, chief amongst which was a proposed attack on Ascalon, still held by the Muslims.

Other writers were more direct in their accusations surrounding the treachery at the siege of Damascus. A German tradition, emanating in Würzburg and first recorded in the anonymous *Annales Herbipolenses*, attributes the failure to the greed, deceit and envy of the Templars whom it was said took a huge bribe to give aid to the besieged. Later, John of Würzburg, who visited the Holy Land in 1160s, was sure there had been an accusation of treachery against the Templars during this siege but he was not sure of its veracity. John of Salisbury, writing from the papal court and perhaps having spoken to returning French crusaders, knew of the accusations of treachery but wrote that King Louis had always sought to 'exonerate the brothers of the Temple'. Many in the West later thought that the blame lay with the 'men of Jerusalem', as some sources called them, with the crusaders receiving money for lifting the siege which then turned out to be false coin, a frequently repeated story. However, the author of the twelfth-century German *Casus Monasterii Petrishusensis* simply blamed 'certain knights of God'. For the English chronicler Ralph Coggeshall (who died in 1216) the Templars had been bribed by Nur ed-Din. Gervase of Canterbury, writing around the same time (he died in 1210), says the Templars had accepted three jars of gold besants from the Damascenes but after they lifted the siege and looked into the jars the Templars found them to be full of only copper pieces. The chronicle ascribed to Ernoul and Bernard the Treasurer amplifies the false coin bribe into packhorse loads received by both the Templars and Hospitallers.

We cannot be sure of the Templar involvement in the disastrous decision made at Damascus. They were not the only accused by any means and the stories of false coins are later embellishments whose authors were writing at a time when the Templars were facing a different set of criticisms than they were in 1148. But the doubt is uncomfortable. Unlike the French and German royal armies, the order was a permanent feature in the military landscape of Outremer, as were the local Frankish baronage. It seems unlikely that the Templars had nothing to say when the potential fate of a captured Damascus was discussed around the camp fires.

Robert of Craon did not live long after the end of the Second Crusade. He died on 13 January 1149 and was replaced as Grand Master by the man who had already proven himself as a capable military leader, Everard des Barres. It was almost certainly the influence of the French king which led to the promotion, perhaps in part as a reward for the great rescue mission in Asia Minor. Everard came West with King Louis to France in the aftermath of the Second Crusade, leaving behind him his seneschal Andrew of Montbard, Bernard of Clairvaux's uncle, who was in charge of the order during the Master's absence. But all was not well in the East and it was not long before Andrew was compelled to appeal for his Master's return. In a letter written to Everard by Andrew, the seneschal complained of a lack of knights, sergeants and money within the Order of the Temple without which he could not 'relieve our mother, the Oriental church, miserably weighed down'. The trigger for all this urgency had been the continuing and inexorable rise of Nur ed-Din and in particular an event which had seen the worst nightmares of Prince Raymond of Antioch become a horrific reality.

After some initial success against Nur ed-Din Prince Raymond of Antioch had become emboldened. He had allied himself in November 1148 with the Kurdish leader of the Assassins Ali ibn Wafa and between them they had stormed the plain of the Aswad at Famiya on the road from Antioch to Marash. Nur ed-Din's commander, a Kurd called Shirkuh, had failed to get involved in the battle and the result was a resounding victory for Antioch. However, Nur ed-Din had rebounded in the spring of 1149 by defeating Raymond at Baghras and then turned south to besiege Inab, a Christian fortress east of the Orontes. Raymond and Ali ibn Wafa marched to the rescue, but with a surprisingly small force which Nur ed-Din took to be only the advanced guard of the enemy. Therefore, he retreated from Inab for a short while. It became apparent to Nur ed-Din that the force was not receiving reinforcements and his scouts had reported that the Franks and their ally had camped in an exposed hollow, a place called the 'walled fountain' between Apamea and Rugia. The Muslim army surrounded Raymond's camp on the night of 28 June 1149 and during the desperate break-out attempt the next morning the Franks perished as they tried to charge up a rocky incline. The Assassin leader was killed and many Antiochene noblemen. Raymond was slain, his killer being the commander Shirkuh who through this act had restored himself to the favour of Nur ed-Din. Raymond's severed head was triumphantly sent by Nur ed-Din to the Caliph of Baghdad as the remaining leaders of Outremer contemplated the horror and significance of what had occurred.

In response to the disaster at Inab, the Patriarch of Antioch had sent to King Baldwin for urgent help. The Templars had gathered 120 knights and 1,000 squires and sergeants to assist Baldwin's drive to the north, no mean undertaking given the pressure on resources. But the borrowing had been heavy;. 7,000 besants were raised in Acre and a further 1,000 in Jerusalem. The Templars constituted the main bulk of Baldwin's force and their arrival in the north seems to have persuaded Nur ed-Din to treat with the Franks and accept a truce. Antioch, though saved, would have its territories greatly reduced as a result. But Andrew of Montbard's letter revealed a desperate situation for the Templars. 'The great part of those we led to the succour of Antioch are dead', he wrote.

How the Templars received reinforcements is not known, but Everard de Barres was back in the Holy Land by the spring of 1152 and he cannot have failed to bring men with him. However, towards the end of 1152, in a surprising move, Everard simply resigned from his position. He is later to be found as a monk of Clairvaux and was still there as late as 1176. His replacement as Grand Master of the Templars, a Burgundian called Bernard of Tremelay, would play a vital role in the kingdom's affairs. The Kingdom of Jerusalem, buoyed by a surprise victory of the citizens of Jerusalem over an Ortoqid Turcoman army which appeared quite unexpectedly on its doorstep in the autumn of 1152, now turned its attention to the problem of Egypt and in particular to the Fatimid city of Ascalon, a thorn in their side for so many years.

A Christian assault on Ascalon had been made possible by a number of factors, not least of which was the emergence from his mother Melisende's shadow of Baldwin III. As well as this, the changeable politics of the region had produced a seemingly unlikely Damascene alliance with the Franks. But there was something more physically obvious in the landscape of Outremer which enabled the Franks to think about a thrust towards Egypt. During the winter of 1149–50 the Templars had been granted the largely deserted settlement at Gaza to fortify. This castle, constructed on an eminence within the city, complemented the already existing crusader castles at Bethgibelin, Ibelin and Blanchegarde and it was the first castle to be granted to the Templars within the Kingdom of Jerusalem itself. Situated around 10 miles to the south of Ascalon, Gaza completed a landward encirclement of the Fatimid city. The establishment of the Templars at Gaza even met with the approval of William of Tyre. The king and the lords of the realm had spent great energy in the construction work and 'by general consent' Gaza and its adjacent district was committed to the Templars to hold in perpetuity. William of Tyre was no friend of the Templars, but he saw the value of the stronghold at Gaza from the date of its foundation down to his own time. He describes this frontier fort and its custodians with emphatic praise:

> This charge the brothers, brave men and valiant warriors, have faithfully and wisely guarded even to this time. Again and again they have vigorously assaulted Ascalon, sometimes openly and again by attacks from ambush. As a result, those enemies who formerly overran and desolated the whole region

and made themselves dreaded by the Christians, now consider themselves most fortunate if, by entreaties or money, they can obtain a temporary peace and permission to dwell quietly within their walls.

William went on to say how Gaza served to protect the entire district and not just threaten Ascalon. He mentions how the Egyptians who had been accustomed to sending reinforcements to Ascalon three or four times a year, had launched a violent assault on the new fortification to no avail in 1150. This failure dispirited the Muslims of Ascalon and their fear of being ambushed in the lands around Gaza forced them to only attempt supplying Ascalon by sea in the future. They were, as William says, 'in fear of the Knights'. But William's assertions that Ascalon was subdued are not entirely true. The renowned Muslim man of letters Usama ibn Munqidh had based himself there on his way back from an unsuccessful diplomatic visit to Nur ed-Din made on behalf of the Egyptian government. From Ascalon Usama fought a number of battles with the Franks but he turned back to Egypt after a time. With the reduction of Muslim raiding in the area and the decrease in frequency of supplies and reinforcements into Ascalon from Egypt came an increasing vulnerability for the doomed Fatimid city. What happened next at Ascalon, however, would further blemish the reputation of the Templars.

Chapter 8

Siege of Ascalon, 1153

In Cairo political murders and constant intrigue had greatly weakened the Fatimid leadership for decades. The Caliph al-Hafiz had appointed his own son Hasan to the position of vizier only to have him executed for disloyalty in 1135. After this, there had been a series of viziers whose rules had brought chaos and carnage to the streets whilst al-Hafiz clung to power until his death in 1149. His son al-Zafir succeeded him but immediately there was civil war between his generals and further intrigue when one of them was murdered. Against this background it might seem that Frankish victory in the south was inevitable. The impending attack against Ascalon, however, would be anything but easy.

Ascalon was a formidable fortification, complete with numerous towers and thick masonry walls forming a giant semi-circle with its back against the sea. Set in a low-lying basin, its four gates were protected by huge towers. Inside, there were numerous deep wells and although the city was not a port as such, it could still receive supplies from the sea. The Franks knew just how strong the place would be, which is why King Baldwin's roll-call included most of the nobility of the kingdom, the Masters of both the Hospital (Raymond du Puy) and the Temple (Bernard of Tremelay), the Patriarch of Jerusalem and a number of abbots, archbishops and bishops as well as a huge assortment of siege equipment. A great part of the strength of the realm was at Ascalon, says William of Tyre and yet the number of defenders within the walls was double the besiegers' numbers.

William of Tyre's account of the siege is perhaps the most critical of the role played by the Templars and his opinions seem to have had some influence over both his audience and later historians. Once again, says William, as at Damascus, the surrounding orchards were initially targeted. But with the withdrawal of the citizens from the outlying areas to within the walls of the city a greater plan was announced, that there would be a full-scale siege, a development which William ascribes to divine mercy. The call went out and reinforcements arrived. On 25 January 1153 the Frankish army camped outside the walls pitching their tents in circular formations. Amongst them was Fulcher the Patriarch with the relic of the True Cross. Alongside the king and the military orders were the secular forces of Hugh of Ibelin, Philip of Nablus, Humphrey of Toron, Simon of Tiberias, Gerard of Sidon, Guy of Beirut,

Maurice of Montreal, Reynald of Châtillon and Walter of Saint-Omer. The last two in this list were serving as stipendiaries for pay, indicating that the others had answered the call as part of their feudal obligations.

The operation in the orchards did nothing to reduce the city. The siege began to drag out, with small actions interrupting the tedium. The blockade was also conducted by sea. Gerard of Sidon was given command of a fleet of fifteen ships, his job to prevent supplies getting in and anyone getting out of Ascalon. By Easter 1153 the pilgrim ships from the West were arriving on the shores of the kingdom. Many of their ships, fighting men and devout non-combatants were all brought into the effort against Ascalon enticed by the king's money. The king also purchased numerous ships which then had their masts dismantled and from these basic pieces a huge siege tower was constructed. It was very tall and well protected against fire, says William of Tyre. It was also covered inside and out with hides and wickerwork. Other devices were constructed. More stone-throwing siege engines were built and some covered sheds to protect the men who were to work away at levelling the embankment so that the siege tower could be brought up to the wall. When this was put in position, the pace of the action accelerated. Many defenders rushed to the section of the wall where it had been placed and there were daily encounters and acts of bravery on both sides, but still there was no great progress for the Christians save a slightly favourable attritional rate.

After five months it looked as if Ascalon would lose its fight against the Franks. Then, from Egypt came a fleet of seventy galleys packed with arms, men and food. It sailed into Ascalon and was only temporarily delayed by Gerard of Sidon's fleet which soon withdrew before it. The reinforcements were added to the defence of the city and fought enthusiastically at first. But Baldwin's forces remained encamped around Ascalon and the great siege tower was beginning to have an effect. The citizens within Ascalon began to prepare kindling wood and anything they could set fire to, to throw down between the tower and the walls. Pitch and oil were added to the debris and ignited. A great wind from the east blew up and pressed the fiercely burning fireball against the walls of the town itself. This firestorm raged all night against the wall, and when the morning of 16 August 1153 broke, a section of the wall between two towers collapsed with a thunderous crash that woke the besiegers in their tents. Part of the great tower had also been hit by the debris from the collapsing wall. William of Tyre says that the Franks rushed to the breach, with the Templars under Bernard of Tremelay getting there first. The Grand Master was refusing to allow anyone other than his own men to enter the breach: 'It was charged that he kept the rest back in order that his own people, being the first to enter, might obtain the greater and richer portion of the spoils and plunder.' William of Tyre seemed certain of the Templar motives. Forty of them entered the breach, but the citizens saw that they were cut off from their comrades and fell upon them, slaying them to a man. The defenders rallied, filled in the breach with timber and other material and hung the bodies of the slain over the walls shouting abuse at the Franks as they did so. The incident had cost Bernard of Tremelay his life.

The Franks held council in the king's tent. It was resolved to continue with the siege despite what had happened, with Raymond du Puy the Hospitaller Grand Master the most vocal advocate. The bombardments started once again and by 22 August 1153 the citizens could take it no more. Their terms were that they should be allowed to depart the city in safety. This they were allowed to do. Baldwin entered Ascalon as the last of the Muslims were trickling away to Egypt. This great historic city was given to the king's brother, Amalric, Count of Jaffa and its mosque converted into the Cathedral of St Paul. It was certainly a huge moment in the short life of the Kingdom of Jerusalem, but William of Tyre's account taints the Templars.

There are, in fact, other accounts of the siege which raise further possibilities about what may have happened. None of the Muslim accounts even mention the role of the Templars, but the European ones do. The chronicle of Sigebert of Gembloux recounts how the Templars rushed into the breach and got as far as the city square where they made a stand. The narrow streets and high walls meant the Templars were quickly surrounded and killed and their bodies hung on the walls. Three days later the city was taken. This account was copied by a chronicler from Afflingem in the Duchy of Brabant who added 'a man who was present, and remained in the army throughout the siege, narrated all he knew to us'. In this version, then, we have the Templars advancing too far into the city, but we are not given the reason. In *The Annals of Egmont* is another account possibly based on eyewitness testimony from Scandinavian pilgrims brought to the siege from Acre by Baldwin. Here, the Templars are accused of greed by rushing into the city, but the overall length of the siege is attributed to the treachery of the Palestinian Frankish nobility. The Templars were said to have been reluctant to attack Ascalon because of the money they had made out of the raiding of the caravans which came to supply the city every six weeks or so. However, when the breach was made in the walls during the siege, it was not the Templars who first went into it, but other young men who were ambushed and killed. This, in turn, angered the Templars who launched a dawn attack, killing many, and then withdrew. Only after the unmasking of the Palestinian nobles' treachery is the city taken much later on. The treachery, however, is not explained. A possible interpretation which has been put forward, is that the Templars were indeed the first into the breach, but got separated from the rest and were subsequently surrounded, killed and hung from the walls. The Palestinian nobility then did not allow their men to follow-up, possibly heaping suspicion on themselves. By the time William of Tyre was writing it was politically necessary to protect the nobility from any accusation.

The idea of Templar greed may have a foundation in the papal sanction afforded to them in the bull *Omne datum optimum*. We might recall that the right to convert spoils from the infidel to their own use was bestowed upon the order. Whatever the truth of the Templar rush to the breach at Ascalon, Bernard of Tremelay was killed in the siege. He would be replaced as Grand Master by the already active and experienced Andrew of Montbard. For the Templars, the loss of forty brothers did not impact upon the strong position the order held in Gaza. Moreover, the eyes of the King of Jerusalem still remained stubbornly fixed on Egypt.

Chapter 9

The Struggle for Egypt, 1154–68

On 18 April 1154 Nur ed-Din set his army at the gates of Damascus and began a siege. Behind the walls was Mujir ed-Din who had planned an attack on Banyas with Nur ed-Din which might have diverted Frankish resources away from Ascalon had it not dissolved into arguments and recriminations. Mujir ed-Din had been a friend of the Franks, seeking to use them as protectors against his own enemies, but this met with the disapproval of the citizens of Damascus and of Nur ed-Din and Ayub, Emir of Baalbek and also Shirkuh, Ayub's brother. When Shirkuh was sent to Damascus as Nur ed-Din's ambassador he was refused counsel by Mujir ed-Din and this was the final straw for Nur ed-Din. The siege only lasted a week and the appeal by Mujir ed-Din for help from the Franks came too late. On 24 April 1154 a Jewish woman let the attackers into the Jewish quarter of Damascus and this was followed by the citizens opening the east gate. Mujir fled to the citadel but could not hold out. He was, however, offered his life and the emirate of Homs but was later deposed by Nur ed-Din for plotting to regain Damascus. To Baghdad he went, with his tail between his legs. In his stead, Ayub was appointed as governor of Damascus and Nur ed-Din returned triumphantly to Aleppo contemplating territorial gains which would now stretch along the eastern frontiers of Outremer. In the long run, the impact of the taking of Damascus by Nur ed-Din would eclipse Baldwin's triumph at Ascalon, but for now he was content to continue the truce between Damascus and Jerusalem.

In June 1154 an event occurred in Egypt which provides another example of Templar strategy in the region. In April, the vizier Ibn Abbas and his son Nasr al-Din conspired to murder the Caliph al-Zafir. But the plan backfired on them both and Ibn Abbas went on to kill the Caliph's brothers as if to implicate them. In May 1154 Ibn Abbas and his son fled Cairo having placed the Caliph's 5-year-old son al-Fa'iz on the throne. They headed for Damascus. They managed to out-distance some angry pursuers who eventually returned to Egypt as the perused fled across the desert. For the fugitives, things would get much worse. According to Usama ibn Munqidh, who was actually in the party, they were attacked on 7 June 1154 in the mountains by a Christian ambush at al-Muwaylih. Usama managed to escape. William of Tyre says that the vizier Ibn Abbas was killed and Nasr al-Din and countless of the entourage's riches were captured. However, Usama says that the entourage had lost much of what it wanted to bring with them during the panic in Cairo. William states that amongst those who carried out the attack on the party were the Templars, who came away with the greater part of the riches. 'There fell to them by lot', he says, Nasr himself. They held him for many days. He had professed a desire to become Christian and had already learned Latin and had been instructed in the rudiments of the Christian faith. But the Templars sold him for 60,000 pieces of gold to the Egyptians whose intention it was to kill him. William continues, 'Heavily chained hand and foot, he was placed in an iron cage upon the back of a camel and carried to Egypt, where, to satisfy their savage passions, the people literally tore him to pieces bit by bit with their teeth.'

If William of Tyre implies Templar cupidity, then Walter Map – no friend of the Temple – makes the case more explicit, by saying that their devotion to warfare was greater than anything else. He says the Templars refused to listen to Nasr when he spoke of the instability of his own religion. The Egyptians paid dearly for him to be returned in the hope they could dissuade him from his apostasy but then shot him with arrows. Perhaps Usama's account of the fate of Nasr al-Din is more accurate. He says that it was the Caliph's four widows who personally mutilated him and that he was hanged and his body swung from the Zawila Gate for two years.

The elderly Andrew of Montbard lasted only until January 1156 as Grand Master. He had been much preoccupied with treading a careful line in the disputes between Melisende and Baldwin within the Kingdom of Jerusalem. After his death he was succeeded by Bertrand of Blancfort whose tenure would see a reforming zeal within the order, and would also reveal much about how the Templars related to the king and to the Hospitallers.

Bertrand, whom William of Tyre calls 'a religious and God-fearing man', had been Grand Master for only about a year when a military disaster befell him. Nur ed-Din had invaded the Buqaia via Baalbek in response to Baldwin III breaking their treaty. Baldwin had attacked a group of Muslim shepherds on the frontier territory around Banyas. In May 1157 Nur ed-Din came from Damascus to Banyas and besieged it. He was successful insofar as the besieged Humphrey of Toron retreated to the citadel. From here, Humphrey sent out to Baldwin for help and so the king came with a combined infantry and cavalry force with its customary Templar contingent. Nur ed-Din then adopted a scorched earth policy by torching Banyas before retreating in the face of the king's army. According to William of Tyre, Baldwin III reconstructed Banyas building by building. Somewhere in the landscape lurked Nur ed-Din, waiting. With Banyas restored Baldwin headed south towards Tiberias accompanied only by his cavalry squadrons. He had already dismissed his infantry and had been further weakened by the need to strengthen the Banyas garrison from his own forces. His army camped overnight by a lake. They were careless in their disposition, says William of Tyre, not paying any attention to the precautions and camp regulations which military discipline demanded. Worse still, some of the nobles such as Philip of Nablus had already parted company with the king's host. The Muslims capitalised on the mistake and set themselves in ambush at Jacob's Ford awaiting the crossing of the Jordan by the Christian army. On 18 June Baldwin's army was pounced upon, still unprepared. Knights could not form up quickly enough as the enemy set about them, fighting in loose pockets here and there. Whilst the Muslims were cutting down Frankish knights, thinking they had even slaughtered the king himself, Baldwin managed to escape to a hill and then fled to the castle at Safad. But behind him he had left a disastrous scene. Five days later, the Muslims paraded their prisoners in Damascus. Amongst them were Odo of Saint-Amand, now the King's Marshal but later to be a Grand Master of the Templars, and Bertrand of Blancfort. Odo would be released in March 1159, but Bertrand only obtained his freedom at the end of May 1159 thanks to the Byzantine Emperor Manuel striking a deal with Nur ed-Din for the release of prisoners. It is perhaps surprising that a royal army with a Templar contingent could have left itself so open to attack in a dangerous landscape. Soon, perhaps partly as a result of Bertrand's grim experience, the Templars would add the Hierarchical Statutes to their Rule (between the years 1165–87), part of which set down the disciplines for camping and marching (see pp. 163–70).

It is not known how the Templars reacted to the incarceration of their Grand Master between 1157 and 1159. When Baldwin won a vital battle against Nur ed-Din at Butaiha in 1158 it seems unlikely there was no Templar contingent. When Baldwin III died on 10 February 1162 and was succeeded eight days later as king by his younger brother Amalric, the Count of Jaffa and inheritor of Ascalon, the race to control a rapidly declining Egyptian Caliphate became paramount. Here again the Templars would play their part.

Amalric's early reign was characterised by a friendly policy towards the Byzantine Emperor. Such an approach would leave him able to concentrate Frankish resources to the south. By 1163 the situation in Egypt was in political melt-down. In 1160 Baldwin III had been promised a yearly tribute of 160,000 dinars by the Egyptians but it had never materialised. In September 1163 Amalric took this non-payment as the cue to act. In Egypt a new vizier, the former governor of Upper Egypt named Shawar, had risen against a background of intrigue and murder. He was now ousted by his Arab chamberlain Dhirgham, who began a reign of terror against all opponents which left his army short of senior officials, who had been caught in the bloodbath. Amalric invaded Egypt with an army which laid siege to Pelusium, but the Nile was in flood and Dhirgham broke some dykes to force the Christians into retreat. Whilst this was happening Nur ed-Din had seized an opportunity to attack the County of Tripoli. William of Tyre, however, says he was careless in the area and fell prey to some quick-thinking Templar response. There followed an action involving the forces of Hugh, Count of Lusignan and Geoffrey Martel who were both returning with their retinues from pilgrimage. They were en route to Antioch under the escort of the Templars led by the renowned former Anglo-Norman warrior Gilbert de Lacy, who had joined the order late in his career and brought with him, as many other

Templars did, a great deal of experience. The encounter is described as being a surprise attack on Nur ed-Din and his forces which resulted in him fleeing barefoot from the battle and even abandoning his baggage and his sword. Many people attribute the depictions of mounted knights charging and marching to war on the murals of the Templar chapel at Cressac as a memorial to this Templar inspired victory (Fig. 5, p. 166 and Fig. 9, p. 178).

After cooling his heels for a while Nur ed-Din received an unexpected visitor from Egypt. It was the ousted Shawar. The deposed vizier offered numerous favourable terms to Nur ed-Din if he would bring an army to Egypt to overthrow Dhirgham. By April 1164 Nur ed-Din had finally made up his mind. He sent an army commanded by his trusted general Shirkuh to Egypt. With Shirkuh was his 27-year-old nephew, a Kurd named Salah ad-Din Yusuf ibn Ayyub, whose ultimate impact on the warfare and politics of the era was nothing short of seismic. To the men of the West, he simply became known as Saladin.

Shirkuh and Saladin were at Pelusium and had defeated Dhirgham's brother before Amalric could answer Dhirgham's call for help, made with the knowledge of such a huge force approaching. Although he successfully defeated his enemy once, Dhirgham was soon killed by an arrow from one of his own men. By May 1164 Shawar was back in power. Predictably, Shawar renounced his Syrian alliance. He no longer wanted Shirkuh in his lands. Shirkuh had seized Bilbeis and Shawar sent to Amalric for help, offering huge inducements of money and further presents for the horses of the military orders who were with him. Amalric gathered an army which included a large Templar contingent and marched to Faqus on the Nile where he met up with Shawar. They marched together on Bilbeis and besieged Shirkuh there. For three months the fortification held out. Then, Amalric decided to raise the siege because Nur ed-Din had taken advantage of his absence in the north by attacking Antioch and besieging Harenc (Harim).

The reason for Amalric's distraction was also a heavy blow to the Temple. Many Templars were with the king in Egypt, but some were not. Nur ed-Din's invasion had prompted an alliance against him which included the Lord of Harenc, Reynald of Saint-Valery, Hugh of Lusignan, Raymond of Tripoli, Thoros of Armenia and the Byzantine general Constantine Coloman. Taking the lead as the Muslims began to retreat was Bohemond III, the Prince of Antioch with 600 knights. On 10 August 1164 Bohemond caught up with Nur ed-Din's forces at Artah and ignoring the advice of Thoros attacked headlong charging straight into an ambush brought about by the use of a feigned flight. It was a disaster. The Muslim army of Mosul surrounded the smaller crusader army. Bohemond, Raymond of Tripoli, Constantine Coloman and Hugh of Lusignan were captured and taken to Aleppo where Constantine Coloman was almost immediately ransomed. Thoros and his brother Mleh (a man who had taken Templar vows but would abandon Christianity altogether) managed to escape. In a letter to King Louis VII of France, Geoffrey Fulcher, Preceptor of the Temple, explained to the French king what had happened:

He [Nur ed-Din] assembled a countless multitude and started to besiege the town of Harenc in the territory of Antioch. When this came to the notice of our Prince Bohemond, a young man of good character, who took after his famous father in every respect, he did not hesitate to confront such a horde. Despite attacking them with the vigour of his father he was overcome and taken prisoner . . .

The rest of the army was almost entirely slaughtered or taken prisoner, despite its formidable size. Sixty of the brotherhood's bravest knights fell beneath the sword as well as client brothers and turcopoles, and only a mere seven avoided death.

Geoffrey goes on to mention to Louis VII that Amalric had gone to Egypt with 'the rest of our brothers' and warns that the remnants of Christendom may be destroyed. He also hints that Bertrand of Blancfort was with Amalric, as he gives Louis the starkest of warnings: 'Do not expect any other messengers from here because in the absence of the king and the master, we do not dare send any fighting man in these difficult circumstances.'

In Egypt, it had become impossible for Amalric to stay. He raised the siege of Bilbeis on the condition that Shirkuh evacuated Egypt. Shirkuh agreed to this and the two armies marched parallel to each other across the Sinai, leaving Shawar in control of his domain. Amalric came to Tripoli and later to Antioch. Bohemond was at last ransomed and Antioch did not fall. Amalric and the Templars would return again to Egypt, but for a while the focus of attention was once again on the Outremer states. Nur ed-Din had not attacked the vulnerable Antioch but instead in October 1164 had switched to besieging Banyas whose lord Humphrey II of Toron was absent with the king. The fortification did indeed fall to Nur ed-Din, prompting another Templar letter, this time from the Grand Master Bertrand of Blancfort to King Louis VII of France telling him of the development. But the dire warnings of these Templar letters would not lead to immediate disaster in the East, although the tone of Geoffrey Fulcher's letter perhaps shows well the pressure on resources under which the order operated.

William of Tyre includes a curious episode at around this time involving a serious falling out between the Templars and the king, although according to some its appearance in his great work may be a later insertion. In a passage which is only vaguely dated and in which the locations are no less ambiguous William tells of some 'impregnable' caves taken by Shirkuh, one being the cave of Tyre near Sidon and the other 'lying beyond Jordan on the borders of Arabia'. Both these places fell through the 'treachery' of the garrisons. The latter was apparently surrendered to Shirkuh by the Templars in whose care it had been placed. Amalric had heard the fortified cave was under threat and had headed out with a company of knights to relieve the garrison only to be told when he was encamped beyond the Jordan that it had already fallen to the enemy. The king was furious and William of Tyre says that he 'caused about twelve of the Templars responsible for the surrender to be hanged from a gallows'. It has been speculated that there is probably a compelling reason for the king's anger. It concerns the strategic value of the land around which the cave was situated, and the king's keen interest in it. Philip of Milly, Lord of Nablus had joined the Templars in January 1166. The king had approved a grant of a good part of Philip's fief of Oultrejordain (lands 'beyond' or 'over' the Jordan) to the Templars on or around the occasion of his joining, as Philip had necessarily donated his wealth to the order. It is possible that the cave fortress was part of this. A specific grant of the castle of Ahamant (probably Amman) 'with all its territory and half of all that Philip of Nablus held in Buqaia on the day he joined the house of the Temple' still exists and it is dated to 17 January 1166. The Templars were to hold the lands under the same conditions that their new brother had held them. Ahamant was one of several Frankish fortifications beyond the Jordan which included Kerak, Montréal and 'Ain Mousa (near Petra), all to the south. It was in frontier territory. The loss of the mysterious cave fortress, probably in late 1166, so soon after its transferral to the Templars will have irked the king and was probably compounded by the fact that the area around it contained iron mines, sugar cane plantations, wheat and cereals and production centres for olive oil, not to mention the caravans which passed through. A tentative identification of the cave has been suggested. Beha ed-Din, Saladin's biographer, calls it Akaf, which may be identical with the grotto of Kaf, south-east of Amman. However, there are no medieval remains at this predominantly Roman period site. The episode remains enigmatic.

Towards the end of 1166 Shirkuh persuaded Nur ed-Din to turn Syrian attentions once more to Egypt. Nur ed-Din this time supplied numerous troops from Aleppo and Shirkuh – along with Saladin – set out from Damascus in January 1167. To Shawar it was obvious what the intentions were, so he sent again for Amalric. At Nablus the king convened a council of his barons and a full-scale expedition was announced to save Shawar from being overwhelmed by the forces of Shirkuh and Saladin. But Shirkuh had stolen a march on the Franks. He was already in Sinai and Amalric's cavalry detachment sent in haste to find Shirkuh reported no success. Shirkuh, suffering sandstorms and other difficulties, reached the Nile at Atfih and travelled along the West Bank to Giza where he set up camp. Amalric for his part had set out on 30 January 1167, using forced marches to get to Egypt. He arrived in the Nile Delta from the north-east and was escorted to a camp on the east bank of the Nile by Shawar himself, whose initial fear and reluctance was replaced by a warm sense of relief at the arrival of a large Christian force. Here, Shawar made a pact with Amalric, having already refused the offer from Shirkuh of an alliance against the Christians. The Franks would receive 400,000 besants, half to be paid immediately and the other half to be paid on the promise that the king's army would not leave Egypt until Shirkuh had been driven out. In order to confirm this treaty Hugh, Lord of Caesarea and the Templar Geoffrey Fulcher were sent into Cairo, their purpose to gain the Caliph's personal endorsement of the arrangement. It was a surreal journey through mysterious alleys and corridors for Geoffrey and his companion. Through throngs of chanting, armed Ethiopians they walked. Beneath gilded ceilings and above stone floors, across open courtyards they paced to meet with the Caliph, in awe of the sheer magnificence of their surroundings. The place resounded with the sounds of fountains and the noise of the exotic animals in the menageries. It shone with silk and golden wall hangings. Behind one golden curtain sat the young Caliph Adid. Geoffrey Fulcher was witness to the extraordinary diplomatic drama which unfolded. Hugh required of the Caliph a bare handshake, which was essential to the ratification of their deal. Although the young Caliph was agreeable to the terms of the treaty, he was reluctant to shake the hand of the Frankish lord. His courtiers were quite horrified that Hugh should even speak to their Caliph let alone demand a handshake. But eventually with a nervous smile the Caliph offered his ungloved hand and the deal was confirmed.

Geoffrey Fulcher and Hugh, Lord of Caesarea retired to their own army. Their experience had been an education. Their arrangement with the Caliph had been remarkably successful. The exact nature of Geoffrey's contribution is unknown, but as a representative of both the king and the Order of the Temple he was clearly a highly important player, and the agreement he managed to broker carried much weight with the Templars.

A month of stalemate between the Franks and Shirkuh followed. But then, after a failed bridge-building exercise, Amalric made a move. He sent a unit to attack one of Shirkuh's attachments on an island in the delta. As a result, 500 men perished in the waters around the island and after he learned of his men's fate, it was all Shirkuh could do to effect an escape to the south, up river, whilst Amalric's force was hindered by a whirlwind. Amalric and Shawar soon followed the enemy but Amalric arranged for Shawar's son Kamil and Hugh of Ibelin to lead a garrison force into Cairo to protect mutual Egyptian and Frankish interest there. It was an uncomfortable moment for many Egyptian warriors as Hugh's Franks became increasingly familiar with the innermost courtyards and sanctuaries in what was a hallowed area of the palace. Christians had not been so numerous in Cairo for many centuries. But the needs were great. Shirkuh was still a threat.

William of Tyre records that he had heard that Amalric's army only had 374 knights in addition to its more numerous Egyptian allies and an unknown number of turcopoles. Somewhere in this army, although William does not record it, were the Templars. What William does record, however, is that Philip of Nablus had joined the army along with Humphrey of Toron during the period of the stalemate. He went on to say that the 'effeminate' Egyptians and the supporting turcopoles did little good in the encounter which was now to occur. Shirkuh's forces were well armed and armoured. He had 12,000 Turks and 10,000 or 11,000 Arabs. They had camped at Ashmunein amidst the ruins of ancient Hermopolis, intending to cross the Nile and head north again. On seeing the Frankish army, Shirkuh decided to give battle. He had been persuaded to do this by Saladin. Amalric for his part, had been visited by a vision of St Bernard of Clairvaux who had given him great encouragement. What followed, on the morning of 18 March 1167, was confusion in the dusty desert landscape. The uneven ground was broken by hills of sand and depressions, making visibility difficult. The forces formed up in their 'battalions', says William, at Beben, which means 'the gates' (due to the closeness of the surrounding hills providing a gateway through the topography). This place was 10 miles from Lamonia.

Shirkuh had seized the sandy hills either side of the gateway. The Franks found it difficult because of the soft ground to advance against these positions. The central Frankish command thus advanced directly against Shirkuh's division and put it to flight, including Shirkuh himself. Less fortunate though was Hugh, Lord of Caesarea whose command fragmented on contact with Saladin's force. Hugh was subsequently cut off and taken prisoner by Saladin along with many others. The remainder fell on the field. The flanking Turks on the higher ground were now free to come down and surround the Frankish baggage train, taking all they could and putting the guards to flight. All of this had been achieved in a maelstrom of sand and dust. 'The only witnesses', says William, 'were the fighters themselves, for no one else could see it'. The battle, he says, was indecisive. But in reality, Shirkuh would have been more pleased with the result. Unopposed, he took his recovered forces to Alexandria and successfully besieged the place. Amalric, however, retreated first to Lamonia where he picked up reinforcements and then returned to Cairo. When he counted his men he found himself short of a hundred knights.

Amalric and Shawar regrouped once again. They took their force to Alexandria and blockaded it, cutting off its vital supplies coming from Upper Egypt via the Nile. A Pisan fleet had been requisitioned to assist the crusaders. For a month it continued, the bread running low inside Alexandria. To the annoyance of Amalric, Shirkuh decided to escape with his own contingent up river, slipping past the Franks to do so. He left Saladin behind with around 1,000 men. He was briefly pursued, but Amalric was persuaded to concentrate his efforts on Alexandria. Saladin's situation had become increasingly desperate and he had even called for Shirkuh's return. But Shirkuh himself had realised that the campaign had reached stalemate. As he returned to approach Alexandria he requested Hugh of Caesarea (now his prisoner) to carry a message of peace to Amalric. Hugh refused, mindful that he might be perceived as simply wanting his liberty above all else. Instead, Arnulf of Turbessel, another prisoner who was also captured at Ashmunein, was put forward for the job. The suggestion which Arnulf carried from Shirkuh to Amalric was that they should both evacuate Egypt, Franks and Turks alike. The Alexandrians were not to be punished for initially siding with the Turks, although in the aftermath of the agreement, this is what happened. The prisoners could also be exchanged. The arrangement suited Amalric, who could thus walk into Alexandria as Saladin parted from it, secure in the knowledge that when he himself left Egypt, he would not be in breach of the original agreement with the Caliphate which brought so much money with it. Ibn al-Athir says at this point the Franks paid the Turks 50,000 dinars and also promised to leave the country. He also says that they installed a Frankish garrison to prevent Nur ed-Din from one day attempting to recover the city. The Franks he said received 100,000 dinars from the Egyptians as well.

On 4 August 1167 Saladin was escorted out of Alexandria with great pomp and respect. He had even been given a guard during his time with the Frankish camp whilst the negotiations were taking place, and it was here that his reputation as a noble warrior amongst the Franks was fostered. He seemed to them to be much like themselves in outlook. Amalric entered Alexandria and raised his banner high above the Pharos, the famous lighthouse. He had then gone back to Cairo where the financial side of things was agreed with the Egyptians and a small Frankish garrison was left in the city. Around 10 August 1167 Shirkuh and Saladin left for Damascus, where they arrived in early September. By 20 August the king was back at Ascalon, a city whose capture had made the Egyptian campaign possible.

Although the 1167 campaign in Egypt had been something of a score-draw, there were some reasons for the Franks and indeed the Templars to be cheerful. The negotiations made in the sweltering courtyards of Cairo's royal palaces had brought valuable income into the royal coffers. But there would soon come another controversial episode between the king and the Order of the Temple in which William of Tyre for once sympathised with the Templars. The problem centred on Amalric's desire, after encouragement from the Byzantine Emperor, to annex Egypt outright in 1168. Amalric had married the emperor's grand-nice Maria Comnena not long after his return from Egypt in 1167. Also, the Emperor Manuel had demanded a share in the spoils of the Egyptian enterprise as well as an increasing control over Antioch where the Byzantines had slowly been acquiring power for a number of years. William of Tyre was sent in person to Constantinople to speak with the emperor. Eventually, he returned in the autumn of 1168 carrying news that the emperor wished to divide their conquests in Egypt. But the Frankish nobility had not waited for them. Egypt was once again vulnerable and the Franks knew it. When he wrote about it later, William of Tyre seems less than comfortable with the new Egyptian policy.

According to William of Tyre, Sultan Shawar was said to have been soliciting help from Nur ed-Din and wished to break his treaty with the Franks. There are hints from elsewhere that the sultan's son Kamil was behind the negotiations with the Turks. But William also says that there were many who said that this was not the case and that Shawar had kept to his side of the agreement and that what happened next was contrary to divine law. As far as the Templars are concerned, we know they were at the king's side at least until May 1168 when Bertrand of Blancfort and Geoffrey Fulcher witnessed a royal grant to the Pisans at Acre given in return for their help in the Egyptian campaign of 1167. But in the summer Count William IV of Nevers arrived in Outremer with a large army and this may have swayed the Frankish nobility. This new aggressive policy adopted in the autumn of 1168 troubled William of Tyre as it did the Templars. Gilbert of Assailly, the Grand Master of the Hospitallers, was a man heavily in debt. It was he who was the 'prime-mover' of the campaign, says William. He had spent money on men and arms to support an arrangement with Amalric that if Egypt should fall, ancient Pelusium should become the property of the Hospital. William says that the Templars refused to take part in the campaign or to follow the king or to supply troops. This was because the arrangement either seemed unfaithful, or because it had been championed by a rival house.

All this politicking had taken place at a council convened by the king in Jerusalem. The Hospitaller argument that swift action should be taken against Egypt won the day despite the fact that the king may well have been waiting for Byzantine help. So, backed by a new influx of crusading knights from the Count of Nevers, the Frankish army set out from Ascalon on 20 October, arriving at Bilbeis ten days later. But there are problems with William of Tyre's account of Templars refusing to take part. The great historian, by his own admission, had not been present when it was all discussed. First, there are good reasons for Templar dissention. Clearly, the Templars would have been slighted by Gilbert of Assailly's galloping enthusiasm for the venture. They would also have reminded the council that the agreement secured with Shawar in 1167 had been masterminded by Geoffrey Fulcher and backed by the Temple and the king himself. There may have been another area of concern for the Templars and this was not Egypt at all. It could well have been the desire to keep up the protection of northern Outremer, an effort which had recently cost the stretched Templars so many men and horses. But are all these reasons for Templar disapproval enough to suggest that they simply refused to go on the 1168 Egyptian campaign? One school of thought which is drawn from an account of the 1168 campaign by Lambert of Wattrelos suggests that the two orders – the Hospital and Temple – did in fact lead separate contingents on the campaign. Its author stresses how he had heard about the campaign from 'true speaking men'. This account raises the possibility that the Templars, or at least a number of them, did participate after all.

Shawar sent out an ambassador to Amalric at Daron on the Egyptian frontier, but he was bribed. Another ambassador caught up with the Franks not far from Bilbeis. He chastised the king for his perfidy. The king demanded 2 million dinars from Egypt. Not surprisingly, Shawar decided to resist the Christians on this occasion. But by 4 November 1168 Bilbeis had fallen to the Franks and a gruesome massacre ensued, with members of the local Coptic Christian population amongst the victims. The same community suffered once again at the hands of a Christian fleet at Tanis and it seemed the anger of all Egypt (both Muslim and Christian communities) was directed at the Franks. When Amalric finally approached Cairo, an angry Shawar burned its suburbs rather than surrender. For eight days there was a delay when suddenly Shirkuh and Saladin once again appeared in Egypt solicited by Shawar's son and hugely reinforced by Nur ed-Din. Amalric failed to halt the Turks as they emerged from the desert and he allowed them to slip past him. He realised then that he had no choice but to retreat out of Egypt, a process he began on 2 January 1169. Shirkuh and Saladin entered Cairo just days later. Negotiations began as to how Egypt would be parcelled out. After some time, Shawar was seized by Saladin and Shirkuh had him decapitated. Shirkuh took over the Egyptian government and took the title of vizier and king. It was still only late January 1169. Crucially, Shirkuh, now master of Egypt, died on 23 March 1169. Saladin, with the Caliph's approval, inherited his titles and his sweeping powers.

With Egypt secured for the forces of Nur ed-Din, the Franks now knew their states were encircled by land and sea. William of Tyre mentions the potential impact upon Outremer's coastal ports and the impact on the free flow of pilgrims to the Holy Land and recalls the desperate embassies sent out to the West seeking aid, all to no avail. Amalric did try again (with Byzantine help) to recover Egypt in 1169, possibly with Templar assistance, but it again came to no good result. Supply problems and heavy rains saw the expedition end in December 1169 with the burning of siege engines around Damietta and a return once again to Ascalon. Then the recriminations began. The Hospitaller Grand Master resigned his post. The Franks and the Byzantines blamed one another for the failures in Egypt. But throughout these months as the Franks looked inward upon themselves, Saladin grew more secure in his seat every day.

Chapter 10

The Assassins

Bertrand of Blancfort died in January 1169. He was succeeded as Grand Master by Philip of Nablus, a man who had been born in Outremer. Philip was in position by August 1169. He was a very capable military man and had been on campaign in Egypt. It seems likely that he was supportive of the king's Egyptian policies despite the debacle of 1168 and it also seems certain that his appointment as Grand Master of the Templars had royal pressure behind it. The Templars soon saw military action once again when in December 1170 Saladin, with an Egyptian army appeared at Daron, the Frankish coastal fortress in the extreme south of Outremer, about 4 miles from Gaza. He was intent, says William of Tyre, to lay waste the land of Palestine. Amalric, alarmed at the appearance of such a force, went with the Patriarch and a small mounted force of 250 knights, a fragment of the True Cross, and about 2,000 infantry, to Ascalon, where he arrived on 18 December. He then moved on to the fortress at Gaza where he acquired some of Philip's Templars. He left Miles of Plancy in charge of the castle. Amalric and the Templars marched on Daron and resisted an assault by the Egyptian army thanks to an unusual density of formation, according to William of Tyre. Having temporarily relieved the pressure the king's army set up camp at Daron. There were several individual and group combats during the day, but then Saladin raised the siege of Daron and instead marched upon Gaza. The lower part of the township around Gaza still had many citizens in it at the time of the Egyptian assault. Miles of Plancy, whom William of Tyre elsewhere in his history says was a degenerate and shameful brawler and troublemaker, had not secured their protection inside the citadel, but instead had encouraged these poorly armed farmers to fight. They were surprised and cut down outside, some sixty-five youthful men from Mahumaria near Jerusalem were amongst the casualties. But then Saladin, who knew he could not take the citadel itself, retreated and sent his forces elsewhere to campaign around the head of the Gulf of Aqaba.

For Philip of Nablus, there would not be much more campaigning. Early in 1171 he led an embassy to Constantinople, resigning his post in order to do so. By April he was dead. His replacement as Grand Master, again due to royal pressure, was Odo of Saint-Amand, the former king's marshal who had suffered imprisonment at the hands of the Muslims in the late 1150s (see p. 43). Odo had also been castellan of Jerusalem and a butler under both Baldwin III and Amalric. He had performed diplomatic missions for the king. But if this level of royal involvement in appointing

3. The Castle at Masyaf in the Jebel al-Sariya, the main castle of the Assassins under the Old Man of the Mountain. The Assassins' main strategy of murdering the leaders of their enemies was of no use against the Templars, whom they knew would simply replace their dead with the same kind.

Templar Grand Masters was designed to reap rewards for the king, he was to be sorely disappointed. Trouble between the Order of the Temple and the King of Jerusalem flared up once again in a dramatic way over the matter of the terrible fate of an Assassin envoy.

The Assassins, whom we have previously encountered (see pp. 22, 35), had been relatively quiet in recent years. A sect shrouded in mystery and legend, these Nizari Ismailis represented a branch of Shia Islam. In its adherence to the line descended from Ali, Muhammad's cousin, and through other practices, the sect was a natural enemy of Sunni Muslims who recognised Abu Bakr, an early Muslim convert, as the Prophet's true successor. Because of their geographical location their fear of Sunni Islam had become all the more acute during the rise to Power of Nur ed-Din and the fall of Christian Edessa in 1144. By the 1170s the sect will also have been aware, after the death of the last Fatimid Caliph in Egypt in 1171 and the rise of Saladin, of the dangers to their own branch of Islam from the Sunni world.

The Assassins had established themselves in the fortress at Alamut in Persia in the late eleventh century, but by the 1170s they had numerous strongholds in the coastal mountains of the Jebel al-Sariya and found themselves bounded by the great Templar and Hospitaller strongholds of Tortosa, Chastel Blanc, Margat and Crac des Chevaliers. Their sometimes accommodating and conciliatory approach towards relations with the Christians might be partially explained by this geography. From these mountain strongholds of which Masyaf was the main headquarters Rashid al-Din Sinan had led this branch of the movement since the 1160s. This mysterious man was known to the Franks as 'The Old Man of the Mountain'. His Assassins are thought by some to have taken their name from the word Hashishiyun, meaning 'those who consume Hashish', although the drug was supposedly given only to the self-sacrificing agents of death, the fida'is, whose missions usually resulted in their own death after performing very public murders – always with a knife – having infiltrated enemy strongholds. Others have argued that the drug-taking element is something of a misnomer and that an alternative explanation for the name 'Assassin' exists, being based upon their founder Hassan Ibn Sabbah's naming of his disciples as Asasiyun, meaning people who are faithful to the asas, or foundation of the faith. However, the drug-taking story seems to have survived at least until the time of the medieval explorer Marco Polo (c.1254–1324) who recalls it in his own writings.

The Assassins adopted a policy of tyrant elimination. This approach drew from a religious belief that one day 'the guided one' would appear and overthrow the tyrants ranged against them. There was always a forward-looking messianic element to their beliefs. In a way, these political killings, aimed at the enemy's tyrannical leadership, made up for their small numbers and inability to put large conventional armies into the field. Their victims were mainly Muslims, although they did in 1152 murder Count Raymond II of Tripoli (1137–52) after which they found themselves paying an annual tribute of 2,000 besants to the Templars. It was this tribute money which seemed to play an important part in the events of 1173.

William of Tyre explains the impact of what happened. It was 'a dreadful affair fraught with dire consequences to the kingdom and the church'. At this time the Assassins appointed an 'eloquent man' with a 'very sharp brain' to rule them. This man began to collect the Gospel books and the records of the apostolic law. He studied them and compared what he found to things 'he had drunk in with his mother's milk' and decided to renounce Islam. He tore down Islamic places of prayer and permitted the drinking of wine and eating of pork. But after some time, wishing to gain a greater understanding of the Christian religion, he sent one of his own wise men called Abdullah to King Amalric. This man carried secret propositions, says William. Chief amongst these was that if the Templars, who had castles adjacent to Assassins' territory, were willing to forego the annual payment to them of 2,000 besants, and would 'observe brotherly kindness toward them' then the Assassins would embrace the faith of Christ and receive baptism.

The king, says William, was happy to receive the embassy and grant him his requests. 'He was even prepared, it is said, to compensate the brethren from his own treasury for the two thousand gold pieces, the amount of the annual tribute which the Assassins asked to have remitted.' Amalric then sent Abdullah back to his master to finalise the arrangement. Abdullah was given a guide and bodyguard to go with him. The Assassin envoy was therefore under royal protection. But when the party had passed Tripoli and was about to enter its own land 'suddenly some of the Knights of the Temple rushed upon the party with drawn swords and killed the envoy'. Because the envoy had been travelling under the royal promise of safe conduct the Templars brought upon themselves the charge of treason. The king was furious. Summoning his barons he told them of how he perceived this to be an insult to his authority. It was decided to send two noblemen, Seiher of Mamedum and Godechaux of Turholt, to demand from Odo of Saint-Amand, the Templar Grand Master, that satisfaction be paid to the king for such a sacrilegious act. Undeserved infamy, says William, had been brought upon Christianity. It had been a one-eyed man, a Templar called Walter of Mesnil, who had committed the crime with the knowledge of his brothers. This 'worthless man', as William calls him, was protected by Odo more than he deserved. Odo sent a message to Amalric stating that he (Odo) had given Walter a penance and was in the process of sending him to Rome to answer to the Pope. Because of this, argued Odo, in the Pope's name, nobody was to lay violent hands on Walter. The letter contained other incendiary words which did nothing to placate the king.

Amalric travelled quickly to Sidon where he knew the Templar chapter to be. There he found Odo and Walter. He had Walter dragged unceremoniously from the house and sent him in chains to Tyre to be incarcerated. Somehow, and with great diplomatic difficulty, the king was able to explain to the Assassins that Jerusalem had played no part in the murder of the envoy. Curiously, in dealing with the Templars Amalric, according to William of Tyre, left the matter in abeyance right up until his death. This man, who had hanged Templars from the gallows for less (see p. 45), was apparently hatching a plan. William of Tyre, deeply suspicious of the Temple, puts it this way: 'It is said, however, that if he had recovered from that last illness [the king died of dysentery on 1 July 1174 not long after the passing of Nur ed-Din], Amalric had intended to take up the matter with the kings and princes of the earth, through envoys of high degree, when it would have been given most careful consideration.' But such a royal assault on the privileges and perceived arrogance of the Templars was a matter for the distant future. As for the murder of the Assassin envoy, Walter Map, writing in 1182, is less than forgiving. He says that the Old Man of the Mountain had asked the Patriarch of Jerusalem for a copy of the gospels. This was sent to him along with a man who could make sense of them. The man and the gospels were equally well received and the Assassin leader duly despatched 'an eminent respectable pagan' to the Patriarch to bring back priests and deacons who would be able to baptise them and give them the sacraments. But the pagan was ambushed en route 'by the Templars of the city' and killed. The Old Man, on hearing of the event, put a stop to his Christian devotion. The Patriarch and the king could not exact revenge on the Templars because Rome was in the ascendancy over the Patriarch and the king, says Map. He also says this deed was done 'so that peace and harmony would not come about through the disappearance of the Muslim religion, for they say that Assassins are the prime movers of the Muslims' lack of Christian religious beliefs'.

Here then, is a hint of an alternative motive. Map does not mention the tribute money. Map's Templars do not want peace to break out, because the Templars, who existed for warfare, feared peace. But it is possible that the Templars did not trust the

Assassins and their promises to convert to Christianity. If Amalric really had offered the Temple recompense for the loss of the annual tribute money, then their motive for carrying out the deed would seem weak. The Old Man's swift reversal of policy after hearing of the murder of his envoy might tend to support the Templars' wariness. It seems the Templars had a wider goal in mind. It is also worth bearing in mind the fear which the Assassins had of the Templars. The Assassin policy of 'tyrannicide' was hopeless against them. The Assassins knew only too well that a murdered Templar would simply be replaced. So, despite William of Tyre's horror and King Amalric's fury, it is arguable that the ambush of the Assassin envoy was carried out in the best interests of the Christian cause, by a deeply committed brotherhood.

The Assassins were not entertained again by Jerusalem after the death of Amalric. Nor were there overtures coming from the mountains. This is perhaps best explained by the fact that Raymond III, Count of Tripoli (1152–87) after a time became the regent for Baldwin IV, the young leper king and son of Amalric. Raymond's father had been murdered by the Assassins. But the episode of the murder of the Assassin envoy certainly seems to have sewn some discord between the king and the Templars. The Assassins would continue their work until well into the thirteenth century, finally succumbing to Mongol Hordes which swept across the region. So too would the Templars continue their work as they entered a new and dangerous era against the background of the continuing rise of Saladin.

Chapter 11

The Battle of Montgisard, 1177

Odo of Saint-Amand is one of the Templar Grand Masters about whom there is some understanding of his personality. King Amalric had found him to be a surprisingly headstrong defender of the order. Superficially at least, the falling out between Amalric and Odo over the killing of the Assassin envoy had borne some resemblance to the famous dispute in English history which occurred about the same time between King Henry II (1154–89) and his Archbishop of Canterbury Thomas à Becket. But like so many Grand Masters of the Order of the Temple, and most unlike Thomas, Odo was as much a military man as a devout man of the cloth. No doubt hardened by his experience of imprisonment (p. 43), Odo had already demonstrated as the King's Marshal a sound military career based on a role which saw him oversee the logistical needs of the royal army of which the provision of horses, the management of mercenaries and the distribution of spoils were key parts. It had been an office second only to the constable of the kingdom, whose own role was the most important behind the king himself. Odo's forthright and bellicose character did not endear him to William of Tyre, who thought him overly proud and blamed him for causing the death in battle of William's own brother Ralph in what would prove to be one of Odo's final acts in 1179 (see p. 66). The invective is palpable. William calls him 'a wicked man, haughty and arrogant, in whose nostrils dwelt the spirit of fury, one who neither feared God nor revered man'.

Odo, however, was the sort of Templar leader who although he came to the position quite late in his career, was made of exactly the sort of stock which the role required. Much maligned, his memory is tarnished by William of Tyre's understandable prejudice. But Odo was responsible for what would come to be thought of as the Templars' most decisive field action as part of the royal army. It would only be a temporary check on the inexorable rise of Saladin, but it would be one which the great man himself would long remember.

By 1177 the threats to Baldwin IV's kingdom were many. Factional infighting had hardly helped. But Saladin's gains had been impressive and now threatened to envelop Outremer. Towards the end of 1174 he had triumphed over Damascus and only narrowly failed to take Aleppo. Two important prisoners, Reynald of Châtillon and Joscelin III of Edessa (whose ancestral land was no longer in Christian hands), were also released about this time. Both would soon feature again in the politics and warfare of the land. As early as the spring of 1176 Saladin had been confident enough to call himself ruler of both Egypt and Syria. There had been some setbacks along the way for him. For example, he had curiously lost his nerve in the face of an Assassin threat and headed back to Damascus. Also, Count Raymond of Tripoli had raided the Buqaia and fought Saladin's governor of Baalbek after which Baldwin IV and the royal army joined him to defeat Saladin's brother Turan Shah and the Damascene garrison. By September 1176 Saladin himself was back in Egypt.

It would be a year before Saladin took his chance. The Byzantines had been greatly weakened by a military disaster at the Battle of Myriocephalum in September 1176, although they still had a fleet to threaten Egypt with. But it was the arrival in the Holy Land of Philip, Count of Flanders which would present Saladin with an opportunity. The baronage had high hopes of Philip spearheading a campaign against Egypt but Philip hesitated and stated that he had really only come for the pilgrimage and to marry-off his two cousins. After a very public falling out with the baronage during which Baldwin of Ibelin chastised the count, Philip left Jerusalem for Tripoli and an expectant Byzantine fleet sailed home disappointed. But Philip did agree to assist Count Raymond in an expedition against Hama, and crucially the young King Baldwin IV provided a hundred royal troops to assist. So too did the Hospitallers and a 'large number' of Templars. The campaigns in the north were ponderous and inconclusive, but they had the effect of tying up some valuable crusader resources in both the secular armies and the military orders. The siege of Hama was eventually raised and Philip and Raymond then joined with Bohemond of Antioch to attack Harenc (Harim).

Saladin moved into northern Sinai with a large army, arriving at a deserted Al-Arish. Here, he left part of his 'heavy baggage', according to William of Tyre, and some garrison troops and moved on with 'the lighter armed troops and the more experienced fighters' to take his army around the Frankish forts of Daron and Gaza arriving suddenly near Ascalon. William of Tyre claims to have researched the numbers involved. He concluded that the invading army consisted of 26,000 light armed cavalry in addition to those mounted on beasts of burden. Of these 8,000 were Toassin warriors (heavy Turkic cavalry recruited as Mamelukes) and the other 18,000 were heavy cavalry lancers from North Africa. Around Saladin himself, he says, there were elite Mameluke bodyguard warriors dressed in yellow robes over their armour ready to fight to the last.

King Baldwin had received intelligence of Saladin's movements and with what forces he had at his disposal had already strengthened Ascalon, although some of Baldwin's first responders to his call-out had been taken prisoner by Saladin. Those Templars who had not gone north had been redirected to Gaza where they expected Saladin's blow to fall. The king marched out from Ascalon to face Saladin's force as he was angered by the ravaging on his own doorstep. But the opposition was a far larger force than Baldwin's and his advisors recommended caution. There was an uncomfortable stand off during which some individual combats took place but by nightfall the Christians retired to the city once more. This had the effect of imbuing Saladin and his forces with great confidence, thinking that Baldwin was no longer a threat. Consequently, the Muslims wandered about the land and were no longer in any sort of battle array. Saladin headed out towards Jerusalem and thus cut the Frankish communication lines between the city and the coast. One of his men, a Mameluke called Jevelino, had ridden as far as the deserted Ramla and burnt it. He also attacked Lydda (Lod) whose citizens fled into a church. The whole plain was awash with enemy troops, deep in the heart of the Kingdom of Jerusalem. The citizens of Jerusalem had retired to the citadel of David in fear. It was too much for Baldwin, who sent to Gaza for Templar help. Together the king and his small army took the northern coastal path intent on arriving at Ibelin and swinging round and coming on the enemy in the plains from the north, hoping to catch Saladin unaware. On St Catherine's Day, 25 November 1177, Saladin's forces were crossing a ravine to the south-east of Ramla when the Franks and the Templars came onto them.

There is little recorded in the sources of the tactical dispositions. It is not entirely clear where the Battle of Montgisard took place. The hill of Montgisard is sometimes identified with Tel Gezer, about 5 miles south-east of Ramla. This place seems the most likely site given the proximity of Ramla, Lydda and Jerusalem and the obvious intent of Saladin's army. Ibn al-Athir places the battle near Ramla without being specific and also says that Saladin's baggage train was mired. We might assume that Imad ad-Din al Isfahani's (Saladin's secretary) Tell es-Safiya (the Frankish castle at Blanchegarde) is a little off the mark, being about 22 miles to the east of Ascalon and about 22 miles to the south of Ramla. What all the sources agree upon is that surprise was achieved by the Franks. It is possible that Baldwin and the Templars, by shadowing the enemy on its northern flank, had pressed its superior numbers into a difficult geographical location where its numerical advantage was nullified. Despite the intention of Saladin to advance on Jerusalem, the route through Montgisard was not the ideal choice. It was a constricted place and close to a nearby marsh. Whatever the circumstances of the route taken, it is clear that as the Franks approached the enemy, Saladin and his disparate forces were not expecting them.

With Baldwin was Odo of Saint-Amand and just eighty of his brethren. Also with the king was Reynald of Châtillon, Baldwin and Balian of Ibelin, Reynald of Sidon and Count Joscelin. They numbered only 375 according to William of Tyre. Albert, the Bishop of Bethlehem carried the True Cross into battle. It was the eighth hour of the day. Saladin hurriedly tried to recall many of his men who were away from the camp. The king's army 'drew up their forces in battle array and arranged their lines according to military rules, disposing in proper order those who were to make the first attack and the reserves who were to come to their aid'. Then, William of Tyre simply adds that the battle was at first indecisive until Saladin's lines were broken and he was forced to flee after a 'terrible slaughter'. Ralph of Diss provides further evidence for the Templar contribution, apparently given to him by an eyewitness. Odo of Saint-Amand, he says 'like another Judas Maccabaeus', went into battle:

Spurring all together, as one man, they made a charge, turning neither to the left nor to the right. Recognising the battalion in which Saladin commanded many knights, they manfully approached it, immediately penetrated it, incessantly knocked down, scattered, struck and crushed. Saladin was smitten with admiration, seeing his men dispersed everywhere, everywhere turned in flight, everywhere given to the mouth of the sword. He took thought for his own safety and fled, throwing off his mailshirt for speed, mounted a racing camel and barely escaped with a few of his men.

William of Tyre says that at the beginning of the battle the Franks lost some four or five knights and some foot soldiers. His mention of infantrymen might indicate that numbers were in fact greater on the Frankish side than just the 375 knights. The Egyptians were thoroughly routed and pursued to the nearby swamp. Here, they cast off their armour and arms as many of them were cut down in their attempt to flee. For 12 miles the carnage continued. The ignominy was great for Saladin. Mounted on his camel and surrounded by little more than a hundred men, he headed back to Egypt with his army in disarray all over the landscape. His small force was harassed by Bedouin all the way home. Captives were constantly being brought to the Franks from the forests and mountains to which they had escaped. Baldwin travelled back to Ascalon where after four days he received a huge amount of plunder from his victorious forces.

There can be little doubt that the victory against all odds was an impressive one. For Imad ad-Din Saladin's defeat was 'disastrous' and 'a terrible catastrophe'. But for the Christians it brought relief for Jerusalem and admiration for the young leper king who had just come of age. It also gave rise to great admiration for Odo and the Templars.

Chapter 12

Marj Ayyun and the Siege of Chastellet, 1179

For many months Saladin remained in Egypt and he did not return to Syria until the spring of 1178. Having stabilised his position in Egypt after the potentially dangerous political consequences of Montgisard, he came to Damascus. Within a day's march south-west of Damascus, just 10 miles from Banyas there existed a ford across the Upper Jordan situated between Lake Huleh and the Sea of Galilee. The ford (now the site of the Daughters of Jacob Bridge, but then known as Jacob's Ford) was important for both practical military reasons and for religious ones. It was of equal significance to both Baldwin IV and Saladin. Odo of Saint-Amand knew the area well. He had been taken prisoner around here himself in 1157. This place was 'where Jacob, returning from Mesopotamia divided his people into two bands and sent messengers to his brother . . .', says William of Tyre, quoting from Genesis (32:10).

Saladin and Baldwin had agreed a truce, although by August 1178 this was already being broken by a Frankish army which went to besiege Hama. But according to the chronicler Ernoul, Baldwin agreed on something else: he undertook not to fortify Jacob's Ford. It would appear that this agreement distressed the Templars who campaigned successfully for Baldwin to change his mind. We might well understand the Templars' concerns. This was an era when the military orders were growing in confidence and in their increasing roles as the stalwart defenders of the crusader states. The Templars had great knowledge and experience of the concept of frontier defence and just to the south of the ford stood numerous Templar fortifications and their dependant territories. And here, at Jacob's Ford was a gaping hole in the border defence of the kingdom. Between 1167 and 1168 King Amalric had already granted to the Temple the fortification at Safad, about 9 miles to the south-west. Imad ad-Din calls this place a 'nest of evil', but the Templars were unable to successfully defend the gap in the frontier from a position so deep into the kingdom.

Between October 1178 and March 1179 the Templar castle of Chastellet was built. Although still under construction by March 1179, it was an impressive fortification. Situated on a low hill just north of the ford, Chastellet dominated the crossing point and also the local lands. But this was disputed territory and Saladin, who was preoccupied until the spring of 1179 besieging Baalbek, was aghast when he was told that Chastellet was being constructed in defiance of his agreement with Baldwin IV. William of Tyre describes the castle as a square shape with thick walls of suitable height. Qadi al-Fadil (Saladin's administrator), whose description of it is captured in a letter to Baghdad gathered together with other documents by the later writer Abu Shama, details the castle's imposing structure:

> The width of the wall surpassed ten cubits; it was built of stones of enormous size of which each block was seven cubits more or less; the number of these dressed stones exceeded 20,000, and each stone put in place and sealed into the masonry did not come out at less than four dinars, and even more. Between the two walls extended a line of massive blocks raised up to the proud summit of the mountains. The lime . . . which was poured around the stone in order to seal it was mixed and incorporated into it, giving it a strength and solidity superior to that of the stone itself, and frustrating, with more success than that of metal, all attempts by the enemy to destroy it.

Other sources mention a citadel or tower within the enclosure, or at its western side. Modern archaeological excavations have revealed much about the castle. It was an elongated rectangular shape with an angular curved wall at its northern end. The circumference wall seems to have been fully completed but its parallel inner wall only joined the outer wall by a barrel vault in the south-east section of the castle and it was this area that a huge 5m-diameter baking oven was discovered. The shape and layout is reminiscent of the earlier phases of the great Hospitaller castle at Crac des Chevaliers. But Chastellet was also similar in essence to Kerak, a castle in the south-east of Baldwin's kingdom. Here, we might have the origin of Saladin's fear. Kerak would soon become a huge thorn in the side for Saladin. Writing about the year 1183 and captured in the collection of Abu Shama, Ibn Shaddad said of it, 'This place caused considerable damage to the Muslims because it closed until then the route from Egypt and obliged the caravans to move under the protection of an army corps.' At that time Reynald of Châtillon embraced an aggressive pro-active policy from Kerak. With the Templars installed at Chastellet within just a two-day march of Damascus itself, Saladin must have feared an equally aggressive crusader policy being adopted uncomfortably close to the heart of his power. Moreover, Ibn Abi Tayy, quoted by Abu Shama, specifically stated that the garrison at the Templar castle was furnished with victuals and weapons of all kinds in order that they could pillage Muslim caravans. It is possible that the Templar's lobbying for the building of the castle was at least partially motivated by this economic consideration.

Saladin at first offered Baldwin IV 60,000 dinars to dismantle the castle at Jacob's Ford. Then he increased the offer, reaching the sum of 100,000 dinars, but was refused by the Frankish king. Saladin's nephew, Taqi al-Din, advised him to use

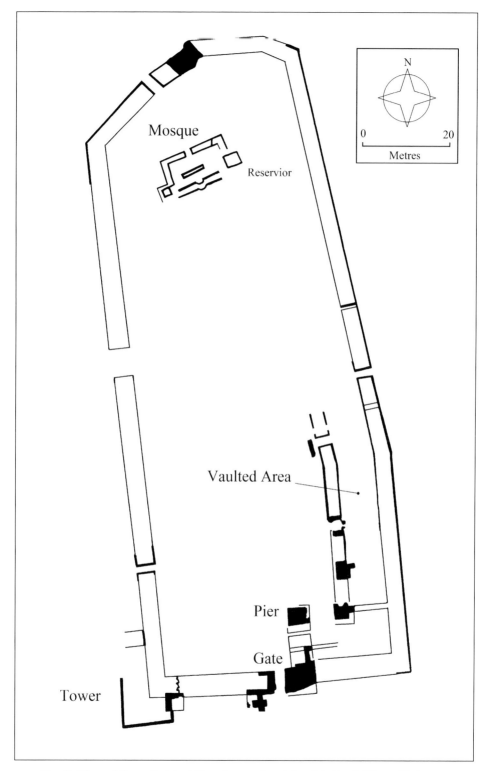

Fig. 2. Plan of the unfinished Templar castle at Jacob's Ford (Chastellet).

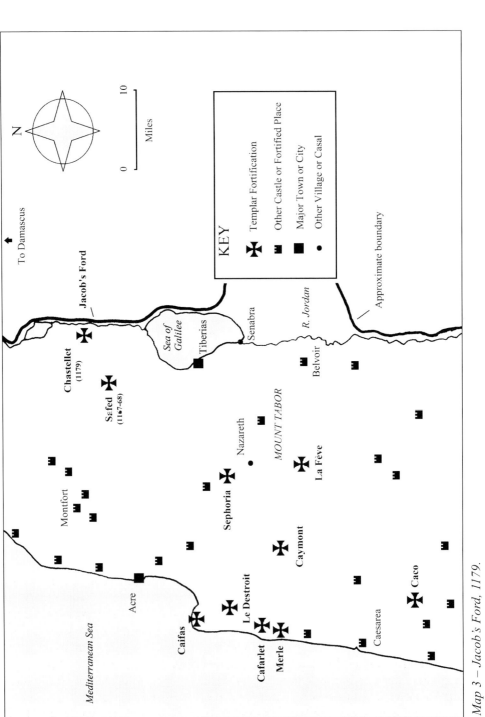

Map 3 – Jacob's Ford, 1179.

the money to equip troops instead. The Templar castle would have to be taken by force if the king would not comply. Campaigning in the area began in April 1179 when Baldwin IV took an army up to the area around the forest of Banyas to capitalise on the seasonal movement of flocks which had come from the plains of Damascus. But Saladin had sent out another of his nephews, Faruk-Shah, who encountered Baldwin on 10 April in a narrow place and ambushed his force. Humphrey of Toron, the widely respected King's Constable since 1151, was mortally wounded in the fight and Baldwin only narrowly managed to escape thanks to Humphrey's heroic holding action in the face of a heavy onslaught. Humphrey was himself recused by his men and taken to Chastellet where he remained for ten days until he died of his wounds. He was taken to his new castle at Hunin and buried with great ceremony. Saladin, as if triggered by the death of such an important elder statesman, now aspired to attack Chastellet, where he arrived in May. His army began its assault on the new fortress with a storm of arrow fire, but one of Saladin's prominent emirs was killed by the return fire from the walls of the castle. It was enough – for now – to convince Saladin to raise the siege.

Saladin retired to the region around Banyas and conducted a campaign of plunder, burning and slaughter. But it was not all destruction. He had many camel loads of sheaths brought back to his camp as he was acutely aware of the need to seize the harvest. Baldwin headed to Tiberias with all the men he could muster, summoning Raymond III of Tripoli to join him. They then moved on to Toron via Safad. Odo and his Templars were amongst the royal army. At Toron the king learned that Saladin had sent out a light cavalry force to plunder around Sidon. This force was under the command of Faruk-Shah and when it tried to return to Saladin's camp on 10 June 1179, it was defeated by the Frankish army at Marj Ayyun (the valley of the springs) between the Litani and the Upper Jordan. The knights in the Frankish army had descended from their hilltop position a little faster than the infantry, but waited on the plain for several hours. The encounter with Faruk-Shah's men whilst it was a defeat for the Muslims after a fashion resulted in some of their force getting back to Saladin's camp. Saladin himself, after arranging for the safe disposal of his baggage train, headed out to counter-attack. Some of the crusader contingents were chasing the scattered light forces of Faruk-Shah whilst others were collecting loot. Count Raymond, Odo of Saint-Amand and the Templars moved to high ground between the Marj Ayyun and the Litani Gorge. Meanwhile, Saladin fell on some of the pursuers of his nephew's defeated forces and overcame them. But it was when Saladin managed to surprise the cavalry forces still at a distance from the resting infantry that disaster struck. William of Tyre explicitly states that the mounted forces (which must have included Raymond and the Templars) had no time to form up. They fought bravely but their lack of cohesion meant only one outcome. They decided to turn and flee and chose to do so down a rocky defile. Many were trapped and surrounded whilst others managed to escape and make a difficult journey to Beaufort Castle, some 5 miles to the south-west. Other escapees managed to head towards Sidon and encountered along the way Lord Reynald of Sidon and his men whom they told of the disaster. Much to William of Tyre's anger, Reynald did not continue on to help, preferring instead to go back to Sidon. Had he ventured onwards he might have saved the many fugitives who were later rounded up from their hiding places by the Muslims.

William of Tyre's brother Ralph had been killed at Marj Ayyun and William held Odo responsible for his death. The king and Raymond of Tripoli escaped. Odo of Saint-Amand did not. For a second time in his military career (see p. 43) he was taken prisoner along with 270 other knights, says Imad ad-Din. Baldwin of Ibelin (who was later released on the promise he would find a huge ransom) and Hugh of Galilee were amongst them. But Odo died a year later, still in captivity, refusing to be ransomed. According to Abu Shama, his body was handed over in exchange for the release of a Muslim prisoner held by the Christians.

With the king's forces in some considerable disorder and the Templars without a Grand Master, Saladin was able to turn his attention once again to the problem of the castle at Jacob's Ford. But it would take time. His preliminary attack in May had taught him that he needed more resources to do the job. And with a new pressure upon him in the form of a recently arrived crusader force in the Holy Land under Henry I of Champagne, Saladin knew that the elimination of Chastellet was a race against time. The siege began on 24 August. He brought considerable numbers with him. The plain overflowed with troops, says Imad ad-Din. The land all around was scoured for wood and vine poles for the palisades to protect the siege engines he had brought with him. Surprisingly, the castle's outer walls were scaled by the end of the first day, but the situation inside the compound was very different. Fires had been lit behind each gate to deter the attackers. Saladin got his miners to undermine the tower by digging beneath it and placing wooden supports within the tunnel which were then fired. The tunnel was 30 cubits in depth for a wall of 9 cubits in thickness. However, due to a miscalculation, these fires did not bring the wall down and Saladin was compelled to offer a dinar to anyone who could bring a skin of water to put the fires out so that his engineers could try again. By dawn on Thursday 29 August, ever mindful of Baldwin's approaching army now at Tiberias, the Muslims watched as the walls of Chastellet crumbled. Imad ad-Din has a striking account of the event and its consequences:

> The Franks had piled up wood behind the wall which crumbled; the current of air which penetrated at the moment of its fall spread the fire, their tents and several combatants were prey to the flames; the remainder who were in the region of the fire implored amnesty. As soon as the flames were extinguished, the troops penetrated the place, killing, taking prisoners, and seizing important booty, [including] 100,000 pieces of iron arms of all types and victuals in quantity. The captives were taken to the sultan, who executed the apostates and the bowmen; of around 700 prisoners, the greater part were massacred en route by the volunteer troops, the remainder taken to Damascus.

Amongst those executed were eighty Templars. Qadi al-Fadil provides a haunting account of the despair of the Templar commander of the castle who knew that all was lost: 'When the flames reached his side, he threw himself into a hole full of fire without fear of the intense heat and, from this brazier, he was immediately thrown into another [that of Hell]'.

Baldwin received the shocking news at Tiberias. It was too late. Not only was Saladin now ravaging around the northern part of the kingdom, he was systematically dismantling the castle which had so preoccupied his mind. In their fury the Muslims had thrown many of the dead bodies of the enemy into the cistern. Other corpses were simply lying about. The result was an outbreak of disease amongst the attackers which cost Saladin the lives of ten of his emirs. But the victory was entirely Saladin's. The new Frankish arrivals did not come to the aid of Chastellet, instead they went home.

Weapon Injuries at Jacob's Ford

Since 1993 archaeological excavations have taken place at the Templar castle at Vadum Iacob, also known as Jacob's Ford or Chastellet. The discovery of five human skeletons bearing signs of battle damage has given insight into the horrors of hand-to-hand combat. Found in a layer of ash beneath the remains of the only completed building in the castle, these five male individuals ranged from 20 to 40 years in age. They were all the defenders of the castle. None had been formally buried and all were positioned randomly.

Individual 1
30–40 years old. Discovered with an iron arrowhead in the left side of his pelvic area. This wound theoretically may have been fatal.

Individual 2
20–30 years old. Discovered with an iron arrowhead at the outer edge of the left humerus.

Individual 3
30–40 years old. This male was badly wounded. His left arm was cut off at the elbow and his forearm was nowhere to be found, indicating that he may have made it to his resting place whilst injured. If this amputation by a bladed item was not fatal, then the slash to the skull which penetrated his brain and split his cranium in two would have been. This latter injury implies no helmet was worn, or it was stripped from him before the blow. He was found with non-fatal wounds to his face suggesting a glancing blow with a sword to his cheek before he died. Three arrowheads in the neck area may not have been fatal.

Individual 4

25–30 years old. This male sustained a wound from a bladed weapon to the top of the left shoulder.

Individual 5

25-30 years old. No skeletal injuries. He Presumably died of soft flesh wounds.

It is not clear who these defenders were, if they were Templars or servants. They clearly tried to defend themselves. Cut down by swords and peppered with arrows, these men's bodies stand as grim testimony to the fury of crusader warfare in 1179.

The crusades are full of pivotal moments, but this catastrophe for the Templars and the Franks at Chastellet marks the first of the great punctuation marks in the story of the loss of the Holy Land. By the later part of 1179 the Templars had lost numerous brothers and also its bellicose Grand Master and a spectacular fortress which could have brought them great power, money and regional influence had it not been raised to the ground. This was also a year (after many other similar years) of drought and disease and poor harvests. No castle would be erected again at Jacob's Ford. The castle at Safad would be isolated and dwindle in its regional influence until well into the next century. Nothing was habitable in this land except for the already established towns. Throughout 1180 Saladin's nephew Faruk-Shah would keep up the devastation of the region which the building of Chastellet had been partly designed to prevent. Drought and warfare had brought the region to its knees. Despite further incursions that year into Christian territory, even Saladin knew he needed respite. A two-year truce (on both land and sea) was agreed between Baldwin and Saladin in May 1180. To William of Tyre's disappointment, it was a truce on equal terms, something hitherto unprecedented. But Raymond's Tripoli was not included. In the summer Saladin invaded the land of Tripoli and the Templars were kept 'shut up in their strongholds'. The Hospitallers remained in their fortress at Crac des Chevaliers. Gathering crops and stealing animals, Saladin continued unchallenged in the countryside. An Egyptian fleet moored on the island of Arwad (Ru'ad) just off the Templar stronghold at Tortosa sent a shiver through Outremer and succeeded in torching a building above the harbour. But Saladin sent it home and concluded a truce with Raymond of Tripoli. As Saladin headed back eastwards to concentrate his energies against Aleppo and other Islamic leaders, one thing was surely certain. The Kingdom of Jerusalem was vulnerable.

Chapter 13

The Springs of Cresson and the Battle of the Horns of Hattin, 1187

Odo of Saint-Amand's death was followed by the election in 1181 of Arnold of Torroja as Grand Master. It was an appointment representing a departure from the leadership of Odo. Since 1167 Arnold had been Master in Spain and Provence and had a huge amount of experience. He had also given vineyards and other property to the order from his family estates near Lerida. His approach was to be more that of an arbitrator in crusading politics than an outright warlike figure, intervening in 1181 in the affairs of Antioch and again in 1184 in Acre. But these politics in the 1180s were hugely complex and in part led to the disasters which were to befall Jerusalem in 1187. The great Frankish families of the Courtenays and the Ibelins were at loggerheads and one high-profile casualty of the infighting was William of Tyre, who failed to prevent the election of Heraclius as Patriarch, a post to which he might have felt entitled himself. William of Tyre, to whom we owe so much of our knowledge, fled to Rome in 1182 or 1183 under excommunication. His life is obscure after this but he may have died as late as 1186.

Arnold of Torroja's tenure did not last long. He served for only three years (1181–4) during which Baldwin IV's leprosy got worse and the kingdom's factions grew further apart. Arnold and the new Patriarch Heraclius and the Master of the Hospital, Roger des Moulins, had travelled to Italy, France and England (where Heraclius consecrated the new Temple Church in London) to garner support for the Christians of the east as Saladin's fortunes rose greater by the month. Arnold would die in Verona in 1184 and was succeeded as Templar Grand Master by Gerard of Ridefort, one of the order's most charismatic, yet controversial figures. As for Saladin, his wars against other Muslims in the north had largely gone in his favour and by the autumn of 1183 he held Aleppo and Damascus which when added to his huge Egyptian empire made him very powerful indeed. Although Saladin had been rebuffed by the Christians the previous year in a battle near to the Hospitaller castle at Belvoir, Outremer was still surrounded by the combined forces of one man.

The kingdom was divided over how best to combat Saladin. Some sought accommodation, such as the dying Baldwin IV and Raymond III of Tripoli. Others wished for a more aggressive policy and one man in particular hoped to lead the charge. Reynald of Châtillon was a constant thorn in Saladin's side. Now the Lord of Oultrejourdain, in 1181, he had broken the truce between Christians and Muslims. He had destroyed a Muslim caravan carrying goods to Mecca and Baldwin was unable to force any compensation for Saladin. Even Saladin's capture of 1,500 pilgrims blown off course near Damietta in Egypt had not persuaded Reynald to hand over his stolen goods. In 1182 Reynald had launched an audacious Red Sea naval expedition, again designed to enrich himself from captured merchandise and to threaten the cities at the very heart of Islam.

In 1183 King Baldwin's illness was so acute that he had lost the use of his arms and legs. His sister Sibylla and the Patriarch persuaded him to hand the regency to Sibylla's husband, Guy of Lusignan. Guy was left in charge of nearly all the kingdom except for Jerusalem itself which was reserved for the king. However, after some hesitation in the field against Saladin's larger army and suffering accusations of weakness, Guy then fell out with the ailing Baldwin IV who chose his heir to be his young nephew, the future Baldwin V. In March 1185 Baldwin IV died and his successor the young Baldwin V died the following year at only around 9 years old. Factionalism reared its head once again. Raymond of Tripoli had been appointed the boy's regent and felt entitled to remain so, although he refused the personal guardianship of the boy. The barons of the kingdom had sworn that if the child had died before the age of 10 Raymond should keep the regency until a new king was chosen through the arbitration of the kings of France and England, the Holy Roman Emperor and the Pope. But Sibylla, the boy's mother and the sister of the leper king, claimed control for herself and her husband, Guy of Lusignan, the man who would become king. The hawkish lobby was again in the ascendancy. Reynald of Châtillon, Gerard of Ridefort and Heraclius were set against the more moderate Raymond of Tripoli and Balian of Ibelin. When the barons of the land slowly trickled away from Raymond and joined Sibylla and Guy, the Count of Tripoli may have harboured thoughts of taking the throne for himself. He had tried to secure an alternative in the form of the Princess Isabella and her husband, Humphrey of Toron, but was defeated by Humphrey's treachery. However, something much darker for the fate of all Outremer was waiting. This would prove to be the wrong time for a disunited kingdom.

Gerard of Ridefort

Gerard was either a Flemish or an Anglo-Norman knight who had come to Jerusalem to seek his fortune and by 1179 had risen to become Marshal of the kingdom. He seems first to have served under Raymond III of Tripoli and felt entitled to an heiress in marriage in return, but the woman Gerard wanted (the daughter of the Lord of Botron) was apparently handed by Raymond to a Pisan merchant instead. Whether this tale is true or not, Gerard soon joined the Templars and became seneschal by 1183. He was firmly set against Raymond III and their enmity did no favours at all for the future of the Kingdom of Jerusalem. Gerard is often accused of being headstrong and bellicose. He did, however, have a curious knack for survival. At the Springs of Cresson on 1 May 1187 he defied both his own Marshal and the Master of the Hospital who both died in the battle they had warned against fighting. Gerard survived. At Hattin that year, the most disastrous defeat of them all, Gerard was captured whilst Saladin executed other Templars. Gerard was held prisoner for a year and released only after Jerusalem and other coastal Christian cities had been secured for the Muslims. In September 1187 he gained his freedom in exchange for the surrender of the Templar castle at Gaza. Pugnacious to the last, Gerard died in the fighting outside the city of Acre in October 1189.

There had been another truce with Saladin amidst all this politicking. It is no surprise to discover who broke it. Towards the end of 1186 a huge caravan came up from Cairo escorted by a small Egyptian force. Reynald of Châtillon attacked it and took its merchants and their entourages to Kerak. Once again Reynald refused to return the plunder to Saladin and war seemed inevitable. Raymond made a truce with Saladin for Tripoli and extended it to his wife's area of influence in Galilee. He apparently also arranged for Saladin's support in his own bid for the kingdom. Gerard of Ridefort did not hesitate to agitate for a royal raid into Galilee to bring Raymond to heel. The plan was to march on Tiberias but Balian of Ibelin intervened and argued for a delegation which he would lead to Tiberias to seek a negotiation with Raymond. It would contain the Grand Masters of both the Hospital and the Temple. He would meet their party at the castle at La Fève the next day. On the night of 20 April 1187 whilst the Masters of the Temple and Hospital headed out to La Fève, Raymond received a Muslim envoy at Banyas asking his permission to send a reconnaissance party of Mameluke slave troops through Galilee, a request he could hardly refuse since his treaty with Saladin. He wanted them gone within a day however, and wanted no town or village harmed. Raymond then sent out a message across his land that the Mameluke party would be passing through and that there was nothing for folk to fear, so long as they remained inside their walls with their flocks. When he learned of the expected delegation from Jerusalem, he sent out the same warning to them too.

Early in the morning of 1 May 1187 7,000 Mameluke warriors passed through Raymond's territory. Balian headed out to La Fève later the same morning. When he got there he was met with a peculiar sight. The castle was all but empty with the tents of the Templars still in evidence. Balian's groom, Ernoul, walked through the building and could find nobody except two warriors lying speechless in the upper galleries. Balian had not received Raymond's message. Gerard of Ridefort had probably received word on the night of 30 April. Confused, Balian headed out along the road to Nazareth. A blooded Templar rode up to him shouting about a great disaster. Gerard, it seems, had acted as quickly as he could and true to character

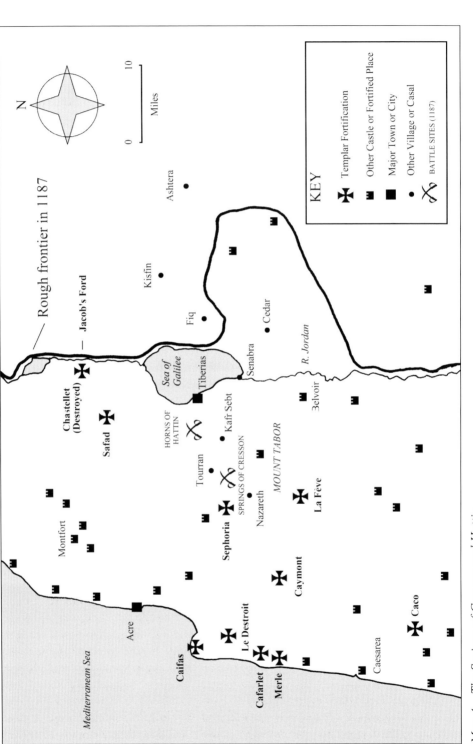

Map 4 – The Springs of Cresson and Hattin.

quickly sought out the enemy. He gathered forces from Templar garrisons at La Fève and Caco (Qaqun) and amongst the king's secular knights at Nazareth he found a further forty men. From Caco came the Marshal of the Temple James of Mailly with ninety knights.

Gerard of Ridefort and his force spotted the Mamelukes not far from Nazareth watering their horses at the Springs of Cresson (Ayn Juzah). He had with him around 130 knights, an unknown number of turcopoles and perhaps a few hundred infantry. Roger des Moulins and James of Mailly suggested a retreat due to the sheer size of the enemy but Gerard poured scorn on his own marshal and told him 'you love your blond head too well to want to lose it', to which the reply came 'I shall die in battle like a brave man. It is you that will flee as a traitor'. Of course these words are posthumously placed in James's mouth but according to the *Itinerarium* (the Chronicle of the Third Crusade) it was the dashing and brave James of Mailly whose actions were worthy of note in an encounter which is described as an 'unexpected' battle.

> So Saladin . . . sent the emir of Edessa, Manafaradin [also known as Kukburi] . . . on ahead with 7000 Turks to ravage the Holy Land. Now, when this Manafaradin advanced into the Tiberias region, he happened to encounter the Master of the Temple Gerard of Ridefort, and the Master of the Hospital Roger des Moulins. In the unexpected battle which followed he put the former to flight and killed the other.
>
> A certain Templar – a knight by profession, of Touraine by nation, Jakelin [James] de Mailly by name brought all the enemy assault on himself through his outstanding courage.

We do not know what the Templar Grand Master saw when he got to the springs. Armies of this period in this landscape moved from water to water and so finding the enemy here made perfect sense. The Christian force had charged into the enemy hoping to catch it off balance perhaps in the same way Montgisard had been won ten years earlier. The problem was that in so doing, the mounted knights left behind their infantry and although the Arab sources indicate that the initial encounter was closely fought, the lack of a successful breakthrough meant an increasing chance of the knights becoming overwhelmed. Dildirim al Yaruqi's Allepan troops held off the attack to allow their comrades to come in with a counter-attack. James of Mailly had found himself surrounded after up to 500 of his army had been killed or captured. He continued to fight, much to the admiration of the enemy who pitied him and urged him to surrender. He had been riding a white horse which reminded the author of the *Itinerarium* of St George. On the ground where he fell there had been stubble before the battle which was now trampled to dust, so furious was James's defence.

All but three Templars lost their lives in this attack. Gerard was one of the survivors. We cannot be certain whether Gerard was caught unawares by the Muslim presence or to what extent he precipitated a risky attack. The Mamelukes do not seem to have harmed a single town or city and thus kept to their agreement with Raymond. However, on their way from the Springs of Cresson they sported the heads of Templar knights at the tips of their lances. The 'unexpected' nature of the encounter might have saved Gerard from some embarrassment. Perhaps he was only doing what any Grand Master of the Temple would do when faced with an enemy force on his doorstep. But what happened next in the scorched landscape of Galilee would paint a different picture of him.

Balian went on to Tiberias without Gerard. The Master of the Temple had sustained serious wounds at the Springs of Cresson. Raymond of Tripoli was horrified at the news. He resolved to break his treaty with Saladin and ride to Jerusalem to reconcile himself with King Guy. Guy was magnanimous and for a moment it seemed that the rifts were heeled. Saladin, however, was amassing a huge army beyond the kingdom's frontiers. To counter this Guy called out all his tenants-in-chief to meet him at Acre with their forces. The Templars and the Hospitallers brought their contingents but in doing so the Templars had left their garrisons across the kingdom depleted. They did, however, bring money which was their share of that which was sent to the military orders by Henry II of England in atonement for the infamous murder of Archbishop Thomas à Becket of Canterbury. By the end of June 1187 the Christian force amounted to 1,200 knights, an unknown number of turcopoles and around 10,000 infantry. On 26 June 1187 Saladin was at Ashtera in Hauran. He placed himself at the centre of his army with his nephew, Taqi al-Din, on the right and Manafaradin (Kukburi) on the left. To Kisfin, through Fiq and then round the south of the Sea of Galilee they marched into Christian territory. His army was around 18,000 in number and comprised a vast array of Muslim allies and their Mameluke slave troops. On 1 July 1187 he crossed the Jordan at Senabra. The next day he divided his force in two and camped with one half at Kafr Sebt whilst the remainder attacked Tiberias, which very quickly fell to him, leaving Raymond's Countess Eschiva stranded in her castle, although she did manage to get a message out describing her plight.

It was the heat of summer. This meant that conditions were punishing and any army in the field enduring this searing heat would surely run low on water and supplies unless it moved from one source to another. Even Raymond argued for a defensive posture. Besides, he argued, Antioch had not yet sent its promised contingents. Raymond complained the army could not last half a day without water and that men and beasts would surely suffer if they ventured out. But Gerard of Ridefort and Reynald of Châtillon accused Raymond of cowardice and made an argument for quick action. Guy listened. The Christians moved out to Sephoria. Here, at least, was water and grazing for the horses. But Eschiva's desperate messages still came from the surrounded castle at Tiberias. Her sons were in the Christian army and tearfully argued for action, but for the moment Guy held at Sephoria. Gerard took it upon himself to go to the king's tent in person and told Guy directly that Raymond was a traitor and that to neglect the opportunity to avenge the deaths at the Springs of Cresson and abandon Tiberias would be a stain upon his and the Templars' honour. Whatever Gerard of Ridefort had in terms of personality, he had it in abundance. Guy was persuaded to alter his plan and he sent messages out that the army would march out to Tiberias at dawn.

The route chosen to Tiberias by the Christians (apparently by Raymond) was the northernmost option via the Galilean hills, as Saladin had already blocked the southern route which led along the western shores of the Sea of Galilee from Senabra by placing his camp at Kafr Sebt. Saladin marched to Hattin to block the Christians. He had the advantage of having water supplies close to hand. This would be the exact opposite of the circumstances Raymond of Tripoli had hoped for in his earlier talks with Guy. On the morning of 3 July the Christians set out in the rising heat to cross the scorched hills. They marched with their cavalry in the centre of each division, surrounded by an infantry box or screen. In the van was Raymond of Tripoli, as this was his domain and such was the Frankish custom. Second was the king, Guy. And third were the military orders with Reynald and Balian.

The column was harassed by Muslim detachments under Saladin's general Manafaradin (Kukburi) who poured missile fire into the van and rear guards. It is possible Saladin had prior knowledge of its movements. The missile fire was a common Muslim tactic and its effects were withering. The strain of constantly having to counter-charge the harassers must have been great. The Templars sent out to King Guy that they could go no further that day, after constantly having to react to the provocation. By afternoon, the army was at a plateau above Hattin. In front of them were two peaks, the Horns of Hattin, beyond which the ground fell away to the Sea of Galilee. Here Guy made camp. It was a fateful decision. Receiving news of this from his position in the van of the army, Raymond of Tripoli proclaimed 'the kingdom is finished!'. But still the army camped there, hoping to find water from a nearby source which when the well was discovered, was found to be dry. Worse yet, Saladin had ordered his volunteers (the Muttawiya troops) to set fire to the scrub on the hillside. The acrid smoke blew into the Christian camp.

Some Frankish foragers seeking water were easily picked off in the darkness as Saladin set his camps around the stranded army. Saladin had based himself to the south of the Christians around the hills at a village called Lubia. Thirsty, tired and with morale at a low ebb, the Christians awoke the next morning preparing to march again to find water. Saladin watched carefully not knowing if they would charge directly at him (as some had urged King Guy to do) or try to reach the Hattin spring. But as Saladin began to receive some deserters from the Franks, he decided to press the Christians from all sides. Once again, the Templars counter-charged from the rear guard. Raymond of Tripoli did the same in the van and for a short while it might have seemed the Franks could break out. At this time, however, the protective screen of Christian infantry began to lose heart and drift to the east in search of water, only to find themselves shepherded onto the rocky Horns of Hattin. King Guy attempted to set up another camp west of the Horns but there was confusion amidst the smoke and only a few tents were erected. Then, Raymond, who is often accused of treachery, made a successful break out through the Muslim lines of Taqi al-Din's division who parted before Raymond, allowing Raymond's cavalry to charge down a gorge with little possibility of returning to the fray. Elsewhere in the Christian army, the infantry and remaining cavalry units were parted from one another around the Horns.

Guy set his tent on the larger flat-topped southern Horn, or possibly in the saddle between the two Horns. Here on the Horns, the True Cross was finally captured by Taqi al-Din's division. Further cavalry charges and counter-charges occurred but the Christian cavalrymen by now were reduced to exhausted heavy infantrymen due to the loss of their mounts. Then, as Saladin and Taqi al-Din closed in, the royal tent was found and cut down. King Guy, Reynald of Châtillon and Gerard of Ridefort were amongst the captured men. Balian had managed to escape.

The king and his surviving barons were brought to Saladin's tent. During their meeting, Saladin handed King Guy a cup of iced water in a symbolic move which indicated his life was to be spared. Guy handed the drink to Reynald of Châtillon, but this displeased Saladin as he had other plans for Reynald. He either killed him then and there, or had his servants do it for him. Either way, Saladin avenged the wrongs done to Islam by Reynald. For the Christians, the disaster was almost indescribable. Saladin rode out to Tiberias and took the city. By 6 July the Christian prisoners were in Damascus.

The captured Templars and Hospitallers had been given the choice of conversion or execution and virtually all of them took the road of martyrdom. The other prisoners were ransomed or sold into slavery. Jerusalem was at the mercy of Saladin. Brother Terricus, who styled himself the Grand Commander of the remaining Templars, wrote to the West. In the wake of Hattin, 230 Templars had been beheaded, he said. This was not counting the sixty lost at the Springs of Cresson. Terricus goes on to say that he himself had escaped the field along with Reginald of Sidon and Balian of Ibelin.

Soon, with the garrisons of the kingdom depleted, many of the strongholds and cities would fall one by one. Tyre would only be saved by the chance arrival of a crusader fleet under Conrad of Montferrat, assisted by the Templars and Hospitallers, during which eleven Muslim galleys were captured. Acre fell on 10 July, Sidon on 29 July, Beirut on 6 August, and on 2 October 1187 the unthinkable would happen in Jerusalem. Eighty years on from the First Crusade, and after a great siege in which Balian famously strove in vain, the Temple Mount was surrendered to Saladin and the cross built upon the Dome of the Rock was dismantled and dragged around the streets for two days, according to a letter to King Henry II of England from Terricus. Al-Aqsa mosque and the Dome of the Rock were cleansed with rose water and much dismantling and rebuilding took place on Temple Mount. The Christians were forced to leave the city. Those who had been ransomed were assembled in three groups, one with Balain and the Patriarch Heraclius, another with the Hospitallers and another with the Templars. To the coast they went, turning their back on the Holy City. Some went to Antioch, some to Tyre and others to Tripoli. For the Templars, it had meant the loss of the holiest of places. Their very reason for existence had been compromised. But despite their losses they were far from

4. *Al-Aqsa Mosque from the Dome of the Rock. The Templars were based here for less than seventy years, losing it in 1187 to Saladin.*

5. *Aerial view of Al-Aqsa Mosque on Temple Mount, Jerusalem. Israel. Showing the southern end of the platform overlooking the concealed 'Solomon's Stables' where the Templars kept their horses. Theoderich, a twelfth-century German pilgrim, said 'a single shot from a crossbow would hardly reach from one end of this building to the other'.*

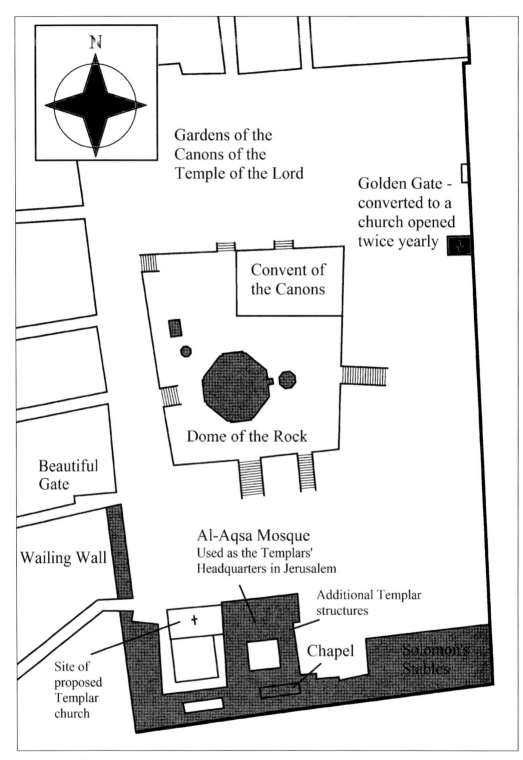

Fig. 3. Temple Mount before 1187.

finished. They had some of their larger castles intact, including their great enclave at Tortosa. But if the fortunes of Outremer were to turn in favour of the Christians, they would need someone to bring fresh men and impetus from the West. Once again, the response to a calamity in the Holy Land would be the business of kings.

Brother Terricus appears to have stepped aside for the released Gerard of Ridefort. King Guy had also been released from captivity by the summer of 1188 and by August 1189 both he and the Templar Grand Master were beneath the walls of Acre. Gerard had been busy, though. He had successfully defended the Templar tower at Tortosa in 3 July 1188 forcing Saladin to turn his attention to the north and concentrate on taking Baghras and Darbsak. But on 4 October 1189 Gerard perished at Acre in the fighting. He was arrayed with his Templars in the left flank of the crusader army facing Saladin's forces who had come to break the siege. The *Itinerarium* records that Gerard had led his Templar knights 'who are second to none in renown and devoted to slaughter' in a charge which had penetrated enemy lines and gone in too far. As a result, he was surrounded in the bitter fighting, but refused to be persuaded to break off, shouting defiantly that it would be shameful to his order to do so. In the same passage, the author of the *Itinerarium* states that if the rest of the Christians had behaved in a similar way, the result may have been different. Arab sources, however, record that Gerard was captured and executed.

Gerard's replacement as Grand Master was Robert of Sablé, whose appointment had the guiding hand of the new King of England Richard I ('the Lionheart') whose vassal Robert had been. Robert was to be one of the main commanders of the fleet of the Third Crusade (1189–92). Richard I was one of the central figures of the new crusade, but the armies he led from the West came into a much-changed land beyond the seas. Gerard of Ridefort had gone and so too had Raymond of Tripoli, succumbing to pleurisy near the end of 1187. Moreover, the Christian territories had remarkably shrunk. Richard and the Templars would work closely together to recover what they could of the diminished Outremer states.

Chapter 14

The Third Crusade,
1189–92

The bad news travelled to the West and the response was one of shock. Ultimately, after some lengthy preparation, the Third Crusade was launched. The ageing German Emperor Frederick Barbarossa had set out with a huge army but had died whilst crossing Asia Minor in June 1190. King Philip II of France (1180–1223) and King Richard arrived with their forces in April and June 1191 respectively. On his way to the Holy Land, Richard came to Cyprus and conquered the island. Lacking the resources to manage it, he later sold the whole island to the Templars who could only afford to put a down payment of 40,000 besants towards the 100,000 price tag. Their subsequent rule was troubled by a lack of resources of their own. They had just twenty brother knights and a hundred men at arms there. Soon, the Templars faced a revolt and they decided to hand the island back to Richard. In turn, the English king sold the island once again to King Guy, whose descendants would rule it for several centuries.

The crusaders finally captured Acre after a long siege on 12 July 1191. At one stage during the siege the Templars' deployed a trebuchet or other type of stonethrower which wrought much damage along with that of the Hospitallers. King Philip left the Holy Land within three weeks of the reclaiming of Acre but Richard stayed on. His goal was to march to Jerusalem but before doing so he cruelly massacred 2,700 of his Muslim prisoners. It is not clear why this happened. Some wrote that Richard had set a time limit on a deal with Saladin which included the return to the Christians of the True Cross and monetary payment and that this limit had expired. Others said that Saladin had executed his Christian hostages days before and so the act was justifiable revenge.

On 22 August the crusaders marched out of Acre. Richard had organised his army to cooperate with a naval force stacked with supplies of additional troops, meat, wine, biscuit and flour. He remained close to the coast and the army could only move at the speed of its slowest component, the baggage train on foot. To the right he kept the sea and to his left he kept an infantry screen with missile capability. He was constantly shadowed by Saladin whose horsemen kept up their close harassment. In a surprisingly descriptive account the author of the *Itinerarium* says that the enemy tactics reminded him of an 'infuriating fly which flies away if you drive it off and returns when you stop'. The descriptions of the crusading army on the march are vivid. The Normans and the English attended the army standard, which was on wheels. The Duke of Burgundy and the remaining French troops took the rear guard and King Richard was in the van. When the column ran into difficulties of cohesion in narrow places, the Turks rushed in and picked off the baggage carts. Richard himself had to lead a relieving charge.

Day after day, the slow march continued with constant harassment. Three days after a stop at Caifas the army once again drew up in battalions. On this day, the Templars formed the van and the Hospitallers the rear. They got as far as Destroit and camped again to await the naval supply ships which they had out-paced. It was here that Richard made the decision to place the Templars in the rear guard for the next stage of operations. His concerns were that the enemy was increasing the number of its attritional attacks. By 30 August the heat was unbearable. People in the army were dropping in large numbers, but they struggled on to Caesarea. By 3 September the army was passing through wasteland and was harassed once again from the rear during which action the Templars, constantly repelling the enemy, were said to have lost many horses. Richard himself received a minor wound in the action. By 5 September the army passed through the forest of Arsuf and came onto the plain. Richard now met with Saladin's brother, Al-Adil, and took Humphrey of Toron as an interpreter. But Al-Adil broke away from the talks refusing to acknowledge King Richard's demands for the return to the Christians of the whole of Palestine.

The army reached the River Rochetailie and stayed there until the morning of 7 September. It became apparent at daybreak that the enemy had blocked the road ahead. Richard organised the deployment. Twelve squadrons were formed into five battalions. The Templars were at the front again. Behind them were the Bretons and the Angevins and then King Guy with the Poitevin troops. The Anglo-Normans made up the fourth battalion and accompanied the royal standard. At the rear were the Hospitallers. The detachments, it was said, kept themselves 'so closely together that an apple thrown into their midst would not fall to the ground without touching people or horses'. Bringing up the very rear were units of archers and crossbowmen. The baggage train was placed between the army and the sea and Henry of Champagne performed a guarding role in this respect.

The attack began against a background of tumultuous noise as Saladin's army bore down on the crusaders. Bedouins, slave troops and Turks poured missiles into the Christians. The impression given is that of the Christian army still being on the move, with its rear guard of crossbowmen looking nervously over their shoulders and firing into the enemy to keep them at bay. Keeping the arrows of the Turks at a distance was paramount. If they came too close the damage could be great. However, at Arsuf Beha ed-Din (Saladin's biographer) records the Frankish infantry marching along with up to ten arrows stuck in their armour, indicating that the range of the horse archers was at its outer limit. Here also at the rear, or what was to become the left flank of the army, the Hospitallers took many casualties. Richard did not permit them to charge yet. But it was the marshal of the Hospital and another knight who could bear it no longer. They charged out towards the enemy. It was a huge turning point as it triggered much of the rest of the army to charge as well, including the King of England. The spectacle of an entire army switching to the offensive in an instant and tearing into the enemy cannot have failed to impress. 'For two miles', says the author of the *Itinerarium*, 'there was nothing to see except people running away'.

There would be more counter-attacks, but as the army gathered around its royal standard, the battle was clearly won. The Templars and the Hospitallers are both mentioned in the immediate aftermath of the Battle of Arsuf. Between them they sent out some knights and turcopoles to look for the body of James of Avesnes, a much-loved warrior who had distinguished himself both at the siege of Acre and here at Arsuf, before perishing. They found him covered in blood. They washed him and brought him to Guy and Richard who assisted in his burial. The army then slowly headed out to Jaffa on the coast, whilst Saladin licked his wounds and headed to Ascalon to demolish it. The crusaders spent some time in Jaffa during which their attentions were focussed on the pleasures the city had to offer. There followed a period of diplomacy with Al-Adil in which the Christian demands included that Al-Adil should marry Richard's sister and live in Jerusalem, giving the Christians full access to the Holy City. There were separate overtures to the Muslims from other great crusaders and lords in the region such as Conrad of Montferrat and Reynald of Sidon, although nothing really came of these.

Saladin disbanded half his army when the rains came in November and Richard began to move on for Jerusalem, heading out from Jaffa to Ramla, where he stayed for six weeks. By 3 January the army had reached the rain-drenched land around Fort Beit-Nuba, 12 miles from the Holy City. Whilst many in the army wanted to capture Jerusalem, a note of caution was sounded by the Templars, Hospitallers and the native Franks. Even if Jerusalem was taken, they argued, the Muslim army beyond it would surely attack it once more. Moreover, the pilgrims in their entourage would soon depart the city to return home, leaving it weakened. Richard was persuaded. He decided to retreat. Soon, he went to Ascalon and rebuilt it. The whole project took four months. Politics began to take several quick turns. There was uproar in Acre during a dispute between the Pisan and Genoese factions there. Also, Conrad of Montferrat, very much a thorn in the English king's side, had been elected as King of Jerusalem instead of Guy. Within days, however, Conrad was murdered by two Assassins and Henry II of Champagne stepped into the void and married the Princess Isabella (the half-sister of Sibylla who had died in an epidemic in 1190) on 5 May 1192. In that same month Guy landed in Cyprus to take the government there.

In March 1192 Al-Adil had offered the Christians the chance to keep their conquests and have a right of pilgrimage to Jerusalem. As well as this, the True Cross would be restored. Beirut would be theirs too, provided it was dismantled. But as May came there was still no ratification of the agreement. Richard therefore moved south to Daron and took it after a five-day siege. It was Saladin's last fort on the Palestinian coast. The Third Crusade still had more campaigning left in it. There was an attack by Saladin on Jaffa which Richard came to repel with an amphibious landing, followed later by a heroic and hard-fought improvised defence outside the walls of the city in August 1192. By September, however, a treaty was finally signed, with both sides counting the costs of the war. Being a king, Richard refused to swear his oath. This was done by the Grand Masters of Templars and the Hospitallers instead. The coastal cities as far south as Jaffa were to once again be Christian. The holy sites could be visited once more. Ascalon, however, would be demolished.

Richard returned to Acre, distracted by the news of his brother John's misdeeds in England. He set sail from the Holy Land on 9 October 1192 but was forced by adverse weather to land at Corfu. Because this was the territory of the Byzantine Emperor Isaac Angelus, Richard, accompanied by four Templar attendants in a pirate boat, allegedly disguised himself as a Templar. This vessel was subsequently wrecked. Soon, however, this great crusading warrior-king would spend a year in prison at the hands of the Holy Roman Emperor Henry VI, after being captured by his old arch enemy Duke Leopold of Austria whose banners Richard had symbolically torn down when he first had come to Acre. But in the lands beyond the sea Richard had left a legacy. There was life left in Outremer yet and the West still had the stomach for the fight. The Templars, always close to Richard the Lionheart, would have their role to play in protecting the gains made in the crusade, but there was much ground to make up.

Chapter 15

Stalemate,
1192–1216

Saladin died in 1193 and on his death Islam's unity faded. His sons began to quarrel with each other and with other enemies too. Even Saladin's brother, the redoubtable Al-Adil, could not hold things together as Cairo and Damascus drifted apart. This was to be a period of truces and political manoeuvrings as opposed to any outright conquests. Guy of Lusignan had died in 1194 and was succeeded by his younger brother, Amalric, who married Isabella (Henry of Champagne having died in 1197). But Amalric died in 1205 and left no direct successor and the inheritance fell to Maria, Isabella's daughter by Conrad of Montferrat. John of Ibelin played the role of Regent and then in 1208 when Maria reached 17 years of age a husband, John of Brienne, was found for her.

As for the Templars, by 1194 Robert of Sablé, the Templar Grand Master, had died and was replaced by Gilbert Erail (1194–1200) who was living in Spain when he learned of his election. He was certainly at Acre in the Templars' house in 1198 when he heard a council accept the Teutonic Knights as an order of the church. Much of his time in office and that of his more bellicose successor, Philip of Plessis (1201–9), was taken up by disputes with the Hospitallers over rights in the town of Vilania, which Pope Innocent III felt obliged to settle. There were also ongoing issues with the complex position in the northern marches where the Templars had lost so much ground in the aftermath of Hattin.

In 1188 Saladin had taken both Darbsak and Baghras from the Templars. In 1191 whilst besieging Acre, he sent a force to Baghras to have it dismantled. Just as soon as he had done so, Leo, the Roupenid Prince of Lesser Armenia, came down to re-occupy it. He kept hold of it, despite the fact Bohemond III of Antioch had demanded its return to the Templars. Bohemond even appealed to Saladin, although he was too busy to intervene. The Templars had allied themselves with Bohemond of Tripoli, son of Bohemond III, and had suffered some attacks on their properties by the Armenians, which included an ambush in a narrow pass costing one Templar his life and seriously wounding the new Grand Master, William of Chartres (1210–c.1219). This brought the wrath of Pope Innocent III into play, who excommunicated Leo, who in turn eventually restored Templar lands. However,

Baghras itself was not restored to the order until 1216 when Leo had put Raymond-Roupen on the throne at Antioch.

As Grand Master, Philip of Plessis reported in a letter to the abbots of Cistercian houses of Europe two assaults against Christian territory made by Al-Adil despite the fact that Saladin's brother had signed a five-year and eight-month truce with Amalric II in July 1198. These attacks occurred in November 1201 and June 1202 respectively. According to the Templar Grand Master they had involved huge armies drawn from across the Muslim world. In 1209, it is probable that Philip of Plessis's objections to a renewal of another five-year truce made in 1204 with the Muslims was partly inspired by the Franks' experience of these attacks. In any event, the hawks won the argument, although there was no grand-scale campaigning as a result.

During this period the crusading movement in general took something of a turn in feeling and fortune. The main objective of the new Fourth Crusade was to be Egypt, for the same strategic reasons as it had been in the twelfth century. However, this grand adventure was diverted by the Venetians (who supplied the ships) to Constantinople, which was sacked in 1204. It led to a Latin rule at Constantinople which lasted until 1261 and brought much disgrace upon those Christians who had sacked one of the greatest Christian cities on earth. Furthermore, the Albigensian Crusade, which got underway in 1209 and which was murderously ranged against the Cathar heretics of southern France, did little to enhance the image of crusading in the long term. Nor did the harrowing and disastrous Children's Crusade of 1212 have any impact on the expansion or consolidation of Christian lands in Outremer. And for all his magnificent efforts in promoting the concept of crusading, Pope Innocent III did not see Jerusalem re-captured in his lifetime. He died on 16 July 1216.

Chapter 16

The Fifth Crusade, 1217–21

Plans for the Fifth Crusade were already underway before Innocent III died. His successor Honorius III (1216–27) continued the preparations. There was Templar involvement from the start, with much of the funding being handled by the Templar treasurer Haimard at the order's house in Paris. The plan had initially been to meet up in Cyprus, but the different parties eventually arrived in Acre independently. These were King Hugh I of Cyprus (1205–18), Duke Leopold VI of Austria (1198–1230) and King Andrew II of Hungary (1205–35). In November 1217 there was some unimpressive Palestinian campaigning, which whilst it brought some victories for the crusaders resulted in little more than King Andrew adding to his Christian relic collection before deciding to return home. Leopold, however, stayed. Only the previous month the Templar Grand Master had written to Honorius III explaining that it would be the Christians' intention to march on Damietta in Egypt, as opposed to an earlier design on Damascus. At around this time, too, the crusaders began work on the huge castle at 'Atlit, which became known as Château Pèlerin (Pilgrims' Castle), a project keenly recorded by Oliver of Paderborn (see pp. 197–9). In April and May 1218 a Frisian fleet arrived at Acre in two phases and the news of further French reinforcements gave heart to the crusading movement and raised the likelihood of a strike at Egypt.

On 24 May 1218 John of Brienne sailed with a crusading army to 'Atlit (Château Pèlerin) and thence to Egypt with the bulk of the force landing six days later near to Damietta. With the force were the Templars, Hospitallers and Teutonic Knights. Later, the force was joined by Cardinal Pelagius, the papal representative and nominal leader of the crusade. Damietta could only be taken by an amphibious action. It would be a long siege full of numerous military actions, both on land and on water. Oliver of Paderborn provides a startling account of the efforts made by the crusaders and paints a very positive and somewhat revealing picture of the Templars in action. The first objective was a chain-tower on an island close to the west bank. A chain was stretched across the main navigable river channel to this tower, behind which was a bridge of boats. The Duke of Austria and the Hospitallers each prepared two ladders on two ships and the Teutonic Knights and the Frisians fortified a third ship with a small fortress on the top of it. The Hospitallers' ladder crashed onto the

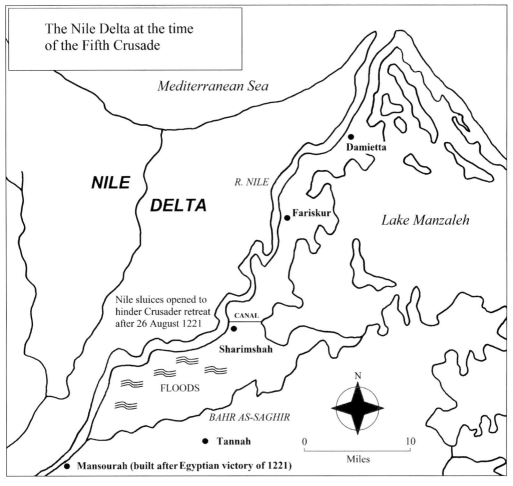

Map 5 – The Nile Delta at the time of the Fifth Crusade.

ships' mast when pressed into action and a similar disaster occurred to the duke's ladder. The other vessel suffered a searing Greek Fire attack (an incendiary syphon which shot a substance capable of burning even when on water), whilst one of the Templars' ships equipped 'with fortified bulwarks' was damaged when alongside the tower. On 24 August 1218 a new contraption was deployed, a siege tower built on two vessels bound together by the Frisians. It too was attacked by Greek Fire from the city which is described as 'like lightning' and a multitude of stones from the machines of the city also targeted it. By 25 August the defenders of the tower were down to their last hundred men, as the crusaders managed to penetrate the tower and win a war of attrition. The Templars had certainly contributed to the naval action, and Oliver of Paderborn later reports the sinking of a Templar vessel in the same campaign.

During the siege of Damietta William of Chartres, the Grand Master, passed away. It is not known quite when, but it was either 26 August 1218 amidst the first amphibious phase of the operation or in 1219 near to the time the city was finally captured. His death did not affect the Templar contribution, however, as his replacement was Peter of Montaigu (c.1219–c.1231), whose own brother, Garin, was Grand Master of the Hospitallers. Peter was another battling Templar warrior from the Auvergne region of France who had been Master in Provence and Spain between 1206 and 1212. He had fought against the Almohads at the pivotal Battle of Las Navas de Tolosa in 1212. There is no discernible change in the Templar commitment after William of Chartres' death in the writings of Oliver of Paderborn.

On 26 October 1218 outside Damietta there was a dawn attack on the camp of the Templars by the Egyptians. The order's rule had a set way of dealing with this (pp. 164–5). Oliver of Paderborn recalls the attack: 'They [the enemy] were driven away by our alert horsemen to the bridge which they had built a short distance from us in the upper part of the river; they were killed to the number of 500, as we learned from deserters.' Later in the campaign in early 1219, Oliver praised the Templar horse-handling capabilities in the muddy and difficult conditions of the delta: 'The Templars, leaders in the ascent of horses, having put up their banners, hurried to the city in a swift march, throwing down the wicked ones who came boldly from the gates to resist those who were advancing.' In July of the same year the brothers were attacked again by the enemy but the response was emphatic and clearly impressed the author: 'The spirit which came upon Gideon animated the Templars. The Master of the Temple with the Marshal and other brothers who were then present, made an attack through a narrow approach and manfully put the unbelievers to flight.'

The Teutonic Knights and some secular forces came to support the Templars, but Oliver of Paderborn was convinced of why this small victory had occurred. 'Thus, on that day', he wrote, 'did God save those who hoped in him through the courage of the Templars . . . [who] committed themselves to the conflict'. But perhaps the most demonstrative account of Templar battlefield commitment came on 29 August 1219 when an attack on an enemy encampment situated between the sea and the river badly backfired due to the indecision of the crusaders. The Templars found themselves having to shore things up. Thirty-three of their number were either killed or captured: 'The army of the Temple, which is usually first to assemble, was last to retreat. Therefore, when it arrived last at our ramparts [i.e. the Christian camp], it stayed without so that it might bring those who were before it back within the walls as soon as possible'. Encapsulated within this brief statement is all that was good about the Templars at war. Early preparedness, quick reactions, steadfast commitment, fighting to the last, huge personal sacrifice and devotion to the protection of fellow Christians.

Al-Adil died shortly after the news of the fall of the outer tower at Damietta. He was succeeded in Egypt by his elder son, al-Kamil, and in Syria by his younger son, al-Mu'azzam. Al-Kamil, in October 1219, made an astonishing offer to cede Jerusalem, return the True Cross and cede Galilee and Palestine in exchange for a Christian withdrawal from Egypt. But Pelagius and the Templars rejected this, believing perhaps correctly that Jerusalem could not be held with Outremer in its current state. Many of the castles of Galilee had been dismantled. To take Jerusalem back now, with the buffer zone of Oultrejourdain also missing, would be to adopt a position of weakness and vulnerability. Al-Kamil knew that his own position was weak too. In Damietta the garrison was suffering from sickness. On 5 November 1219 the Christian army penetrated an unmanned part of the defences and took the city. The Fifth Crusade had taken its objective. But there then followed arguments about how to govern the place. King John and the Templars and Hospitallers wanted it to become part of the Kingdom of Jerusalem but Pelagius wanted it for the Church. It was decided that the king could govern it until the Holy Roman Emperor Frederick II arrived on a long-anticipated crusade. But the immediate aftermath of the taking of Damietta was characterised by delay and quarrels. The Italian merchant contingents squabbled with the other crusader leaders over the division of spoils and had to be driven out at one stage by the military orders. The opportunity to march on Cairo quickly was squandered.

By September 1220 the Templar Grand Master Peter of Montaigu was able to construct a letter to Nicholas, Bishop of Elne written against the background of more absentees from the crusader camps. Leopold of Austria had long since departed before Damietta was even taken and King John had been distracted enough in March 1220 to successfully seek permission to leave the crusade and attend to Armenian succession affairs. Moreover, for the Templars in the same month, there was another emergency in Palestine. Al-Mu'azzam had fallen on Caesarea and besieged the new Templar castle at 'Atlit (Château Pèlerin), from which he did not withdraw until November 1220. Peter had to rush his Templars back from Egypt. However, Peter's letter, written in September of that troubled year, still has something to say about the strategy of the Fifth Crusade. The wisdom of an advance on Cairo was now questionable. Whilst Peter acknowledged that there had been an influx of fresh crusader resources sufficient enough to garrison some castles and also hold Damietta, he disagreed with Pelagius that there were sufficient resources available for a push on Cairo. The barons took the same view. The sultan, he said had 'built bridges on both parts of the river to impede the Christians, [and] was waiting there with such a large number of armed men that the greatest danger would have threatened any of the faithful who had pushed forward'.

And so it dragged on. Still there was no arrival of Frederick II, although he did send Duke Louis of Bavaria in the spring of 1221. The news of this impending arrival of a sizable force prompted elation in the heart of Pelagius and fear in that of al-Kamil, who came up with a new peace proposal. Jerusalem would be ceded and money given in compensation for its dismantlement. A thirty-year truce would be agreed and the Christians would have all Palestine bar Oultrejourdain. Pope Honorius had told Pelagius not to reject any peace proposals without first referring to Rome, but Pelagius chose not to heed the instruction. When the duke's army arrived, the offer had already been rejected. The Templars had been in favour of accepting this second deal and it is not difficult to see why. The added bonus of a long peace must have been very appealing.

What happened next in Egypt was a catastrophe. Pelagius and Duke Louis's arguments for quick action based on the impending Nile floods had won the day. By 6 July 1221 a somewhat pessimistic King John was back in Egypt with an army. Six days later Pelagius moved the army out to Fariskur, leaving a garrison at Damietta. The Muslims marched to Sharimshah and then retired before the Christians, taking up prepared positions at Talkha. On 20 July the crusaders took Sharimshah and King John wanted to stay there, fearful of the arrival of the floods. Pelagius would have none of it. The army would advance. This was the last mistake. A canal to the south of Sharimshah came into the river from another branch. The Christians had not defended it, perhaps because it was yet to flood. But it very soon did. As it was doing so, the armies of al-Kamil's brothers crossed it near to Lake Manzaleh and took up a position to the rear of the crusaders blocking their retreat to Damietta. With a large army in front of them the crusaders were surrounded and supplies began to run low. The Christians had reached as far as the Bahr as-Saghir. It was too far.

On Thursday, 26 August it had been decided that a retreat was the only option, despite the difficulties. There was little cohesion and much burning of stores too heavy to carry which gave the Muslims a clear visible indication of the Christians' intention to retreat. Peter and his Templars had returned to the crusade from Palestine and were with the army during this retreat. The march was commenced at night, says the Templar Grand Master, in a letter to Alan Martel, preceptor in England (written in September 1221). The Muslims then 'cut through the embankment of the Nile, the water rushed along several unknown passages and ancient channels, and encompassed us on all sides'. Peter goes on to show how the crusaders were outwitted by the enemy: 'Destitute of provisions, the army of Christ could neither proceed further nor retreat nor flee anywhere, nor could it fight with the sultan on account of the lake between the waters. It was trapped like a fish in a net.'

Many retreating crusaders were killed in the flooded landscape whilst others waded through the mud in vain. Some of the army were not even in a fit state to stand up, having drunk all their wine rather than carry it back to Damietta. The military orders, however, did manage to drive back the sultan's Nubian infantry, but by August 28, amidst scenes of devastation, desertion and despair, Pelagius gave in.

The terms were not nearly as generous as the two previous offers. There would be an eight-year truce, an exchange of prisoners on all sides and the return of Damietta to the sultan. The True Cross would also be given back. Peter of Montaigu was sent back to Damietta along with the Grand Master of the Teutonic Knights to explain the terms to the garrison. Henry, the Count of Malta had just arrived there with forty ships and the crusaders were deeply unhappy at the news and there was some brief rioting in the town directed against the military orders and King John.

The Templars discussed the possibility of strengthening the defences of the city instead of surrendering it, but the resources were not there to do this. Also, the food was now running out and a fresh Muslim army would soon arrive. By 8 September the crusaders were aboard their ships. Having supplied the Christians with loaves and flour for fifteen days as part of the agreement, the sultan entered Damietta. The crusaders sailed away without the True Cross which could not apparently be found but which always seemed to be a useful bargaining chip in the negotiations. Perhaps the crusaders were mindful of the offers they had turned down before the disasters in Egypt. Perhaps they were mindful too of the absence of Frederick II, whose men would surely have made a difference.

Chapter 17

The Sixth Crusade of Frederick II of Germany, 1228–9

There was still support for the military orders even after the disaster at Damietta. Philip II of France in his will of 1222 left 2,000 marks each to the Temple and the Hospital as well as 50,000 marks for the military upkeep of the Kingdom of Jerusalem. Peter of Montaigu, however, spent much of the rest of his time as Grand Master embroiled with the problems created by the ongoing feud between Frederick II and the papacy. This battle between temporal and spiritual power had been rumbling on for centuries, but with an overbearing character such as Frederick, things began to get worse. As far as the Latin East was concerned, Frederick's failure to appear there was the main grudge. In 1223 the military orders and King John put back another crusade by a couple of years and decided to marry John's daughter, Isabella (also known as Yolande), to Frederick. To them, it was a way of heightening Frederick's interests in the fate of the Kingdom of Jerusalem. The marriage did indeed take place two years later in 1225 and yet the continued delay of the appearance in the East of this new consort of Jerusalem angered the military orders, who complained to Pope Gregory IX (1227–41). Then at long last, in July 1228, Frederick's forces came to Cyprus and by September he was in Acre. But much had happened by then. Isabella had died in May that year having given Frederick a son, the infant Conrad. This meant that Frederick's regency status was now questionable to say the least. Worse, Frederick had fallen ill in the previous September and had sent his fleet ahead to Acre without him. On hearing the news, the unimpressed Pope excommunicated him.

In Acre, word had spread that Frederick had been excommunicated for a second time for setting out on another crusade before being absolved. The Templars and Hospitallers received him warmly until they heard the news. The Templars by now could list amongst their membership some exiled Apulian lords who had no love for the Holy Roman Emperor. As for Frederick, his army was no more than a few thousand at best, and he arrived in the East with the knowledge that an angry Pope was preparing to invade his territories in the West. He would have to play a game of diplomacy if this, the Sixth Crusade, was to be a success.

Frederick's overtures towards al-Kamil were not successful, so in November 1228 he decided to move out in a show of military force with all he could muster. Towards Jaffa they marched, as Richard I had done over thirty years earlier. But this time, because they were following an excommunicate, the military orders did so only at a distance equal to a day's march, something unthinkable during the Third Crusade. By the time the army had reached Arsuf, the military orders had compromised by re-joining the army but not so as to appear being under the emperor's command. But there was to be no glorious fighting like there had been in King Richard's time. Frederick was increasingly concerned about affairs in Italy and al-Kamil was distracted by power struggles with his own kin group, particularly as al-Mu'azzam had died on 11 November 1227 and his son, an-Nasir Dawud, had risen in his place, presenting problems and opportunities in the same instant. And so an agreement was reached with al-Kamil on 18 February 1229.

On the face of it, the treaty might appear to be a triumph of diplomacy but the Templars were incandescent with rage. Although Jerusalem was to be returned to the Christians with Bethlehem, only a narrow corridor running through Lydda to the sea at Jaffa would be granted. And yet the Holy City was to remain more or less unfortified bar some works which Frederick commenced himself. Worse than this, the Temple area was to remain in Muslim hands. There would be no return to their spiritual home for the Templars. The agreement also forbade any improvements to the order's castles at Tortosa and Chastel Blanc. With the Templars still seething at this outcome Frederick entered Jerusalem in March and crowned himself (placing the crown upon his own head) amidst much consternation from all sides. Many of the barons took the view that Frederick, as father of Conrad, was only really the father of a King of Jerusalem at best. Even the Patriarch placed an interdict (an outright ban on certain church services) on the city. Just two days after Frederick's 'coronation' the Patriarch's interdict was formally brought in writing to Jerusalem. It was enough to compel the emperor to leave the Holy City and head out to Jaffa and then to Acre, where he was by 23 March 1229.

In Acre the mood was dark. The barons were angered that the treaty had been made without their consent. There was rioting in the streets and the Templars were in no mood for peace, knowing that the treaty had only been signed with just one of the many Ayyubid leaders of the Muslim world who all had differing designs on the region. There were stories that the emperor even wanted to imprison or kill the Templar Grand Master and this was why the Templars put up such a show of force. There were also counter rumours that the outraged Templars wished to kill Frederick. As if the enmity could get any worse, the Templars had to suffer the indignity of an imperial demand to cede the new castle at 'Atlit (Château Pèlerin) to Frederick's army which came to sit outside it. The Templar response was to simply shut the gates of this impregnable fortress on the emperor and leave him to return to Acre with no result. In Acre itself, Frederick besieged the houses of the Temple and the Patriarch. He placed crossbowmen at strategic places around the city so that no one could get in or out of the Templar complex. But Frederick was rocked by the news that John of Brienne had invaded his states at the head of a papal army. John's career had taken a new turn as he now looked forward to ruling as the Latin Emperor at Constantinople until his death in 1237. It was enough for Frederick to decide to turn for home. On 1 May 1229 he left Acre, trying to steal away in the morning, but he was spotted by a crowd who threw rotten meat at him. He had left two men, Balian of Sidon and Garnier the German, in control of the kingdom, and later from 1231 his *bailli*, or official representative, was to be Richard Filangieri, an imperial marshal who operated mainly from Tyre. Despite his diplomatic achievement, Frederick II must have known of the bitter resentment against him. By June 1229 he was back in Italy and in an act of spite against the military orders who had crossed him, he confiscated many of the properties of the Temple and Hospital and although he was reconciled with the Pope by 1230, this property was not restored until 1239, the very year he was excommunicated yet again by the Pope for failing to hand back the property.

Chapter 18

The Barons' Crusade, 1239–41

Frederick II had left the Holy Land in something of a hurry. The provisions he had made for pilgrims to use the corridor of land into Jerusalem do not seem to have included a realistic plan to protect them. For the Templars it must have seemed like business as usual in a hostile landscape. Even Jerusalem itself was attacked by Muslim fanatics who withdrew at the arrival of Balian of Sidon and Garnier, who managed to restore some stability, but elsewhere roving bands of robbers were once again attacking pilgrims. Although the interdict in Jerusalem was lifted, the politics of the Outremer states were dominated by a factional split between the supporters of 'The Old Lord of Beirut' John of Ibelin (based mainly around the citizens of Acre and the baronage), and the pro-imperialists centred on Tyre and Richard Filangieri. Riots in the streets of Acre and civil war in Cyprus did nothing to secure the future for Outremer. John of Ibelin had been popular in Acre and even became its mayor during these struggles. It is probable that despite the tangled complexity of the power struggles, the local baronage saw John as a de facto ruler of the kingdom at this time. Although the Templars seem to have stood aside during all this, the fact that John ended his days as a Templar in 1236 may indicate there had been a tacit support for the anti-imperialist cause.

Amidst all this turmoil, the Franks were lucky that the vulnerable kingdom was not seriously threatened. Peter of Montaigu had died in around 1231. His replacement was Armand of Périgord (c.1231–c.1244/46) who had been preceptor in Calabria and Sicily and whose appointment may have had imperial influence behind it, although this is by no means certain. The Templars had marched alongside the Hospitallers in 1230 in a combined effort against Hama during which they had been ambushed and defeated. In 1233, in a continuing dispute over the Emir of Hama's failure to pay tribute money to the Hospitallers, the Templars joined with them along with secular knights from Jerusalem, Cyprus and Antioch to conduct a punitive eight-day campaign in order to secure payment. But not all campaigns brought such results. In 1237, when roving bands of Muslims were foraging in the region between 'Atlit (Château Pèlerin) and Acre, Armand called out 120 of his knights. This area would have been considered a crusader heartland, even at this time when the kingdom had shrunk, so Armand's reaction is perhaps understandable. What is less clear is why the leadership ignored the warnings given by Walter of Brienne (the Count of Jaffa) against an attack. The enemy, as it perhaps always had been, was much larger than Armand's army and the subsequent Templar attack left only the Grand Master and nine of his brother knights alive.

There were more losses for the Temple in 1237. The garrison at Baghras undertook a raid on some Turcoman tribesmen east of Lake Antioch which infuriated the Muslim leadership at Aleppo. In retaliation, the forces of Aleppo besieged Baghras which was rescued in a timely fashion by Bohemond V of Antioch, who arranged a truce. However, the Templar Preceptor of Antioch, William of Montferrat, had different ideas. He led his Templars along with many secular knights and barons to the fortification at Darbsak, which had been an important marcher castle for the order. Now in enemy hands, William decided to besiege it with what turned out to be a numerically weak force. Aleppo once again came to the rescue and William was apparently even told of the impending arrival of the Muslim army by Christian captives in Darbsak who had managed to get a message out. In the event, the Templar force was swamped by the enemy and William was killed and many Templars taken captive. It was one of a number of defeats, news of which began to filter back to the West which did nothing for Templar public relations. However, King Henry III of England, when he heard of the news, was moved to send 500 marks of silver to the Templar Master in England for the ransom of the captives. Soon, a new truce was agreed in the region.

The treaty between Frederick II and al-Kamil was due to expire in the autumn of 1239. The sultan had died in 1228 and his heirs were divided. Pope Gregory IX had been preparing for a new crusade and had sent representatives across Europe where their message was responded to by a number of high-ranking noblemen from France and England. Chief amongst these in the first instance was Theobald, King of Navarre and Count of Champagne whose force of around 1,000 men arrived in Acre on 1 September 1239. Armand of Périgord was developing a Grand Strategy in the meantime. He had written to Walter of Avesnes in the summer telling the man who had helped the Templars build 'Atlit (Château Pèlerin) how he saw the divisions amongst the Ayyubid leaders as an opportunity. The new Sultan of Egypt was an unpopular man called al-Adil II, whom Armand branded a coward. He was at loggerheads with the Sultan of Hama. The Lord of Kerak an-Nasir Dawud was set against Damascus. Amidst all this, Armand reported that some Muslim lords were prepared to submit to the Christians and this would be advantageous in the long run for the regaining of territory. It was an elaborate analysis, but by the time Theobald had arrived in Acre, things were already changing. Al-Salih Ismail had seized Damascus from his nephew who in turn had been captured by the Muslim Lord of Kerak.

The crusading barons were different in nature from the previous crusaders of Frederick II's expedition. They had come to fight in the old-fashioned way. They numbered amongst themselves some particularly enthusiastic men such as Henry, Count of Bar. Theobald decided that the southern flank of the kingdom should be made secure before a drive on Damascus could be attempted. To this end, the objectives would be Gaza and Ascalon. They moved out from Acre on 2 November 1239. What happened next provided an example of the increasing difference in attitude between the Franks of the West and those of the East. It also sowed the seeds of Western distrust of the military orders, whose caution was often based on superior knowledge of the political landscape.

The Egyptian sultan had sent a Mameluke emir, Rukn ad-Din to Gaza. Henry of Bar, on hearing news that it might be a small force, kept his plans to attack it secret from all except for a few Western Frankish friends. At night-time on 12 November around 1,500 crusaders got ready to move out to Gaza when news of their preparations broke around the rest of the camp. Theobald, the Count of Brittany (whose recent successful foray against a Muslim caravan in the Jordan valley had probably provoked Henry's warlike stance) and all three masters of the military orders demanded that Henry cease the preparations. He did not listen. His men were subsequently surrounded in the dunes near Gaza by the larger Muslim army and badly mauled, their horses unable to gain a foothold in the sand. Around 600 men were captured and the rest killed, amongst the dead was Henry. One of the prisoners was a poet named Philip of Nanteuil whose scathing attacks cast blame upon the military orders for the debacle at Gaza: 'If the Hospital and the Temple and the brother knights had given a good example of fighting to our men, our great knighthood would not now be in prison nor would the Saracens be alive. But this they never did, which was a great fault and seems like treason.'

The criticism was inaccurate and unfair, but it represented a growing notion in the West (albeit ill-informed) that the military orders had their own agendas in the East. Perhaps the shrinking land mass of the kingdom and the fact that the military orders were holding an increasing proportion of that land had something to do with it. But to Western minds the Templars in particular, who were supposed to fight the enemy wherever they were and whatever the circumstances, were embroiling themselves in the politics of the region and not supporting pious noblemen such as Henry of Bar. To the Templars, charged with nothing less than the military protection of the Holy Land in a time of turbulence, such views were naïve in the extreme. It did not help that the Temple and Hospital were about to embark on alternative policies over the next few years which revolved around which Muslim polity to throw their support behind as the situation moved quickly. In short, the Templars favoured Damascus and the Hospitallers Egypt, but to explain all this to a Westerner at the time was virtually impossible.

Theobald's crusade moved north after the Gaza defeat. As if to add insult to injury, an-Nasir of Kerak stormed the weakly defended Jerusalem and retired eventually to Kerak only after some of the new fortifications built by the crusaders in the Holy City had been dismantled. By the summer of 1240 Theobald had come down to Galilee where he was approached by Al-Salih Ismail of Damascus. Ismail was afraid of a Muslim alliance against him based on the strength of Egypt. The Templars had much to gain from an alliance with Damascus. The castles at Beaufort and Safad and the territories dependent upon them would be in Christian hands once again, if the negotiations followed their promised course. Safad in particular was a considerable concession for the Templars. They would be restored to an area they had dominated in the years before Hattin and their subsequent rebuilding of the castle at this time attracted much comment (see p. 199).

But the Hospitallers were keener to negotiate with Egypt. When the allied army of Theobald and Al-Salih Ismail moved south, many of the Muslim contingent deserted to the Egyptian side. This resulted in a Hospitaller brokered agreement which promised the release of the prisoners of the earlier Gaza encounter and the right to fortify Gaza if they remained neutral henceforth. Theobald accepted the agreement. The Franks of Outremer were disconcerted at his easy break with Damascus.

Many Muslims had also been bewildered at the Damascene alliance. As Theobald departed the Holy Land in September 1240, perhaps rather more swiftly than he had planned after this latest development, there were some who stayed behind. The Templars found themselves encamped near Jaffa with the Count of Nevers. The Duke of Burgundy had stayed too. Ascalon, Beaufort and Safad had come back into the fold, so the crusade had at least been a partial success. But on 11 October 1240 an Englishman, Richard, Earl of Cornwall (brother of Henry III of England) whose sister was married to Frederick II, arrived at Acre.

Richard of Cornwall found Acre in uproar. The Templars and Hospitallers were in open conflict with each other, with Hospitallers moving more towards an imperial line. Richard was, however, an impressive diplomat. He went to Ascalon and consulted with a representative from the Egyptian Sultan Ayub's government. In return for recognising the treaty agreed with the Hospitallers Richard demanded confirmation of the Christian territories in Galilee granted by Ismail and furthermore demanded that Belvoir, Mount Tabor and Tiberias were added to the agreement. He also finally secured the return of the Frankish prisoners from Gaza. In May 1241 Richard left Palestine rightly pleased with himself, as too was his brother-in-law, Frederick II. West of the Jordan the kingdom was almost as large as it had once been in the years before Hattin, with the exception Gaza, Hebron, Nablus and other minor Samarian settlements. But these diplomatic successes masked the discord which still ran through the Outremer.

The Templars for their part had been irked by the agreement with Egypt. Ascalon had been given to imperial representatives before Richard's departure and not, as might have been expected, to the Temple. In the spring of 1242 they launched an attack on Hebron which brought a retaliation from an-Nasir of Kerak who blocked the road to Jerusalem and exacted tolls on the Christian pilgrims. This was enough to anger the Templars whose core function was the protection of these very pilgrims. They attacked Nablus in October 1242 and destroyed its great mosque and massacred many of the people there. It was an uncharacteristic slaughter which the Templars seem to have commemorated in a fresco at their church at San Bevignate in Perugia. The reasons for such an overt celebration of a massacre which included many Christian as well as Muslim souls is not entirely clear.

What is clearer is that the Templars' Grand Strategy seemed to be gaining the ascendancy over the Hospitallers and imperialists. The Templars had thrown their support behind Alice, Queen Dowager of Cyprus as regent of Jerusalem over Conrad, Frederick II's son, who perhaps had a greater right to rule than Alice. However, like his father, Conrad was rather reluctant to turn up in the East, and had instead sent an old enemy of the Templars in his place, one Thomas of Aquino, Count of Accera. Thomas some years ago had kept some war booty from the order. However, the barons' acceptance of Alice and their ultimate driving out of imperialist forces at Tyre in 1243, gave the Templars renewed vigour. Armand of Périgord wrote late in 1243 to the English Templar Preceptor Robert of Sanford in London and explained the order's policy in the East. He was also able to rejoice at a remarkable piece of diplomacy which had seen the Temple play off one Muslim faction against another as offers from each camp poured in. The result was a triumphant Christian return to the Temple area in Jerusalem, as the Muslims pulled out of the area. 'To the joy of angels and men', he wrote, 'Jerusalem is now inhabited by Christians alone … in those spots where the name of the Lord has not been invoked for fifty-six years, now, blessed be God, the Divine Mysteries are daily celebrated'. How this bargaining position of strength had been reached by the Templars is not clear, but the blistering attack on Nablus the previous year, as well as some enigmatic mentions of actions around Gaza, may have demonstrated to Ismail, Ayub and an-Nasir that the Templars were of a single mind when it came to the matter of protecting the Holy Land.

In his letter, the Grand Master had been concerned about the lack of concord and unity amongst the Christians and felt as though the whole burden of the defence of the Holy Land was falling once again to the Templars and a few dedicated barons. Armand had something to say about military plans as well. The Sultan of Egypt could not be trusted. He had kept Templar emissaries sent to Cairo in 1243 for six months in virtual imprisonment, something Armand saw as a delaying tactic so the sultan could overcome his opponents, particularly Ismail. Hebron, Gaza, Nablus and Daron remained in Muslim hands. Gaza in particular, he saw as the gateway to the kingdom and must be regained. Armand even proposed the building of a new castle on the route between Jaffa and Jerusalem so the kingdom could be more easily defended, but he finished his letter with a prophetic warning that the Sultan of Egypt was 'a most powerful and cunning man'. These developments failed to amuse Frederick II who felt that Templar independent actions had undermined his authority in the East and in particular his 1229 treaty. He may have been right, but when Armand received an angry letter from the emperor threatening to confiscate the order's properties in Italy and Germany, Armand's reaction can only be guessed at.

Chapter 19

La Forbie, 1244

In the spring of 1244 war broke out between Cairo and Damascus. Ayub and Ismail were the main protagonists but an-Nasir and the Prince of Homs, al-Mansur Ibrahim, had also joined forces with Ismail. The Templars had persuaded the barons of the land to support a Damascus alliance. But true to Armand's fears the Egyptian sultan had sought a renewal of an old alliance with a fierce Turkish tribe, the Khwarismians. This group were now raiding around northern Syria and had based themselves near Edessa. Ayub knew that it was their geographical position as much as their ferocity which posed a great threat to Damascus and the Kingdom of Jerusalem, both of which he wanted the Khwarismians to attack. In June 1244 they did just that. They sacked village after village in the region of Damascus but then turned away from the great Muslim city and headed out to Galilee, taking Tiberias and coming through Nablus en route to the Holy City. There were 10,000 of them, far too many for local Christian forces to resist. Even so, the Templars and Hospitallers worked furiously on reinforcing the garrison and new fortifications in Jerusalem. But on 11 July 1244 the Khwarismians overran the outer defences and poured into the streets of the city. As people were brutalised in the streets, the garrison held out and sent for help to their new (and yet reluctant) Muslim ally, an-Nasir. The Lord of Kerak sent some troops who demanded of the Khwarismians that they allow the garrison safe conduct to the coast in return for the surrender of the citadel. The saddest part of the ensuing exodus of 6,000 Christians is what happened to them once they were outside the city on their way to Jaffa. Some who saw Frankish flags flying in Jerusalem attempted to return to it thinking Christian help had arrived. They were cut down in large numbers outside the city. Others were picked off by bandits in the hostile landscape. Just a few hundred reached Jaffa. Inside the city the Church of the Holy Sepulchre was stormed by the Turks, its priests slain and the bones of the kings of Jerusalem strewn around. And then the place was set ablaze. Only after the markets and shops were stripped of their goods and many other churches burned, did the Khwarismians move on to join the Egyptians at Gaza.

The lack of Christian intervention during the Jerusalem massacre was a problem of numbers. The knights of the region were preoccupied by the necessity to guard their own strongpoints lest they be taken. And for this reason they were dispersed around the kingdom near to those strongpoints thus rendering themselves unable to come to the city's aid. A collective letter of September 1244 written to Pope Innocent IV had outlined this problem. However, the allies as a whole did respond. Outside Acre the secular knights of Outremer slowly gathered and were soon joined by al-Mansur Ibrahim of Homs and an-Nasir. The Muslim allies were entertained in the Templar quarter. On 4 October they marched down the coast to the south to Jaffa, although an-Nasir seems to have kept his distance with his Bedouins. The army was larger than any put in the field since Hattin. There were 600 secular knights under the command of Philip of Montfort, Lord of Toron and Tyre, and Walter of Brienne, Count of Jaffa. Armand of Périgord had over 300 of his Templars and the Hospitaller Master William of Châteauneuf had a similar number of his own brethren. The Teutonic Knights provided a little over 400 of their number and also present were the leper knights of the Order of St Lazarus. Along with many thousands of infantry troops there were also the contingents of John and William of Botrun and John of Ham, Constable of Tripoli. The Patriarch Robert, the Archbishop of Tyre and Ralph, Bishop of Ramla were also in the army. The allied commands of al-Mansur Ibrahim and an-Nasir seem to have supplied lightly armed yet numerous contingents of cavalry.

The army marched to Ascalon whilst the Egyptians and Khwarismians marched north of Gaza. They did not stay long around Ascalon and moved out on 17 October towards Gaza but came across the enemy army on a sandy plain a couple of miles to the north-east of the town. The subsequent encounter became known as the Battle of La Forbie (or Hirbiya). Walter, Count of Jaffa appears to have been the most bellicose. His desire to combat the Egyptian army was more powerful than the caution advised by al-Mansur Ibrahim, who suggested they make camp and fortify it. Armand's position is less clear, but being previously opposed to Walter, he might have favoured his Muslim ally's approach. The crusaders and allies divided into three sections. The Christians were on the western or coastal flank and then in the centre were the men of Damascus and Homs and an-Nasir was out on the eastern or left flank of the army.

The battle raged for two days. The Egyptians initially withstood Frankish charges and the first day ended in stalemate at sunset. However, the next day, the Khwarismians targeted the Muslim allies of the Franks and the Damascenes finally turned and fled in disorder. Also, an-Nasir's forces retreated. This had left the 'warriors of the cross', says a joint letter written by the Christians, 'alone to withstand the united attack of the Egyptians and Khwarismians'. During the flight of the Muslim allies, the Christian infantry became mixed up with the knights, making it difficult for the knights to mount effective attacks. Moreover, the sandy plain hindered the grip of the horses. Al-Mansur escaped the field but the Khwarismians were now able to attack the Christians in their flank and the resulting casualties were enormous. Amongst them was Armand of Périgord himself, either captured or killed. William of Rochefort, the new acting Grand Master, reported that only thirty-three Templars and twenty-six Hospitallers managed to escape. The Hospitallers had taken an even dimmer view of those numbers, reporting that just eighteen and sixteen brothers of the Temple and Hospital had escaped respectively. Other dead included the Archbishop of Tyre, the Bishop of Ramla and the two Lords of Botrun. Walter, Count of Jaffa, the Hospitaller Master and the Constable of Tripoli were taken prisoner. Walter was led in captivity to his own Jaffa by the Khwarismians and tortured and paraded before the walls, but the inhabitants held firm and refused to capitulate, so Walter was carried off into captivity once more, later dying as a prisoner. Philip of Montfort and the Patriarch had made it back to Ascalon and had gone on by sea to Jaffa. The losses were said to have been up to as many as 5,000, amongst them all but 3 of the Teutonic Knights' contingent and all of men of the Order of St Lazarus. The commitment of the military orders was clear, hurling themselves into a numerically superior enemy. But it had been a disaster. Already struggling for numbers, the kingdom was once again on its knees and vulnerable. Even the military orders, so reliable and necessary a backbone of Outremer's defences, had been severely depleted by the defeat at La Forbie. Someone had to take the blame, so Frederick II pinned it squarely on the Templars who had not only accommodated the Muslims, but had then been deserted by them on the battlefield. Given the success of the Templar position up to the point of the battle, this criticism is both partisan and inaccurate, but as the defence of Outremer had come to rely upon the military orders, any failures were therefore bound to be their fault. Outremer would never fully recover.

There are hints from Matthew of Paris's chronicle that Armand of Périgord may not have been killed after all and may have been the focus of a failed ransom bid in 1246. During this uncertain period, another Templar, Richard of Bures, may also have stepped in as acting Grand Master, but little is mentioned of him. The next Grand Master, William of Sonnac, Preceptor of Aquitaine, was not elected until 1247. But one thing would be certain, the Templars would eventually replace their losses and remain a viable fighting force. By then, though, Ayub had ascended to supremacy amongst the Muslims, taking Damascus in 1245. His delay in doing so probably saved Outremer from complete extinction with the Franks now penned-in to their coastal cities hurriedly concentrating on their physical defences. And soon the sultan had taken more Christian land and the castles at Tiberias, Mount Tabor, Belvoir and Ascalon, which he completely dismantled. The Franks were hanging on by a thread.

Chapter 20

The Seventh Crusade, 1248–54

Help was a long time in coming. King Louis IX of France (1226–70) had been seriously ill with malaria in December 1244 and had vowed to go on crusade. He was a famously pious man and was canonised in 1297, a generation after his death. But Louis's crusade was three years in the planning and preparation. It was not until 5 June 1249 that the king's forces made landfall in the East, and he came not to Palestine, or to Syria, but led a crusading army once again to Egypt and the Nile Delta. The decision to attack Egypt was made when the crusaders were at Limassol in Cyprus in late September 1248. The Master of the Temple was there alongside his Hospitaller counterpart and many barons of Outremer, all hosted by the Cypriot King Henry. Once the decision was made, probably with memories of how readily Egypt had offered concessions in the face of the crusaders of 1217–21, some veterans of which were present, Louis was keen to set out straight away. However, the Grand Masters of the military orders and the barons dissuaded him, urging caution. Louis was unimpressed by the Templars' own diplomatic efforts in his absence. They had negotiated with the sultan and an offer of territory in return for Frankish military help was in the offing, but Louis would not entertain such negotiations and rebuked the Temple for liaising with the sultan's envoys and forbade them to do so again.

Louis had stayed in Cyprus for around seven months, at the end of which there had been some difficulties raising sufficient shipping from the squabbling Italian merchant states. Also, because of the delay the food was running low. When Louis set out for Egypt from Cyprus he did so with only about a third of his force, the remainder having been scattered by storms in mid-May. He did not wait for the others to re-group. Sultan Ayub, who had been in Damascus and was expecting an attack in Syria, had managed to rearrange his forces and get help to Egypt. He came back to Cairo and at the head of his army he appointed his vizier, Fakhr ad-Din. The sultan was concerned for Damietta, with good historical reasoning. He stiffened its garrison with Bedouin tribesman and placed himself at Ashmun-Tannah. When the landing came, the Franks fought their way up the sandy beach pushing back Fakhr ad-Din's forces who had met them there. The vizier pulled back to Damietta, whose garrison was now very aware of the successful Frankish landing. Fakhr ad-Din decided to evacuate the city of its Muslim populace and the Bedouin garrison followed on soon after, but did not heed their orders to torch the bridge of boats which led to the city. On 6 June 1249 the crusaders more or less walked into the city. William of Sonnac wrote to Robert of Sandford telling him how this happened with the loss of just one of their number. Whilst work commenced on converting Damietta into a Christian city, Louis waited, keen not to repeat the disasters of the Fifth Crusade amidst the rising Nile waters. Cairo or Alexandria might well be the next target, wrote William of Sonnac.

Delay however, has consequences just as serious as precipitate action. Bedouin tribesmen remained at large in the watery landscape ready to pick off wandering Franks. Damietta ran short of food and disease broke out in the crusader camp. The delay also allowed the ageing sultan to deal with the Bedouin emirs who had so ingloriously deserted the city. He executed them. He also disgraced Fakhr ad-Din and the chief Mameluke commander. The Mamelukes were in rebellious mood and had designs on taking over the leadership itself, but Fakhr ad-Din had seen to it that this did not happen and so earned himself a reprieve. The sultan even sent messengers with offers to buy back Damietta from the crusaders in an echo of the past, but Louis would not hear of it. The Egyptians sent troops into a newly built town at Mansourah, founded by al-Kamil in the wake of his victory of 1221. The town's name itself, meant 'victorious'.

By the end of October 1249 the Nile waters had receded and the king's brother, Alfonso of Poitou, had arrived with reinforcements. The debate over Alexandria or Cairo as the focus of the next stage of the campaign continued as Peter, Count of Brittany and a veteran of the Barons' Crusade, argued for a surprise attack on Alexandria thus securing the whole stretch of coastal Egypt for the Franks. But a powerful representation by one of the king's other brothers, Robert of Artois, called for an advance on Cairo, and this argument prevailed. The army set out on 20 November, heading towards Mansourah with William of Sonnac's Templars in the van. But just three days later the Egyptian sultan died.

The sultan's death gave the crusaders heart although the news only slowly leaked out, being carefully managed by the sultan's widow and Fakhr ad-Din, who was now the de facto leader of Egypt's resistance. He kept his forces behind the canals of the delta and harassed the Frankish advance. Near to Fariskur on 7 December 1249 there was an attack against the van of the army, repulsed by the Templars and others, according to John of Joinville, Louis's biographer. However, the subsequent Templar pursuit of the fugitives apparently went against the king's orders and angered him. For their part, the Templars probably felt that they were merely doing what they always did in the van of the army by clearing away the attackers. By 21 December the Franks were camped on the banks of the Bahr as-Saghir canal opposing Mansourah. For six weeks there was a stand-off. A Muslim attempt to pass cavalry to the rear of the crusaders was beaten away by another of the king's brothers, Charles of Anjou. Meanwhile, efforts to bridge the canal were thwarted by the Greek Fire syphons of the enemy whenever the Franks brought up their amphibious machinery to build a dyke. Early in February 1250 a local man approached the crusaders and in exchange for money revealed to them the place where a ford existed across the canal. On 8 February the army marched out, leaving the Duke of Burgundy behind in the camp. In the van were the Templars, Robert of Artois and William Longespée (II), Earl of Salisbury with an English contingent.

The van crossed the canal. What happened next embedded itself in the corporate memory of the Knights Templar for the rest of their existence. Whether we believe Joinville's account (who after all, was on the crusade, but not present in the van), Matthew Paris's account (based partly on a messenger's tale reported to Richard of Cornwall) or the snippets we get from elsewhere including the reported anger of the men of the Earl of Salisbury, there is one person who does not come out of it well. The Count of Artois, says Joinville, immediately attacked the enemy and put them to flight. This sort of thing was the Templars' bread and butter as traditional leaders of the van of a crusading army and it did not sit well with William of Sonnac. The count should have been in the second squadron by the king's own orders. This does not account, however, for the fog of war. The Templars remonstrated with the count but their words were ignored as one of the count's knights who received the complaint was profoundly deaf. Moreover, it was this same knight who continued to urge the advance. Subsequently, the Templars, fearing dishonour, charged after the rampant Count of Artois and on into the restricted streets of Mansourah, where they were trapped and surrounded and brutally slaughtered with losses totalling over 280 Templars, the count himself, and 300 others.

Matthew Paris paints a surprisingly detailed picture and does not mince his words. The count was 'proud and arrogant', he says. He pursued the fleeing enemy into Mansourah and was only pushed back by a volley of missiles. He then turned to the Templar Grand Master and the Earl of Salisbury arguing for a continued attack but was rebuffed by them both. Paris describes William of Sonnac as 'discreet and circumspect', skilled and experienced in matters of warfare. The Templar argued that his men were exhausted and many of his horses injured. Besides, a further attack would reveal to the enemy the relatively weak numbers of the crusaders in relation to their enemy. At this, Robert of Artois flew into a rage and nothing that William Longespée could do to persuade him to see the Grand Master's point of view would help, despite the fact that the Englishman reminded the count that the Templars' experience of Eastern affairs was so much greater than his. It was the count's pride (an accusation usually hurled at the Templars when things went wrong) which led to the disaster in the streets of Mansourah. He did not inform the king of his intentions and went headlong into calamity. The Earl of Salisbury was killed, Robert of Artois drowned trying to escape (or was massacred inside a house, according to another account) and only two Templars and one Hospitaller escaped.

Other accounts vary, but there is some small room for an apologia for the bellicose count. His attack was against the Egyptian camp in the first instance and this assault does seem to have caught them unawares. Fakhr ad-Din was slaughtered by some Templars having just left his ablutions and others were scattered. But in Mansourah itself the advance was doomed. A Mameluke commander had strategically placed troops around the junctions of the streets to pour fire into the oncoming crusaders who came through the gate left open for this very purpose.

William of Sonnac appears to have lost an eye at some stage. He still held his faith in the king and the cause of the crusading army as he returned to assist the king who had fought his way over to the other side. But the Egyptians had brought up more reinforcements and by 11 February the Mameluke onslaughts against the crusaders were relentless. William of Sonnac had built a barricade with broken up captured Saracen engines, says Joinville. But the enemy came up and hurled Greek Fire into it. They encountered the Templars amidst the burning flames. The Grand Master, fighting to the last as so many others had before him, lost a second eye and was slain. 'And you should know . . .', says Joinville, 'that there was at least an acre of land behind the Templars, which was so covered with arrows fired by the Saracens, that none of the ground could be seen'.

The Egyptians eventually retreated but King Louis could go no further. The Seventh Crusade had faltered in the same region as the Fifth. Moreover, Turanshah, the son of the late sultan, had come to aid Egypt and had organised an amphibious force which was intercepting Frankish supply ships behind their own lines. History it seemed, was repeating itself. By April Louis could only realistically contemplate retreat. And this he did under difficult conditions with what remained of the military orders forming the rear guard. It was a muddy disaster with numerous casualties. In time the Franks were surrounded and a huge number of prisoners were taken, including the royal person himself. The terms demanded by the Muslims were nothing less than the exchange of Louis for Damietta and the sum of 500,000 livres for the ransom of the army, although this came down later to 400,000, half to be paid at Damietta and half when the king returned to Acre. However, on 2 May 1250 Turanshah was murdered by members of the regiment of Mamelukes who had so conspicuously defended Mansourah. At the head of the murderous group of warriors was a man whose eventual rise to power would have far-reaching consequences for the Franks of Outremer. He was a Mameluke of Kipchak origin whose name history has shortened to Baibars.

The Mamelukes

Originally military 'slave' warriors, the Mamelukes seized power in Egypt in 1250 at the time of Louis IX's Seventh Crusade. However the term 'slave' is misleading. After a period of training a Mameluke might rise to a number of high administrative posts. Under the Egyptian Sultan Ayub (1240–9) the official use of Mameluke warriors dramatically increased as such men were made available by the displacement caused further east by the Mongol invasions. Ayub's elite regiment of Mamelukes numbered 800 to 1,000 men, many recruited from Kipchak Turkish areas. It was the Mamelukes who surrounded and killed the Count of Artois and many Templars in the streets of Mansourah in 1250. After this, the rise of the Mamelukes was unrelenting. Not only did they sweep to power at the expense of the Ayyubid rulers, it was their armies who overcame the Mongol threat and finally expelled the Franks form Outremer in 1291.

On 6 May Louis IX was released and Damietta handed over, but the king's brother was kept back to ensure payment of the first 200,000 livres. When the crusaders counted their money in Damietta they found themselves to be 30,000 livres short. Joinville reports that he himself went to the Templar commander Stephen of Otricourt for a loan of the money, but to Joinville's anger and annoyance he was refused on the grounds that the wealth the order had brought with them belonged to others who had entrusted it to the Templars and so it was not theirs to give. It was then that Reginald of Vichiers, the Templar Marshal who was acting as Grand Master, came up with a solution. If Joinville and his men were simply to rob the Templars of the money then the knights' honour would remain intact. Once on board the Templar galley which carried the money, Joinville met with further resistance from the Templar treasurer who refused to hand over the keys to the chests, but when Reginald of Vichiers intervened and prevented Joinville from taking a hatchet to the chests, the treasurer relented and handed over the keys. And so the ransom money was paid and Louis, leaving behind numerous imprisoned or dead men ruefully made his way back to Acre, where he arrived on 13 May 1250.

Louis stayed at Acre whilst many senior figures of the crusade sailed home. By July he had been recognised as the de facto ruler of the diminished kingdom. He genuinely seems to have wanted to make amends, concentrating his efforts on diplomacy and the refortification of the remaining crusader coastal cities with the help of the military orders, in particular at Caesarea. He did not leave Outremer until 1254 and being a pious man, never quite rid himself of the crusading urge, coming later in life on crusade to Tunis, where he ended his days in 1270. The Temple seems to have had a mixed relationship with the king. On his arrival at Acre in 1250 Louis had rewarded Reginald of Vichiers for his courtesies by throwing his weight behind the marshal's elevation to Grand Master.

In 1251 the relationship seemed to be going well when some Assassin envoys arrived at Acre and attempted to blackmail the king. They demanded tribute from him as they had done with many other regional rulers. But they added that if the king did not wish to pay them, they would instead accept a cancellation of the tribute money which they themselves had to pay to the military orders. Louis was wise enough not to fall for the ploy and fetched in the Grand Masters of both the Temple and Hospital. Joinville says the Masters had no fear of the Assassins since they knew that their murderous strategy of killing important figures would mean nothing to the military orders who would just replace their head with someone similar. The Masters demanded the envoys state their demands, as it seemed they had temporarily lost their tongues. On hearing these demands, the meeting was put back to the next day. When it was reconvened the Masters launched themselves in a verbal tirade at the envoys. They demanded that the Assassins go back to their leader and return to the king with valuable gifts. Ultimately, the Assassins backed down and brought the gifts and arranged a mutual defence treaty with the Franks.

Reginald of Vichiers stood godfather to Louis's son, Peter, who was born in the Templar stronghold of 'Atlit (Château Pèlerin), but relations were not always cordial between the king and the Temple. In 1252 Reginald sent his Marshal Hugh of Juoy to negotiate an agreement with Damascus. Its new ruler, al-Nasir Yusuf of Aleppo, had risen to power in 1250. The agreement reached would return some land to the order, but when the Marshal and an envoy from Damascus returned Louis flew into a rage that negotiations had taken place without his knowledge. He made the Templars walk barefoot through the camp to his tent. The sultan was to be told that the treaty was not going to be ratified and his envoy was to return with all the relevant documents. For Reginald it was a public humiliation. For Hugh of Juoy, the punishment was banishment from the kingdom. It was no idle threat. Hugh is next heard of in Spain in 1255.

Reginald of Vichiers died in January 1256. He had been Preceptor of Acre in 1240 and Preceptor of France between 1241 and 1248. He had assisted Louis's crusade efforts in both the provision of shipping and in the fighting on the ground. He had helped bail him out of trouble too. Nobody knows what Reginald thought when Louis set sail from Acre in April 1254 to attend to home affairs. What little remained of Outremer was more vulnerable than ever before. There was civil strife brewing amongst the Italian merchant contingents in Acre. The Mamelukes of Egypt were growing more powerful, but their leader Aibek and the ruler of Damascus both separately concluded treaties with the Franks between 1254 and 1255. But everyone in power in the region at the time had good reason to be distracted. The new Templar Grand Master Thomas Bérard (1256–73) would have more than just the civil upheavals in Acre to worry about. The Mongols, for a long time a menace, were now a direct threat to all.

Chapter 21

Mongols and Mamelukes

The Templars were certainly wary of the Mongol threat. In late 1256 Guy of Baisanville, a Templar Commander of Knights, had written to the Bishop of Orléans explaining that the Mongols had invaded many of the Muslim lands and were bearing down upon Jerusalem. In either 1256 or 1257 Thomas Bérard sent twelve brothers to Jerusalem, but four of them soon left the city. As there were Mongols in the countryside, Thomas sent a letter to the Commander ordering him to leave the city and retire to Jaffa. Four brothers, probably those who had left earlier, approached the Commander asking him to obey the instruction but he refused to leave the brothers of the Hospital who were with them. He also refused to order the brothers to stay, creating a loophole which had to be resolved by clause 576 of the Templar Rule. The four then left and returned to their Master pleading for mercy knowing that they had left their commander and banner in the city but had tried to honour the Master's original order. According to clause 576, the brothers escaped harsh punishment. This was the sort of upheaval the threat of the Mongols could have on the protocols of a military order.

The fear Thomas felt was made worse by the damaging events which became known as the wars of Saint Sabas which broke out in Acre at around the same time and which sucked in many important families with ties to each of the groups involved. The Genoese and Venetians were in conflict over the property of the abbey of St Sabas in Acre and the constant flare-ups between these two Italian merchant communities, which also involved the Pisans, did nothing to convince anyone of a Christian united front in the face of a much greater threat. Worse, the Hospitallers sided with the Genoese and the Templars and Teutonic Knights with the Venetians. So fierce was the conflict in the city of Acre that at one point in 1258 Thomas Bérard found himself holed up in the tower of St Lazarus when his own quarter was caught in the crossfire between all three squabbling groups whose siege engines were hurling missiles at one another. The military orders, however, saw sense and agreed to keep the peace by October 1258. Eventually, the Genoese were driven out and went on to help the Byzantines wrest the imperial throne from the Franks in 1261.

The rise of the Mongols was inexorable. The Assassins in their Persian bases had been all but wiped out by the invaders. Early in 1258 Baghdad had fallen and further west Aleppo had succumbed in January 1260. By March even Damascus had capitulated to the Mongol leader Kitbogha. It is no surprise to find Christian leaders sending urgent letters to the West for help. Amongst these was a letter from the prolific Thomas Bérard carried by a Templar messenger to the order's English treasurer, Amadeus Morestello, in London with such a degree of urgency that he made it from Dover to London in a single day. Penned on 4 March 1260, it was read by its shocked recipient on 16 June.

It was not the first time Thomas had informed Amadeus of the 'terrible and awesome arrival of the Tartars [Mongols]'. But now, he says, 'they are here in front of our walls, knocking at our gates'. Their huge numbers were their great advantage and they were irresistible. He goes on to describe the Caliph of Baghdad's (the 'Pope of the Saracens') murder along with members of his family at the hands of the Mongols and lists a long string of places they had taken and destroyed. The people of Antioch only narrowly evaded the same treatment by offering gifts. Thomas complains that there are only three castles in the Kingdom of Jerusalem worthy of withstanding the hordes. 'Atlit (Château Pelerin), the newly rebuilt Safad and the Teutonic Knights' castle at Montfort were up to the task and the order had three more in Antioch and two more in Tripoli. But Thomas devotes much of his letter to describing the perilous financial situation of the Temple, and reminds his reader that the burden of financing the defence of the kingdom 'falls largely on us'. He was concerned the Templars might even 'default completely in respect of the defence of the Holy Land'. Acre was now empty of Italian merchants who despite their squabbling might otherwise have provided the sources for important financial loans. The Templars had had to 'quadruple our expenses on the fortifications since we cannot hire labourers unless we feed them and pay danger money'. The whole of Christendom 'on this side of the sea' seemed to have rushed to Acre for refuge. Only 10,000 marks of silver from the King of England could save the situation, said Thomas.

The Franks were rightly concerned, but, as Thomas had pointed out, each victim or target of the Mongols so far had been part of the Muslim world. The Mameluke power was more or less the only Muslim power left to realistically confront the Mongols. It was now headed up by the new Mameluke Sultan of Egypt Saif ad-Din Qutuz (1259–60). In July 1260 a Mameluke army penetrated into the Gaza region intent on seeking out the Mongol army. The Mongols had recently been weakened by internal dissension which had drawn significant numbers away from the region. At the head of the Mameluke army was Baibars. Looking to gain a strategic advantage over the Mongols who were in Baalbek, Qutuz sent to the Franks for permission to have free passage through their lands and also for any military help. The Franks convened at Acre and granted the free passage but not the additional military help (the Teutonic Knights had argued against it). The Mameluke army came right up to the environs of Acre which Baibars viewed with some interest, suggesting to Qutuz that it might even be taken by surprise. But there was a greater struggle to be had. Qutuz took the army out through Nazareth and came to Ain Jalud on 2 September. The next morning a smaller Mongol army under Kitbogha arrived. The battle that followed was a crushing success for the larger Mameluke force and

1. Temple Mount in Jerusalem looking north, showing the Dome of the Rock and the Western or Wailing Wall. This platform, so revered by three major religions also hosts al-Aqsa Mosque, a building which became the home of the Templars.

2. Statue outside Temple Church, London, England, showing two Templar Knights on one horse, a symbol taken by some to indicate the original Templars' frugality and humility.

3. and 4. Temple Church, London, England. The Templars had their first base in Holborn, a mile north of the current site. By 1161 they were in the 'New Temple' area by the river. The church was consecrated in honour of the Blessed Virgin Mary by the Patriarch of Jerusalem in 1185 when he visited London. The Round Church is the earlier structure, built to recall the Church of the Holy Sepulchre in Jerusalem. The chancel was added in the thirteenth century.

5., 6. and 7. Interior of the Round (nave) of Temple Church, London, England. The effigies on the floor of the church include those of Geoffrey de Mandeville, First Earl of Essex (d.1144); William Marshal, First Earl of Pembroke (d.1219), who joined the Templars near to the end of his life; William Marshal, Second Earl of Pembroke (d.1231); Gilbert Marshal, Fourth Earl of Pembroke (d.1241); and Robert de Roos, Fourth Baron of Hamlake (d.1227).

8. Painted glass window in the spiral staircase at Temple Church, London, showing the familiar Templar symbol of two knights on one horse.

9. Beaufort Castle, commanding the Litani Valley and southern approaches to the Beqa Valley. One of the few Templar castles surviving to a substantial degree. However, it was only in Templar hands between 1260 and 1268, when it fell to the Sultan Baibars.

10. A huge Templar barley barn at Cressing in Essex. This building dates from the early thirteenth century and is one of the few surviving Templar structures in England. Matilda of Boulogne, wife of King Stephen (1135–54), originally granted the order land at Cressing, from which they received a considerable income.

11. Now a tourist attraction, this tunnel was not discovered until 1994. At 350m long, it links the Templar fortifications at Acre to the city's medieval port on the east, passing through the Pisan sector of the city. The base of the tunnel is hewn out of solid rock and the middle and top are of carved stones making a semi-barrelled vault.

12. After the loss of Jerusalem in the wake of the disastrous Battle of Hattin (1187), many cities fell to Saladin. Acre was re-captured during the Third Crusade (1189–92) and became the new headquarters for the Templars, which they held until the siege of 1291. By this time the order had developed a substantial complex of buildings by the shore in the south-west corner of the city. What little survives today is partially submerged.

13. The Templars had a house in Sidon by 1173, but by 1260 they had purchased the entire lordship of Sidon and moved to this grand sea castle, begun in 1227–8 after a period of abandonment by Muslim conquerors in the era after 1187. It was held until it was abandoned in 1291 after the fall of Acre.

14. Tomar, Portugal. The main church of the convent. Now a UNESCO world Heritage site, Tomar became the Templars' headquarters in Portugal after 1160. In 1319 a new order named the Order of Christ received Templar property in the wake of the disbanding of the Templars.

15. Miravet Castle. Granted to the Templars in 1153 by Raymond Berenguer IV (d.1162), Count of Barcelona and ruler of Aragon, this castle was one of the strongest in Catalonia, overlooking the River Ebro.

16. The Horns of Hattin. In July 1187 the crusaders set out in the scorching heat and camped in the waterless landscape. Saladin surrounded and defeated the Christians. After this, many cities and castles fell to the Muslims.

17. Remains of the Templar castle at Tortosa (modern Tartus or Tartous, Syria). Modern superstructures cannot conceal the strength of the original Templar walls. Ashlar blocks rise above a rock-cut talus or slope. The castle comprised a 35m² keep and a double line of walls with towers. It was the regional centre for the Templars.

Baibars who led the van was instrumental in the success. Kitbogha was captured and executed. For the Mamelukes, the victory catapulted their power into the ascendancy in the region.

The new political landscape would now be dominated by the Muslims' desire to turn on the old enemy and ultimately to expel him from the region. Quickly the Muslim cities which had fallen to the Mongols such as Aleppo, Homs, Hama and Damascus had Islamic leaders once more. Mongol attempts to reverse the situation largely failed. As for Qutuz, his decision not to allow Baibars the governorship of Aleppo, cost him his life. The sultan was murdered on his way back to Cairo by Baibars, who elevated himself to the throne.

It may have been a way of taking advantage of the great Muslim victory over the Mongols that the Ibelins and Templars mounted a large-scale raiding expedition in February 1261 which targeted some Turcoman tribesmen in the Jaulan region who had fled from the Mongols. It was a large force drawn from Templar centres at Acre, Safad, 'Atlit (Château Pèlerin) and Beaufort, comprising 900 knights, 1,500 turcopoles and around 3,000 infantry. The expedition was such a disaster that it led to numerous Franks being killed or captured and the Marshal of the Templars, Stephen of Saissy, was one of the few who escaped. The 'Templar of Tyre', a writer who was clearly close to the Master, recorded that the Templars lost all their equipment in the action. He says, 'It was said of him [Stephen of Saissy] that he executed his attacks on the Turks poorly and turned back without striking a blow, either because his courage had failed him, or else voluntarily, because (they said) he bore ill-will to the Lord of Beirut urged on by a mad jealousy over a woman of his country.'

Thomas Bérard was displeased to such an extent that he took the step of depriving the Marshal of his habit and even sent him to the Pope for judgement. It did not much help relations with Baibars when early in 1263 after protracted negotiations John of Jaffa negotiated a peace with the Muslims and an exchange of prisoners that met with Templar and Hospitaller resistance. The orders were reluctant to give up their Muslim prisoners since they were skilled craftsmen who made them a profit. That same year Baibars conducted a punitive campaign against the Franks which saw him fighting beneath the walls of Acre, coming once again uncomfortably close to the seat of Christian power.

Thomas Bérard presided over a diminution of the Templars' base in Outremer even though he fought desperately to avoid it. His letters show that he was even prepared to pawn crosses and incense burners to raise the funds, but he just never had enough money. It is true that some funds came from Louis IX and elsewhere but it would never meet the costs of defence. Also, the papacy was distracted by its struggle to support Charles of Anjou in Sicily at this time. Baibars, with a colossal war machine at his disposal, took slow and systematic advantage of Frankish weakness as he campaigned across the Holy Land. In 1265 Caesarea fell to his siege engines, as did the Hospitaller castle at Arsuf and the town of Haifa. The next year, the prize Templar castle at Safad, so lovingly rebuilt by the order, also fell to Baibars after he resorted to trickery in the face of a seemingly impregnable fortification (see p. 200). Baibars even approached Acre once more in May 1267 carrying before him the captured banners of both the Temple and the Hospital. It was a clever ruse allowing him to get close to the walls, as the sultan knew that military orders' banners were often seen at the van of the Christian army. On this occasion, however, he did not succeed in taking the city. But in 1268 Jaffa fell and so too did the Templar castle at Beaufort. On 18 May 1268 Antioch ominously fell to the Mamelukes prompting a Templar abandonment of Baghras and much of their remaining presence in the Amanus march. In 1271 Chastel Blanc fell to Baibars as well as the Hospitaller stronghold of Crac des Chevaliers after a thirty-six-day siege. The Teutonic Knights fared no better. Montfort also fell in June 1271.

In 1271 the English Prince Edward, son of King Henry III, came to the East, having borrowed 27,974 livres to fund the expedition, which he later paid back with interest. It had been the fall of Antioch that had prompted the move. Edward's army was not as large as it might have been, numbering just around a thousand men in combined arms. He had wanted to join with Louis IX, who had gone to Tunis having been convinced by Charles of Anjou that the Emir of Tunis was susceptible to conversion. But Louis's crusade was a disaster and when Edward arrived there, the French king was dead. Edward continued on and arrived at Acre on 9 May 1271 having sailed via Sicily and Cyprus. He was joined by Prince Bohemond VI of Antioch-Tripoli and by King Hugh III of Cyprus, who had risen through a series of tangled claims and counter claims to the nominal throne of Jerusalem to become king himself, being crowned in 1269.

Prince Edward's subsequent diplomatic approach brought some Mongol intervention which Baibars had no choice but to deal with. There were large-scale incursions in northern Syria. Edward also conducted his own raids with the Templars and Hospitallers (see p. 162) but lacked sufficient numbers for these to make any lasting impact. It was clear that a treaty must be sought and so on 22 May 1272 at Caesarea the leaders of Outremer and the sultan agreed a ten-year treaty after Charles of Anjou (an opponent of King Hugh) had mediated between Edward and Baibars. But Outremer was shrinking by degree. Although Tripoli had been saved by a different treaty the year before, the crusader states were little more than a rump of what they had once been. Edward sailed for England to take the crown there, returning home late in 1272.

Thomas Bérard died in March 1273. His replacement was William of Beaujeu, preceptor of South Italy and Sicily, whose appointment as Grand Master may well have had the active support of Charles of Anjou. William was yet another battling Templar. He had been captured on the disastrous raid for which Stephen of Saissy had been punished in 1261. He had later become Preceptor of Tripoli and had plenty of experience in the Latin East. William was every bit as energetic as any of his predecessors and he travelled to France, England and Spain raising substantial funds for the cause. He also took a Templar contingent to the Council of Lyons in May 1274, convened by Pope Gregory X (1271–6), where the idea of a new crusade was discussed. King James I of Aragon (d.1276), the only attending monarch at the council, was also present and was enthusiastic about a new crusade and offered 500 knights and 2,000 infantry towards the enterprise, but William's delegation took a more cautious line according to the recollections of the king himself. The Grand Master, writes James, spoke of great logistical difficulties. King James left the council a frustrated man and perhaps felt the Templars to be less than enthusiastic. It may have been, however, that William felt that James' offering could be out-matched by Charles of Anjou who was busy manoeuvring himself into a position where he could challenge for the throne of Jerusalem. The final years of the Templars in Outremer were characterised by an adoption of a partisan stance in internal disputes whilst the storm clouds gathered around the remainder of Outremer.

Chapter 22

The Final Stand – Acre, 1291

William of Beaujeu came to Acre late in 1275. King Hugh would feel the effects of the Templar alliance with the Angevin lobby as he was more or less ignored by the order when they bought a small village outside of Acre without referring to him in 1276. Hugh's distrust of the Templars was quite open and he even wrote about it, blaming both them and the Hospitallers for the state of the kingdom. But Hugh wrote from Cyprus, to which he returned on numerous occasions. When he heard that the only other rival claimant to the throne, Maria of Antioch, had sold her stake to Charles of Anjou, he must have been mortified but not surprised. Roger of San Severino, Charles's representative, soon headed out to Acre and to the Templars' house. He began a cosy relationship of mutual cooperation with the Templars and Hugh's subsequent attempts to wrest control away from the Angevin camp met with failure. Hugh did, however, retaliate against the Templars in Cyprus by attacking the castle at Gastria and other Templar houses on the island.

Baibars had died in July 1277. It was a year of change in Outremer. The Muslims descended for a short while into a familiar pattern of power struggles but Baibars had left an inherently strong platform, and within a few years the Mameluke threat was once again great. But in those years the Templars became embroiled in a damaging civil war in Tripoli. Whilst they were probably only doing what they had always done by backing a strong strategy to best protect the Holy Land, their partisan involvement at a time when there was much else to worry about brought some distrust upon the order.

The Civil War in Tripoli lasted from 1277 to 1282. Bartholomew, the Bishop of Tortosa, had run Tripoli on behalf of the young Bohemond VII for a few years up to 1277, when Bohemond came of age. However, Paul of Segni, the Bishop of Tripoli, who had been at the Council of Lyons and was on good terms with William of Beaujeu, was opposed to Bartholomew. Bohemond soon fell out with his cousin and former friend Guy of Embriaco over a marriage proposal. The girl at the heart of it was a local heiress who was soon kidnapped by Guy and handed to his brother John for a bride. Bartholomew, however, had wanted her for his own nephew. Guy knew what he had done would incur the wrath of Bohemond so he ran off to the Templars and joined them. In retaliation Bohemond attacked the Templar house at

Tripoli and cut down a valuable forest of theirs at Montroque. The Templar Grand Master was incensed by this action and led a protest at the walls of Tripoli and then went on to torch the castle at Botrun and besiege Nephin, which did not go to plan and cost him twelve men killed or captured by Bohemond's men. The Templars moved back to Acre whilst Bohemond went looking for Guy. But Guy had thirty Templars with him and there was a battle between himself and Bohemond in which those Templars seem to have played a decisive part. Bohemond's forces were badly mauled and he sued for a year's truce. But in 1278 he was set upon again by Guy and the Templars. It was another defeat, but this time with a naval element. Bohemond's galleys attacked the Templar castle at Sidon, the order's own galleys having been dispersed by bad weather. Hospitaller help came to the Templars and prevented a defeat.

Guy was determined to get the upper hand over Bohemond and had designs on Tripoli itself. In 1282 Guy and his men stole into the Templar house there in a bid to take the town by surprise. But the Spanish Templar preceptor called Reddecouer was not there when they arrived. Suspecting intrigue, the men fled to the Hospitaller house but were spotted. Bohemond promised them safe conduct if they surrendered but then broke his word and had Guy and his immediate company killed and the others blinded.

Outside of Tripoli's internal disputes events moved swiftly and ominously. Charles of Anjou was hampered in his Eastern designs by the wars of the Sicilian Vespers in 1282. The Mameluke power struggles in the wake of Baibars's death resulted in the rise of one very capable commander called Qalawun. At around the same time as Qalawun's star rose, Charles of Anjou died in January 1285. King Hugh's oldest surviving son, John, reigned only very briefly and another son, Henry, succeeded as Henry II (1285–1324), coming to the East in 1286. The situation was perilous for the Franks, but the Templars had played a part in negotiating peace treaties, including one in 1282 which was to last for ten years and ten months and was to feature a ban on re-fortifications in the Tortosa region.

Qalawun, however, seems to have scented blood before these truces could expire. The Hospitaller castle at Marqab fell in 1285 and the important port at Latakia fell in 1287, the same year that Bohemond VII died. By 1289 Qalawun was at the gates of Tripoli where the Grand Master's reputation built up during the Civil War caught up with him. The Genoese lobby had risen to prominence in the town during the turmoil following the Civil War and some envoys had left Tripoli to tell the sultan that should Genoa prevail, the trade of Alexandria might be affected. Qalawun therefore had a pretext for intervention. On hearing through informants that the Mamelukes were closing in on Tripoli, William of Beaujeu sent a message into Tripoli to warn the townsfolk, but his messenger was not believed. Another message was sent to Acre where the Templar Reddecouer's message was this time accepted. The Templars sent a force under Geoffrey of Vendac, the Marshal. Also, the Hospitallers committed a force along with the secular troops of John of Grailly. But it was too late. On 26 April 1289 the sultan's men stormed the walls of Tripoli and amongst the slaughtered citizens was Peter of Moncade, the Templar Commander.

King Henry had managed to organise a truce with the sultan, but when a rabble of Lombard peasants and merchants arrived at Acre in response to panicked appeals for help, they embarked on a rampage around the city slaughtering everyone they thought was Muslim and embarrassing the Frankish authorities and military orders as a result. Qalawun was angry. He insisted that the government of Acre make reparation to him for the slaughter. Nobody quite knew the identity of any of the culprits except the obvious ring leaders. William of Beaujeu suggested emptying all the city's prisons of their Christian prisoners to give to the sultan in recompense. But the Grand Master was overruled. Qalawun had decided that Acre's days as the capital of a shrunken Christian kingdom were numbered.

Whilst the armies of Damascus and Egypt prepared their siege engines once again, William of Beaujeu's Muslim informant, an emir called al-Fakhri, told him that the Muslim plan was to direct an assault against Acre and not, as had been widely reported, to undertake an African expedition. Once again, as he had done at Tripoli, the Grand Master sent a warning into the city and once again he was not believed. William even sent his own envoy to Cairo to negotiate with the sultan who offered Acre respite in return for one Venetian penny per head of population. So William put this proposal before the High Court at Acre amidst apparent scenes of howling derision. The offer was rejected outright and William was hounded by the citizens as he left the hall. Once again they thought the Templars had gone to the Muslims with some underhand dealings about which they knew very little.

The Muslim preparations were slow but thorough. The sultan was no longer making Acre a secret target. He had vowed to rid the city of all Christians. But in November 1290 he died just a few miles outside the city. His son, al-Ashraf Khalil, however, had promised his dying father he would finish the job. Still, he put the assault off to the next spring. Acre's leaders tried to make the most of the respite and sent a delegation to Cairo which included a Templar named Bartholomew Pizan, a Hospitaller and a leading figure of the town who spoke fluent Arabic. Not one of them survived. They were incarcerated by the new sultan and soon perished. Meanwhile, the sultan's preparations continued. Siege engines large and small made their way to Acre, and tens of thousands of troops accompanied them. By 5 April 1291 they were beneath the walls. Any complacency the Templars or the townsfolk might have had was now gone. Within the walls, looking out on the vast array of the armed Muslim regiments were the Templars, Hospitallers (both stationed in the northern suburb of Montmusard), Teutonic Knights and some troops sent by King Henry along with his brother, Amalric. Edward I had also sent some men from England who had accompanied the Swiss Otto of Grandson. The Venetians and Pisans were there too. Mixed in with these were the townsfolk now called to arms, and the Italians who had so rudely precipitated the earlier riots.

King Henry had recently strengthened the walls of the city. There was a double line of outer walls and a single wall separating the main part of the town from

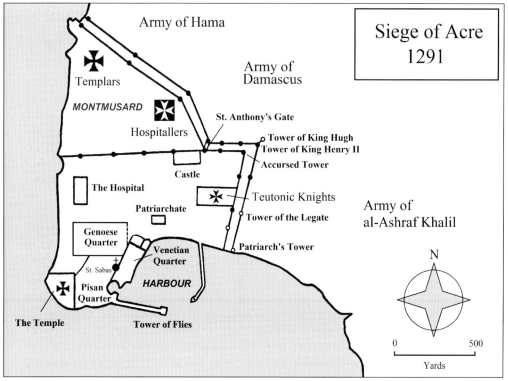

Map 6 – Siege of Acre.

Montmusard. The city's castle was on this single wall near to where it met with the outer walls. Here, the double walls jut out forming a vulnerable and obvious bulge in the defensive line. The Templars found themselves facing out to the north of Montmusard looking down on the Muslim army of Hama encamped by the sea, whilst the Hospitallers faced the army of Damascus. Al-Ashraf Khalil was camped to the south opposite the Tower of the Legate.

The siege was set to last for a good while. The Christians, having control of the sea were able to bring food over from Cyprus, but they could never have enough fighting men. On 6 April the bombardment started from the sultan's engines. Also, his engineers began preparations to undermine sections of the walls, whilst thousands of archers fired their missiles into the battlements. The defenders, however, certainly put up a fight. One Christian ship which had a catapult on board did damage to the sultan's camp, and on 15 April William of Beaujeu conducted a daring night-time raid along with Otto of Grandson on the army of Hama's camp. However, the tactic was not a success. In the murky darkness the Templars' horses got their feet caught in the enemy tent's guy ropes and were thus stricken and their riders captured. Eighteen men were lost. With a similarly disastrous night sortie made by the Hospitallers a few nights later came a decision not to repeat the tactic.

And so the siege dragged on. On 4 May King Henry came to Acre with forty ship loads of troops from Cyprus, mainly infantrymen. They numbered a little over 2,000. But even this was not enough to fully man the vast walls of Acre. Henry decided to send two knights as envoys to speak with the sultan. One was William of Cafran, a Templar, and the other was William of Villiers. They had not come with the keys to the city, they told the sultan. Al-Ashraf Khalil said he would spare the Christians if they surrendered. However, just as the envoys were about to refuse such a demand a huge stone from one of the city's catapults landed near to where they all stood and the sultan immediately took the view that the Christians had no intention of negotiating. In fact, it was only the intervention of a level-headed emir which prevented the sultan from killing the two knights himself. The two men returned to the city empty handed.

By 8 May the Tower of King Hugh, at the tip of the bulge in the defences, was standing precariously. The Christians torched it and began to retreat. The Towers and walls from here to St Anthony's Gate were all beginning to crumble due to the work of the Muslim engineers. A new tower built by Henry II lasted until 15 May but also began to collapse. On the morning of 16 May the Muslims poured into the breach and the defenders fell back onto the inner walls. A concerted attack against St Anthony's Gate, situated on the inner angle of the walls near to the castle, then took place. The Templars and the Hospitallers rushed to its defence and fought bravely. But on the morning of 18 May a general assault was ordered on the entire southern stretch of the defences from St Anthony's Gate to the shore. The Accursed Tower, at the apex of the bulge, was penetrated and the defenders fell back towards St Anthony's Gate. Now, amidst the noise and flames, there was fighting on the streets. William of Beaujeu rushed to the defence. His Templars were joined by the Hospitallers, but the enemy were everywhere. The Templar Grand Master had not had time to properly fix his armour plates (The Templar of Tyre says he had picked up another's armour in haste) and just as he raised his left arm he was struck in the armpit by an enemy spear. He had no shield and the weapon went through him to a 'palm's length'. It came through a gap where his armour plates were not joined. The Master turned towards some Italian crusaders and said 'My Lords, I can do no more, for I am killed: see the wound here!'

The Grand Master was carried back by his men to the Templar quarter, but later died of his wounds. Now the situation was beyond hope. King Henry fled to the ships. Even the wounded Grand Master of the Hospital John of Villiers was dragged onto a ship against his better judgement. At the quayside there were scenes of chaos as people crowded to get onto small craft and sail out to the larger vessels and to safety. Amongst those who capitalised on the desperation of the women and children was a Templar sea captain, Roger of Flor.

Roger of Flor

Roger was the son of a German Falconer and was an enthusiastic sailor from an early age. He found service on a ship of a Templar sergeant from Marseille who had put in at Brindisi. He later joined the Templars as a sergeant himself and took the captaincy of a vessel called *The Falcon*, formerly a fine Genoese ship. The vessel was involved in a mixture of trade and 'piracy' and the order did well from it. At the fall of Acre *The Falcon* was in the harbour and Roger used it to rescue rich women and sailed them away with their treasure to 'Atlit (Château Pèlerin). Although Roger gave a large amount of his proceeds to the order, there was suspicion that he pocketed much himself. His subsequent behaviour, taking *The Falcon* to Marseille and abandoning it, thus escaping the Grand Master's attentions, might implicate him further, as does his new found life as a mercenary leader of the Catalan Company. Roger died serving the Byzantines in 1305.

There was murder everywhere on the streets of Acre. Women and children were either killed or enslaved. Many people fled to the only remaining part of the city in Christian hands. It was now 25 May. The Temple quarter sticks out into the sea at the south-west tip of Acre. Inside this vast complex of Templar fortifications and buildings, Peter of Sevrey, the order's Marshal, and the remaining citizens held on for nearly a week until the sultan offered Peter safety if he and the other citizens were to sail away to Cyprus and leave him with the city. Peter agreed, and a hundred Mamelukes were allowed into the Templar quarter whilst their sultan's banner was hoisted on high. However, these Mamelukes took to molesting the women and mistreating the boys within the area. This provoked a retaliatory attack from the Templars who could hardly allow such open abuse. The enemy banner was ripped down and the Templars slaughtered the offenders. At night Peter sent Theobald Gaudin and a few others away in their ships to Sidon. Theobald had been both a Commander and Turcopolier in the order and had a long history of around three decades in the East. Myths have formed regarding what exactly the man who would soon become the Templars' penultimate Grand Master took with him in the hold of his ship. Legends soon arose that Theobald took the order's treasure, but nothing is known for sure.

Al-Ashraf Khalil knew how determined the Templars were and he knew how difficult their defences were to overcome. So, he once again offered the same deal as before. Peter came out under the promise of safety but when he and his party reached the sultan's tent they were seized and beheaded. The remaining defenders stayed resolute behind the walls. However, these walls were gradually being undermined by the industrious Muslim engineers. By 28 May they were in a state of near collapse. When they did finally disintegrate, the sultan poured men over the rubble. But there were so many of them bearing down upon the shaky structures that a whole section of the fortification came crashing down on everyone, Christian and Muslim alike. Now the sultan's men were inside the complex, the dreadful slaughter began once

6. *The walls of Acre. In 1291 this was the last sight many Christians had of the Holy Land as the Muslim siege forced them to flee. One Templar sea captain, Roger of Flor, benefitted from the desperation by charging a high price to carry people away from danger.*

again. The roof had finally caved in on Outremer. For those Templars who somehow managed to escape, things would never quite be the same again.

Sidon, Tortosa and the castle at 'Atlit (Château Pèlerin) were all that remained in Templar control. Theobald Gaudin was elected as Grand Master at Sidon where the Templars remained for a few weeks. Then a large Mameluke army appeared at the door of the city and the Templars withdrew to the castle on the sea to the north of the harbour which is linked to the mainland by a causeway. Theobald set sail for Cyprus apparently intending to return with reinforcements. Messages soon came to the remaining Templar defenders of Sidon from Cyprus urging them to give in. When the Mamelukes began to build their own crossing towards the castle, the Templars abandoned it and sailed along the coast to Tortosa. Two great centres of Templar power remained. Here, at Tortosa, where for so long the order's knights had held sway in the region and had struck fear into the hearts of enemies, the brothers now prepared to leave. They were gone by 3 August. Their impregnable fortress at 'Atlit (Château Pèlerin) was never taken. It was abandoned on 14 August and subsequently the Mamelukes destroyed it. With the cities of Tyre and Beirut having already fallen, there were no Christian territories left on the mainland. There was just one tiny little island, that of Arwad (Ru'ad) off the coast from Tortosa, where the Templars would play out a final desperate scene in the great drama of the crusades in 1302 (see p. 217). Despite sending out for help to Europe from his base in Cyprus, Theobald Gaudin did not come to the Holy Land again, although he may well have managed to secure a gathering of 400 brothers at a chapter meeting in Cyprus in 1291. He died on 16 April 1292 or 1293. His successor was the last Grand Master of the order, James of Molay, about whom more has been written than any other. Molay would have a long and troubled stewardship but would show that there was still some fighting to be done. Molay's preoccupations would eventually turn to the struggle to defend himself against King Philip IV of France, but at the beginning of his time as Grand Master, and for some years afterwards, he will have been thinking of how the Templars could once again reclaim the Holy Land for Christianity.

Chapter 23

A Brief Introduction to the Reconquista

At the beginning of the twelfth century the Iberian Peninsula was a vibrant place. Centuries of Muslim migration and conquest from North Africa and Christian resistance had led to the formation of a land which was largely Muslim in the South and Christian in the north. Those Christian Lords however, selfishly regarded the winning back of land they considered rightfully Christian as a means to enhance their own power and influence. By the early twelfth century Muslim power, once centred on the caliph, had fractured into small Taifa or 'party' states which did not resist Christian advances in an organised way. Moreover, papal support of Christian aggression in the later eleventh century had resulted in many warriors from Normandy, Aquitaine and Burgundy coming to Spain.

The Christian kingdoms of the north which took to the offensive were León, Castile and Aragon as well as the counties of Portugal and Barcelona. Alfonso VI of León-Castile had captured the centrally located city of Toledo in 1085 and won himself much glory for symbolically restoring the ancient Visigothic capital which had existed before the Muslim invasions. The movement against the Muslim south began to be seen as a crusade when Pope Paschal II (1099–1118) declared that anyone who went against the Moors (the Muslims of the Iberian Peninsula) would have the same remission of sins as if they had gone to Jerusalem.

Although the Muslim leaders were fractured and disunited their military capability was significant. This was further enhanced when at the behest of the rulers of Seville in the south, the Almoravids, a collection of Berber tribes of North Africa, flooded into the land and made some gains, largely for themselves. By the 1140s the power of this new group was on the wane and Iberia became the focus of a significant Western force during the Second Crusade during which Lisbon in the west and Tortosa (not to be confused with Tortosa in Outremer) in the east were captured. After this, a new Muslim group from North Africa, the Almohads began to restore some unity in the south which led to a prolonged period where the Christians adopted a defensive posture until the tide was turned in a great victory in 1212 at the defining battle of Las Navas de Tolosa. Valencia and Seville were not won to the Christians until 1238 and 1248 respectively. However, by 1300 only the mountainous regions of Granada remained in Muslim hands and stayed that way for nearly two more centuries.

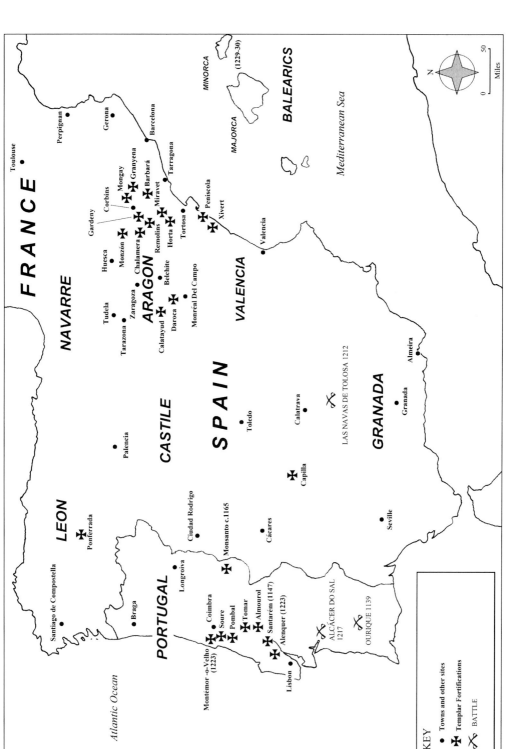

Map 7 – The Iberian Peninsula.

Chapter 24

Portugal

The Templars are to be seen performing an important role, starting particularly early in Portugal. In March 1128 Countess Teresa of Portugal (1097–1128) gave the Templars the recaptured castle at Soure to the south west of Coimbra. Afonso Henriques (d.1185), Teresa's son and successor confirmed this grant a year later stating that it was done partly 'for the love which I have in my heart for you [the Templars] since I am a brother in your fraternity'. This indicates a form of associate status within the order for the count, but it is doubtful at this stage of the Templars' history they could have garrisoned it with a large number of brothers. Afonso however, was an expansionist and planned a push to the south combined with an increasing separatism from Castile. In the south he overcame the Almoravids at Ourique in 1139 and as a result called himself king. Templar participation in the drive is evident in 1144 where they are recorded as being military active around Soure and then in March 1147 they assisted Afonso in the assault on Santarém in the Tagus valley, thus paving the way for the Second Crusade's combined effort on Lisbon which surrendered in October that year. As a reward for their help at Santarém, the Templars were awarded the churches of the city. They had already been granted a pilgrim hospital at Braga by its archbishop in 1145. When Lisbon was taken the churches of Santarém were given to the newly established bishop there and the Templars were compensated with the castle at Cera on the River Tomar. Here, in 1160 Gualdim Pais the Master of the Temple in Portugal founded the town of Tomar. He would soon found the castle at Pombal further north. Later, after 1165, Pais established the order in Monsanto after a grant of a large area was awarded by King Afonso I. In 1171 the Templar defence of the Tagus Valley was further enhanced when they reconstructed the castle at Almourol, a fortification associated with the order since 1129. By now, the Templars had also been awarded a castle at Longroiva by Afonso's brother-in-law Fernand Menendiz, in a seemingly deliberate attempt to hold underpopulated land in a recently recovered region.

Afonso's reign was long and successful. He was succeeded by his son Sancho I (1185–1211), who gained a reputation for repopulating areas around his kingdom. Sancho also gave the Templars further lands and used their centre at Tomar as a storage place for the royal treasure. But the Christians had not had it all their own way. The Almohad caliph al-Mansur struck into Christian Iberia in 1190 causing devastation in Portugal. He forced Santarém to surrender which he then destroyed,

7. *Almourol Castle, Portugal. Situated on a small rocky island in the Tagus river, this picturesque castle was improved by the Templars from 1171 including the provision of ten round towers along the outer walls and a three-storey keep.*

8. *Templar castle and Convent of Christ, Tomar, Portugal. Founded in 1160 by Gualdim Pais, Master from 1157 to 1195, Tomar became the order's Portuguese headquarters.*

before going on to attack the Templars at Tomar, but the Templar resistance was too strong despite the fact they were seriously outnumbered. The caliph came back once again however the following year and took Alcácer do Sal which had been in Christian hands since 1158. It was not recaptured until 1217.

The Templars eventually gained custodianship of two further castles in 1223 after Pope Innocent III had resolved in 1216 that Montémor-o-Velho and Alenquer should be held by the Temple as a neutral party in a dispute between King Afonso II (1211–23) and two of his sisters Sancha and Teresa. The order also embroiled itself in the politics of the Portuguese kingdom. Sancho II (1223–45) was faced with a rebellion from his brother Afonso and the Templars took the side of the king who had been a long term friend of the Master of the Portuguese Temple, Martim Martins. But Sancho was eventually overthrown and the Templars lost some property in the aftermath.

Gualdim Pais, Master in Portugal (1157–95)

Gualdim Pais was the founder of the Templar castle and city of Tomar. He had gained a reputation as a battling Templar during the Siege of Santarém in 1147 and again at Lisbon before going to Outremer and taking part in the Siege of Gaza in 1153. His stalwart defence of Christian Portugal throughout his long career won him admiration even after the Templars were disbanded. In 1319 Templar property was handed to the newly formed Order of Christ, who after a number of years at Castro Marim, came back to Tomar. Pais was buried at the Templar Church of Santa Maria do Olival, where twenty-two other Portuguese Templar masters were buried.

The Templars were deeply committed to the defence of Christian Portugal. When it came to the suppression of the order in the wake of the French King Philip IV's attack on the Templars, the Portuguese monarchy under King Diniz (1279–1325), like their Spanish counterparts, did not turn against the Templars. Instead, a new order was founded called the Order of Christ and in 1319 Templar property was handed to this order. By 1356, after spending some time based in the Algarve, the Order of Christ came back to Tomar. Their subsequent history was a long one and included the exploits of Henry the Navigator (Grand Master from 1418) whose famous caravels with their sails adorned with a red cross, sailed into a new age of discovery.

Chapter 25

Spain

On the eastern side of the Iberian Peninsula the Templars are thought to have gained land in Aragon as early as 1130. Donations came from Raymond Berenguer III, Count of Barcelona (1093–1131) and Count of Provence (1112–31). He joined the Templars as an associate member and in a grant of the castle of Granyena to the Temple dated to 14 July 1130 he handed himself over to the care of Hugh of Rigaud who had responsibility for Templar lands and property in the Provence, Toulouse and Aragon regions. This castle, he says in the grant, was situated 'in the march between myself and the Saracens' and he gave it 'together with the knights who hold this castle for me and with the people living therein'. The implication here is that although the Templars would have the castle they lacked the numbers to fully garrison it from the ranks of their own brotherhood at this time.

Another donation in the region came in 1132 from the Count of Urgel Armengold VI, who gave the order the castle at Barbará 'in the Saracen march'. This was a donation repeated by his Lord Raymond Berenguer IV in 1134. This latter Raymond Berenguer had succeeded his father Raymond Berenguer III in 1131 as Count of Barcelona and ruled to 1162. He also became ruler of Aragon in 1137. Up to this point Aragon had expanded under Alfonso I 'the Battler' (1104–34). His crusading zeal had seen him take Zaragoza, Tudela, Tarazona, Daroca and Calatayud between 1118 and 1120. This same zeal coupled with a need to defend an expanding domain resulted in Alfonso setting up fraternities of knights to fight against the Moors of the peninsula. In 1122 one such foundation was that of the confraternity of Belchite whose members joined for various lengths of time, took no vows, but were instructed 'never to make peace with the pagans' unless they were ruled by Christians. During the late 1120s he also set up a military order at Monréal del Campo in an uncultivated region between Daroca and Valencia, establishing a holy militia on virgin territory which might have prospered but for lack of financial resources.

In 1131 Alfonso left his successors with a headache in the form of his will. Although it was never fully implemented, its dramatic implications took until 1143 to unravel. Alfonso had no heir, so he bequeathed his entire kingdom to the Holy Sepulchre in Jerusalem, the Hospitallers and the Templars. The reasons for such a seismic decision are not clear. It may have been that Alfonso was wary of the ambitions of his Castilian stepson Alfonso VII (1126–57). To keep Castile out of his kingdom the ruler of Aragon may have been trying to embroil the Pope into the succession crisis by trusting the kingdom to those who owed loyalty to Rome. Alternatively, the move may be seen as a genuine attempt to escalate the struggle with the Moors at his frontier. On Alfonso's death in 1134 things played out differently. His younger brother Ramiro, a monk at San Pedro de Huesca, came out of his monastery and fathered a child called Petronilla. Ramiro later returned to his monastery after this remarkable piece of statecraft. In 1137 Petronilla was promised to Raymond Berenguer IV, Count of Barcelona and ruler of Catalonia. They eventually married in 1150 and although Alfonso VII of Castile remained strong, Raymond Berenguer was able to keep a hold on Aragon.

The matter of the will of Alfonso I had to be resolved by Raymond Berenguer IV. He was obliged to compensate the military orders for his takeover of the kingdom. He knew he still needed the Templars and Hospitallers in his expanded Aragonese and Catalonian empire, especially as there was more fighting to be done in the south. Besides, Raymond's father Raymond Berenguer III had joined the Templars before his death in 1131 and Raymond Berenguer IV joined as an associate for one year in around April 1134. At this time he had pledged to permanently maintain ten knights in the order. Twenty-six other Catalan nobles followed suit with similar commitments. In 1137 Raymond wrote to the Templar Grand Master asking that ten knights be sent to him so that he could maintain them from the kingdom's finances. Moreover, he offered Osso, Daroca and Belchite to the order and a tenth part of future conquests. But the carrot was not big enough for Robert of Craon, the Templar Master. He held out for more, even though the Hospitallers and the Canons of the Holy Sepulchre had cut their losses in Spain in 1140. However, it was with a settlement reached in 1143 that Raymond Berenguer IV exorcised the ghost of Alfonso I. This was a final agreement with the Templars, and it was quite some concession.

On 27 November 1143 at Gerona Robert of Craon and the Templars, in return for renouncing their claims received in 'perpetual right' from Raymond Berenguer IV six major castles along with their dependant territories. These were Monzón, Mongay, Chalamera, Barbará (already theirs since 1132), Belchite (subject to an agreement being made with its Lord Lope Sanchéz which did not happen), Remolins and also Corbins 'when God deigns to return it to me'. As if that was not impressive enough, a tenth of royal revenues would be given to the order, plus 1,000 solidi of silver per annum from Zaragoza, plus a fifth of the proceeds gained by chevauchées carried out in the region (see pp. 161–3 for Strategic Raiding) as well as freedom from customs and tolls. Furthermore, the order was granted a fifth part of any future land conquered from the Moors and royal assistance in any castle building the Templars wished to undertake. In an explicit acknowledgement of the Templar Master's role as a military advisor Raymond also stated 'I will not henceforth make peace with the Moors except on your recommendation'. And so, it is no surprise to find that throughout the 1140s and onwards the Templars were more militarily active than before and stood at the side of Raymond on many expeditions including an

9. *Monzón Castle, Aragon, Spain. Captured from the Moors at the end of the eleventh century, the castle was given to the Templars by the Lord of Aragon Raymond Berenguer IV in 1143, along with five others and numerous concessions. The future King James I (1213–76) received his initial schooling here between the ages of 6 and 9.*

attack on Tortosa in 1148. This attack was assisted by veterans of the Lisbon crusade and Genoese naval contingents. The Templars are recorded as specifically assisting in the five month siege by holding the ground between the crusader camps and the river Ebro.

The Templars continued to receive property and rewards from Raymond Berenguer IV such as the grant in 1153 of the castle at Miravet, one of Catalonia's most strongly fortified castles. However, the attitude of Alfonso II (1162–96), was not quite as cordial towards the order and there seems to be a departure from the mood of compensation. Those gifts which were given to the Templars during Alfonso's reign were granted away from the border as if to make sure that the order did not become too geographically powerful. But by the time of the reign of Peter II (1196–1213) the Hospitallers had gained the favour of the Aragonese monarchy to a greater extent than the Templars. That is not to say that the Templars were not militarily active in the thirteenth century. On the contrary, under Peter of Montaigu whom we have observed went on to become Grand Master (c.1219–c.1231) the Templars participated in the Siege of Al-Damus (Ademuz) in 1210 which saw the Almohads lose a key fortress in the run up to the pivotal battle at Las Navas de Tolosa in 1212 in which Peter also participated. Under James I of Aragon (1213–76) the Templars assisted in the capture of the Balearic Islands from the Almohads. The Templar commander of Majorca even gave the advice to the king suggesting the assault on Minorca. The resulting spoils were shared equally with the Hospitallers which caused some friction given that the Templars had done most of the fighting. The Templars were also at the king's side during the gradual conquest of Valencia which was completed by 1238. However, King James regarded the Hospitaller prior in Aragon (Hugh of Forcalquier) as a personal friend and had agitated for his appointment. No such relationship existed between the king and the Templar leadership. In fact, the experience James had when he was a boy at Monzón (between the ages of 6 and 9) where he was educated by the Templars may have affected his later relations with the order.

In 1269 James set out to go on crusade having assembled a fleet at Barcelona. He had the Templars and the Hospitallers with him. His fleet was blown off course in a storm and fetched up on the south coast of France, with the Templars' ship having lost its rudder. James' own vessel had a spare rudder which was sent out to the stricken vessel, but this move was opposed by an advisor to the king who thought the Templars should have brought their own spare.

Towards the end of the Templar era in Aragon, things became complicated for the order as they were expected to assist the monarchy in defending the kingdom against fellow Christians. By now, and since 1244 the kingdom had no border with Islam. Instead, when a French army invaded Aragon in 1285 in a 'crusade' to punish Peter III of Aragon for supporting Sicilian rebels, the military orders were expected to support the Aragonese ruler. And yet, it was the Pope himself who had called the expedition and the King of France who had led it. The adventure ended in a failure and a French retreat, but it serves to highlight the dilemma faced by the Templars when their raison d'être (i.e. a clear and obvious war against a Muslim threat) was missing.

In Castile the Templars were not quite as obvious a presence as they had proven to be in the east and west of the peninsula. They were however, still very much a part of the Reconquista here. In 1157 the Templars had had to abandon the town of Calatrava, claiming that they could not hold it against a Muslim invasion. This curious announcement threatened danger for the newly crowned King Sancho III of Castile (1157–8) who had to look at the protection of his southern borders once again. From this problem eventually rose the solution of home-grown military orders. Here, in 1158 the Order of Calatrava was founded. Similar local military orders were founded by Iberian rulers in the twelfth century providing the Spanish rulers with the benefits of the same rapid response and longevity in the field as the Temple and Hospital could give but also providing a concentration of resources on the peninsula itself instead of losing money and men to the Latin East. The Order of Santiago was established in 1170 by King Ferdinand II of León to protect the city of Cáceres and the Order of Alcántara based at a convent near Ciudad Rodrigo gained papal approval in 1176 becoming a military order in the 1180s. Each of these orders were founded from knightly fraternities. The Templars did receive property in León and Castile however. On the pilgrimage route to Santiago de Compostella they held properties which included the fortress at Ponferrada and in 1236 Fernando III of León and Castile (1217–52) awarded the order the castle at Capilla.

In 1274 at the Second Church Council of Lyons an idea was put forward to amalgamate the military orders. The Spanish contingent objected strongly to this, as would the last Templar Grand Master later in 1307 (see pp. 169–70 and 218). But the Spanish reasons for opposing the move were not the same as those of James of Molay. One military order would be too powerful an organisation in Iberia, they argued. If it were to combine all the local military orders then the struggle against the Moors in Iberia may well play second fiddle to the need to shore up what was rapidly becoming a reversal in the Latin East. James II of Aragon (1291–1327) even argued to the Pope that the Templars should fight the Grenadan Muslims and not be sent to the East. But Iberia had not been the only region outside of Outremer where the Templars had an active interest. In Eastern Europe for example, there was another side to the military history of the Knights Templar.

ON THE EASTERN FRONTIERS OF EUROPE

Chapter 26

A Different Frontier

The Templars performed a role in Eastern Europe which bore little resemblance to that which they undertook in Iberia and the Holy Land. Although Eastern Europe in the twelfth century was another of Christendom's theological, cultural and political frontiers it was markedly different in many respects to Outremer, Spain and Portugal. Here, from the shores of the Baltic across the sparsely populated areas of Central and Eastern Europe the threat of paganism and the opportunities for the expansion of Christendom were the chief concerns of the church and secular landowners alike. The main regions of activity in this regard were in Livonia (modern Latvia), Prussia, Poland and Hungary, the last of which shared a border with the Pagan Cumans. It was not a war of conflicting ideologies battled out between two of history's great faiths as it was in the Levant and Iberia. It was more a battle against chaos, disorder and a brutal antipathy towards the Church. As early as the 1160s and as far west as Schleswig, a priest named Helmod of Lübeck travelled through the remnants of villages which had so long ago been razed by pagans so that the remains of structures barely protruded above the thick undergrowth. Nor was it much different 300 or 400 hundred miles to the north-east where in 1198 Bishop Berthold of Livonia, a former Cistercian who was fleeing the region in desperation, scarcely evaded being killed by an angry crowd.

Despite the fact that both the Templars and the Hospitallers received early grants of land in Central and Eastern Europe they were not brought into the region specifically to fight. Much of their property had been given to them by barons who had been impressed with what they had seen or heard about in the Holy Land and so their establishment in these regions was more to do with supporting their continuing work in the Latin East in return for assistance in colonising land and making it productive. If the Templar role in Eastern Europe was played out more as a landowning interested party, this is not to say there was not a 'crusade' going on here, particularly in the form of the missionary work whose participants needed protecting by a number of military orders. Even as early as 1147 on the eve of the Second Crusade Bernard of Clairvaux had been advocating a crusading movement

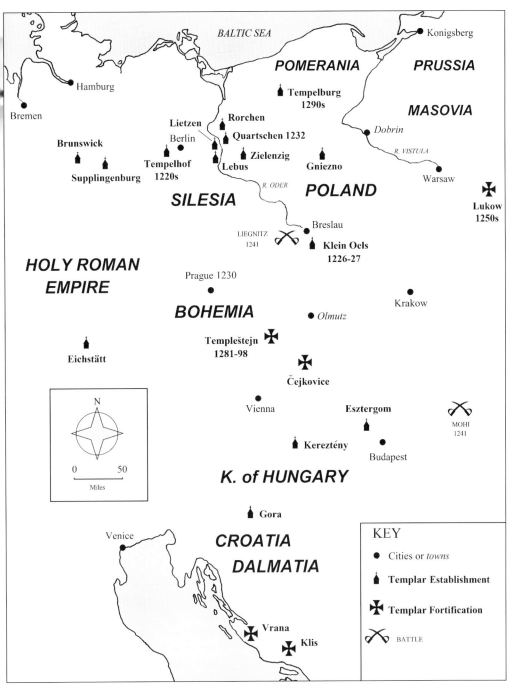

Map 8 – Templar establishments in Central and Eastern Europe.

in the Baltic area. But the main orders who were most militarily active on this front were either locally formed or brought in from that other crusading frontier of Iberia. In the early thirteenth century the Militia of Christ of Livonia, otherwise known as the Order of the Swordbrethren was established at Riga in 1202. Later, along the same model the Order of Dobrin (Dobrzyn) was established in Poland in 1228. The Swordbrethren fared well until their defeat at the Battle of Saule in 1236 after which they were amalgamated into the larger and more widespread Teutonic Knights who themselves had been founded in the 1190s and who based their Rule on that of the Templars. The Order of Dobrin was similarly absorbed by the Teutonic Knights around the same time. Also, at this time further down the River Vistula a convent of the Spanish Order of Calatrava was being established near the Prussian border at Thymau possibly in reaction to the sacking of the Cistercian house of Oliva in 1226.

The Templar presence was not great in the north-east. In Central and Eastern Germany, the donations had been greater, due to the fact that so many important barons had seen the brothers in action whilst on the Third Crusade and again during the German crusade of 1197–8 (such as the Landgrave of Thuringia) and the Fifth Crusade (1217–21) which had also included the Duke of Austria and the King of Hungary. Conversely, in Bohemia and Moravia the donations do not come until around 1230 with the order acquiring a house in Prague in 1230 and a fortified commandery at Čejkovice plus a very late castle at Templštejn (1281–98). In Hungary, where there was a more extensive relationship with the kings of Hungary than there was in Bohemia, there were enough Templar properties to justify 'Hungary' in its widest sense, becoming a Templar province for administrative purposes. In Central Hungary they acquired Kereszteny and Eszetergom and further south in Croatia (Dalmatia) which was then part of the Hungarian Empire the Templars had links to the castle at Vrana where in 1203 the Hungarian king deposited some silver with them and in 1217 King Andrew II (1205–35) is mentioned by Thomas of Split as giving over the castle at Klis to one Pons, Master of the Temple in Hungary because none of his own nobility was prepared to garrison it. Still further south, another castle at Lamia in Thessaly in what had now become Latin Greece after the capture by the Franks of Constantinople in 1204 seems also to have been acquired sometime before 1210, its purpose being for the defence of the empire.

Chapter 27

Battles of Liegnitz (Legnica) and Mohi (Muhi), 1241

Despite the fact that the Templars in Eastern Europe were not there specifically to fight, there is some record of military action. The order held land and was expected to protect it. And so the Templars' reaction to the Mongol invasions of Poland and Hungary was as one would expect it to be, a military one. The Mongols did everything on a grand scale. They had swept across Russia, devastating and conquering. They had also taken Kiev in December 1237. The Mongol leadership had felt that they had also subjugated the Cumans but by 1241 the Cumans had fled to the west of the Carpathian Mountains into Hungary seeking respite from the Mongol hordes. The Mongols demanded that the King of Hungary Béla IV (1235–70) surrender the Cumans, but the king refused the ultimatum. The stage was set for a huge invasion of Eastern Europe. The Mongols' strategic goal was to attack Hungary with a giant army of tens of thousands of their mounted bowmen and lancers, and to do this they created a diversion to the north by invading Poland with another army of many thousands.

The diversionary force was an army in its own right. The Mongol leadership under Batu Khan and Subutai had planned to lead their own armies into Hungary and had sent a third army under leaders Baidar and Kadan into Poland where they sacked and burned Krakow on Palm Sunday 1241. They bypassed Breslau and converged on the city of Liegnitz (modern Legnica) where they were opposed by Duke Henry II of Silesia (1238–41) on the plain known as Walstadt. Henry had up to 25,000 troops with him which included Polish and German knights and men at arms and a very small number of Templars. Early in the morning of 9 April 1241 Henry ordered his German heavy cavalry to charge the oncoming horde, but it did not fare well against a heavy volume of mounted missile fire. Henry tried a second time with the Polish cavalry and the Templars, but this time the Mongols deployed a feigned retreat, drawing the Westerners further into trouble without them being able to make contact with the enemy. Superior mobility meant that the Mongols were able to wheel on each flank of the now spread out cavalry and turn to fire into the flanks. Moreover, they had set up a smoke screen between the lagging infantry and the advanced knights. With the Templars and Polish cavalry engaged out front the Mongols appeared through the smoke and charged into the infantry in great numbers. Henry was amongst them, on his horse and in the panic he fled with his body guards, but was unhorsed and tracked down and beheaded. His head was placed upon a lance and later paraded before Liegnitz. Casualties in the rout were very high but the sources vary. Quite how the Templars fought and lost at Liegnitz is unknown, but the combination of superior Mongol mobility and huge numbers against such a small contingent (even when counted alongside its numerous Polish allies) is a logical explanation. The Master in France, Pons d'Aubon wrote to King Louis IX appealing for help and telling him of the losses. The order lost 500 of its people both at Legnica and in the subsequent raids on three of its villages and 'two towers', amongst which were three knights and two sergeants. To give some idea of the aggression, size and speed of this Mongol army (by no means the largest known) Pons gave the king a grim assessment:

> They have ransacked the land of Duke Henry of Poland [Silesia] and killed him and many of his barons . . . And you should be aware that they spare no-one; they kill everyone poor and rich and small and great . . . And you should be aware that their army is so large, as we have been informed by our Brothers who have escaped from their army, that it is a good eighteen leagues long [approximately 2½ miles] and twelve wide and they ride as far in a day as it is from Paris to the city of Chartres [approximately 46 miles]

Batu Khan had received nine bags of human ears cut off to count the European dead in the wake of Liegnitz, but in Hungary on 11 April 1241, there was worse to come. The Hungarian nobility had been slow to react to the Mongol invasions. There was also blame apportioned to King Béla IV, who prevaricated in the face of the threat whilst Frederick, Duke of Austria and Styria had shown himself to be more willing to face the hordes. Eventually, the Hungarian king took his 15,000-strong army against the Mongols who simply melted away before him. They stopped to await supplies at the flooded River Sajó, near to Mohi unaware that beyond the wooded banks of the river on the other side was a giant Mongol army. The bridge over the Sajó was to be the Mongols' first choice of a route to encircle the Hungarian fortified camp. Béla's brother Koloman, his Archbishop Hugrin and James of Montreal, 'a certain Master of the Knighthood of the Temple' set out from the camp in darkness (see p. 167 for Templar conduct at night) to attack the Mongols and prevent them crossing the bridge before dawn. Though outnumbered, they were partially successful and destroyed more enemy than they lost themselves. However, a large Mongol detachment found a ford to the north and began crossing it early the next morning. Another detachment had built its own bridge and began crossing that. Again, the Templars went out to meet the enemy and again they were outnumbered. Further prevarication by King Béla, who only issued orders to prepare his men at the last minute, meant that the Mongols could complete their crossing. The ensuing battle at Mohi was bitterly fought and the Mongols lost many men, but in the event, won a decisive victory and swarmed all over the Hungarian plain in the aftermath. The Templars are mentioned twice by Thomas of Split in his account of events and each time the reader gets the impression that the brothers were deploying in exactly the way they were meant to fight according to their Rule. It had been the Templars' job to keep watch at night and when they 'heard the shout', they burst out of the camp:

> Then, girded in military arms and grouped in one wedge they rushed boldly into the enemy army and fought with them for some time with much fortitude. But, since they were very few in number in comparison with the infinite multitude of Mongols, who bubbled from the ground everywhere like locusts, they returned to their camp, after killing more than they had lost themselves.

On the second occasion the Templars went out again with the archbishop and with Koloman:

> King Koloman and the Templar with his fellow Latin knights inflicted great slaughter on the enemy. But at last, unable to bear the blows of the multitude, Koloman and the archbishop barely escaped, bitterly wounded, with their men; whilst the Templar Master and the whole army of the Latins fell.

The Templars are often accused of rashness in their response to such situations. They were outnumbered almost everywhere in each theatre of war they encountered. It might seem that such precipitous and predictable actions were unwise. However, this is to misunderstand what the Templars expected of themselves and what others expected them to achieve. If we can understand the mind-set of a Knight Templar then actions such as those at Montgisard (1177), Mohi (1241) and Mansourah (1250) become a little easier to interpret. For this, there is no better place to turn than to the Rule of the Templars and to its exhaustive narrative on how the order organised its war machine, centred upon the mounted knight. But first, by way of introduction, we might ask ourselves why anybody would want to become a Templar in the first place.

Part 3

Military Organisation

Chapter 28

Recruitment and Reception

At a personal level the reasons why anyone would want to join the Templars were varied and complex. To join the order you had to be a freeman, not in bondage and free from serfdom. Typically, this type of entrant was a sergeant, of whom there were many more than brother knights. Concealing an unfree status was not only punishable within the order but ran the risk for the offender of his own Lord one day seeking him out and retrieving him, as apparently happened to a Templar sergeant who had been a serf at the time of Louis IX's Egyptian Crusade. However, to join as a knight and take the iconic white mantle and thus place the dark life behind you, you had to be not only of knightly descent but also as the thirteenth century drew on, be able to demonstrate a legitimate birth. Clause 586 of the Rule, in a section written between 1257 and 1268 which is entitled Further Details on Penances, gives an example of what happens when such a lineage is suspected to be absent. There were men in the order who had said that a certain knight brother was neither the son of a knight nor of knightly lineage, and so the matter was brought before the chapter. The imposter was at Antioch and so the Grand Master sent for him. When the evidence was heard the brother was found guilty of having no knightly heritage and his white mantle was taken from him and replaced by a brown one. He was however, allowed to be a chaplain brother. The offence was considered so serious that even the man who had made the imposter into a brother knight was sent for from overseas and when he came, he pleaded for mercy and said that he had done it under orders from a Commander of Poitou, who was now dead.

That the order appealed to the upper echelons of society is not in doubt. The extraordinary will of Alfonso I of Aragon (1104–34) (see pp. 127–8 above) in which the king bequeathed his entire kingdom to the military orders is perhaps an overtly political example as is the financial donation made by Fulk of Anjou after he had joined the order as an associate member. Some high ranking nobility such as Hugh, Count of Champagne were compelled to join as full members. In Hugh's case his wife's alleged unfaithfulness was a factor. Others took the opportunity to serve temporarily like Fulk for a set period of time (*ad terminum*). Temporary or short-term commitment to the order was not uncommon, particularly in the early decades. The Rule even allowed for it. Clause 66 of the French text of the Primitive Rule specifically required that secular knights desiring to serve for a fixed term should buy a suitable horse and arms and 'everything that will be necessary for such work'.

10. Effigy of William Marshal, Earl of Pembroke (d.1219), Temple Church, London. A close friend of Aimery of Saint-Maur, Master of the Temple in England, William joined the order just before his death. He even had a mantle pre-prepared.

There are examples of successful short term service such as that effected in the year 1148 by Garcia Ortiz in Corbins. By the 1140s however, the practice was less widespread but still not altogether unheard of and in some cases it was still actively promoted.

Some nobility nearing the end of their distinguished political and military careers joined the order on the brink of death, knowing their days were numbered. In England, William Marshal, Earl of Pembroke (d.1219) did just this. So too did John of Ibelin in Outremer in 1236 to the apparent displeasure of his family. Illness may have prompted Gerard of Ridefort, the Templar Grand Master (1185–9) to join, although his failure to secure the hand of the heiress of Botron is given equal measure in the sources. Despite these examples of some high ranking men joining the order it is true to say that comparatively few knights came from the ranks of the upper nobility. The majority were drawn from the middle and lesser nobility and were of modest status. Their motives were varied and there is enough evidence to suggest a variety of different personal reasons for their joining.

Usually a young man's parents might choose for their son to join a holy order, but in the case of the military orders this was less common, although not unknown. William VII of Montpelier's will of 1172 for example, decreed that one of his sons should join the Temple. For those not chosen in this way there were some attractions. Joining the Temple might be perceived as a career opportunity for some lesser knights. It gave them the chance to move around inside the organisation and undertake roles which gave them a certain degree of power, perhaps financial or administrative. Even at the lowly sergeant rank it was possible to hold some important offices within the order. This elevation to positions of power even led to reports of such Templars adopting a lofty attitude towards their secular counterparts on occasion. James of Vitry, Bishop of Acre (1216–28) wrote that some Templars who had come from poorer backgrounds were particularly susceptible to such pride. He also recounted that he had heard of one Templar who had never in his life laid his head on a pillow prior to joining the order. On joining, he got so used to having a pillow that when it was taken away so the cover could be washed he kept the whole house awake with his muttering and complaining. So for some, the idea of an enhanced status in life and some basic creature comforts may have seemed attractive. There were other mundane motives for joining. It may be that a person was already employed in some way by the order such as Hugh of Tadcaster who when giving evidence during the trial of the Templars in 1309 said he had been a Claviger (key keeper) for the order and had subsequently petitioned to join.

Overwhelmingly, the desire to protect the holy places played its part. Some who became Templars may have been pilgrims once themselves and seen the work of the order and decided to join. Others may have joined to see those places for the first time. But another of the driving forces seems to have been the notion of spiritual salvation. In the part of the Rule which covered the Reception procedure (in this case, clause 663) Templars were told that they were joining the order for three different reasons. The first of these was so that they could abandon the evils of this world. The second reason was in order to serve the Lord. The third reason was to be poor and do penance in life for the salvation of the soul. It could be that some postulants (candidates who requested entry) might even take the habit to atone for a particular offence. Joining the Temple as a penance for a crime is referred to in the sources and must have led to discipline problems within the order. The murderers of Archbishop Thomas à Becket of Canterbury (d.1170) sought forgiveness from the Pope in Rome in 1171 and were required to serve in the Holy Land as Templars for a full fourteen years. Similarly, in 1244 Pope Honorius III requested of the Templar Grand Master that he accept into the order for a seven year penance a certain Bertran who had killed a bishop. St Bernard had even encouraged robbers and murderers to fight in the East, selling it as a double blessing whereby the West would rid itself of a criminal and the Holy Land gain a Christian fighter.

Difficulties at home may have motivated some men, as they had for Hugh, Count of Champagne. In 1129 Guy Cornelly of Tilchâtel near Dijon approached the abbot of Saint Bénigne. His wife Rezvinde had contracted leprosy and his daughter seems also to have been afflicted. Guy handed over the care of his wife and daughter to Saint Bénigne and sweetened the deal with the offer of Rezvinde's dowry. Guy took vows to end his life in the service of the Templars in the Holy Land and set off with two horses and one thousand sous in his bag, given to him by the monks of Saint Bénigne. Less financially fortunate however, was Bertrand Guasc. Debt was greatly discouraged in the order, but Bertrand's case was one of simply running out of money. In 1311 he gave this as his reason for having joined the Temple twenty years earlier.

On the matter of the admission of children into the order, the Rule was clear enough, although in reality there were some who did join young. Most religious orders in the early twelfth century would accept children offered by their parents as oblates or affiliates, but under Cistercian influence there was a move away from this as the century progressed and the Templars were no exception to the general movement. There was no minimum age given for joining the order but the hopeful young man who sought admission needed to be of a certain maturity to have the acceptable physical strength for the role. But this is not to say that parents did not wish for their sons to join. Some eager parents will have made an early commitment and waited for their sons to reach maturity.

Although the Primitive Rule advised strongly against the admission of children, young men and boys did find themselves placed in the care of the order. In April 1148 Alfonso-Jordan, Count of Toulouse, whilst on crusade left his fourteen year old son Raymond with the Templars in Jerusalem where he stayed until his father's untimely death changed the political landscape for the young man. Raymond's case does not appear to have involved an obligation to join the order, but it is probable that other boys found themselves in the care of the Templars implicitly to join it when they were older. Around the time of the interrogations of the Templars in the early fourteenth century, some men said they had joined as young as 9 years old, as was the case with one Templar questioned in Cahors in 1307. Others mentioned ages between 11 and 13. But this clearly was not the norm. One historian has pointed out that of the 224 brothers questioned before the papal commissioners in Paris between 1310 and 1311 just thirty-three had joined below the age of 20 and that the average age of entrants had been somewhat older at 27½ years. This would imply that by medieval standards there were some ageing men who were joining the order in the late thirteenth and early fourteenth centuries. However, many of these would not have seen fighting roles and instead would have stayed in the West dedicating themselves to assisting the huge logistical network which supported the defence of the Holy Land. For those older warriors who had joined long enough ago to have seen active military service but were now too old to continue to fight, the Rule made a provision. In clause 338 in the section on Conventual Life, an ageing Templar who found himself in this predicament was obliged to approach the Marshal and offer his equipment to be given up and passed to a brother who could use it. The Marshal in turn was obliged to consult the Master before he did anything with the equipment, but the elderly knight would receive in return for giving up his horses, 'a gentle, ambling horse for his pleasure'.

As for the length of service of a Templar there is some late evidence. From the depositions made at Paris in 1307 it is possible to deduce that length of service could run from less than one month to forty-five years. One-hundred-and-thirty-three Templars gave their length of service of which just thirty-five had been in service for five years or less. The average length of service was a little over fourteen-and-a-half years.

It would seem that in the early years of the Order of the Temple there had been some sort of relaxation of the terms of entry, presumably as pressure mounted to obtain recruits. The original Latin Rule (translated into French between 1136 and 1149) provided for a probationary period after the postulant had made a formal request to enter the order, but this sentence is missing in the equivalent clause of the French translation and the line is moved and somewhat downgraded in tone and meaning, to appear in the clause on forbidding the entry of children where it uses the term 'be put to the test' as opposed to mentioning a probationary period.

Married brothers were permitted in the order, but under certain conditions. It was told to a postulant during the admission procedure that if he lied about his married status and his wife subsequently sought him out in the house, he would be clapped in irons, have the habit taken away from him (a serious punishment) and be forced to work with the slaves before finally being returned to the woman whose right it was to ask for him. The term used for married brothers in the Latin Rule is *fratres conjugati*. They were not to wear the white mantle, however. This is not to say that the arrangements could not work well for both the house and the couple. If the husband died before his wife the Temple was to arrange for a portion of their estate for her maintenance, whilst the order received the rest. Wives, according to clause 433 of the Rule were expected to become a nun, but in another order. This was not always the case in practice and it should not be forgotten that some women were very rich and provided the Templars with a source of income and were often treated with a degree of flexibility.

On women in general however, the Rule was clear enough. 'The company of women is a dangerous thing' says the Rule. Many have been led astray by just this, it goes on to say. Avoiding the embraces of women was paramount. Nor should a brother ever kiss a woman, not even a relative. Sexual intercourse with a woman was a sure way to 'losing the habit' or expulsion. 'Henceforth' says the Primitive Rule, ladies were not to be permitted as sisters into the house of the Temple. That said, there is evidence of sisters later than this. There was one Templar nunnery given to the order in 1272 by Bishop Eberhard of Worms which passed to the Hospital on the dissolution of the Temple and there are records of women living as sisters in Templar commanderies such as Sister Adelheide of Wellheim at Mosbrunnen in the early fourteenth century who had entered as the wife of a brother. There are examples of the giving of women as bondswomen to the order, such as Adam, Marshal of the church of the blessed Stephen of Meaus giving Mathelina (daughter of Theobald) his female surf, to the Templars in 1221. Although women were forbidden to work for the order there are examples of dairymaids being employed such as at Rockley in Wiltshire in England in 1307 (via the tenants) and at a Templar house at Baugy in France.

The Templars were however, a *military* order. They needed fighters in the Holy Land and were always pressed for numbers. This inevitably led to the need to recruit mercenaries. The turcopole was one such. He was a native middle-eastern horseman, first encountered by crusaders in the late eleventh century. Their name from the Greek means 'sons of Turks', possibly indicating they were the product of a union between Greek and Turkish parents. They were at least nominally Christian although many in the crusader states may have been Muslim. They came to represent a useful auxiliary force to the leaders of Outremer and in particular to the military orders. Both the Templars and Hospitallers employed an official called a Turcopolier whose job it was to manage these forces within the military structure of the order. They formed a mounted contingent, mainly with lances as their principal weapon. It would seem that their role in Syria and indeed within the orders was also extended to that of infantrymen, but their mounted role included reconnaissance and would have additionally bolstered the ranks of the cavalry units as light cavalry. The turcopoles, although distantly linked to the Turks, do not seem to have been deployed by the Templars to execute the mounted archery tactics familiar to the Turks during this period, but were rather absorbed into the tactical and strategic methods of the Frankish armies.

It is clear that the recruits were from different ages and social backgrounds, but what was their geographical origin? From seventy-six depositions made in Cyprus in 1310 we have some evidence. Of these Templars only five had entered the order in the crusader states themselves. Four had joined in Cyprus and one in Cilicia. Forty had joined the Templars in France which unsurprisingly provided the bulk of the recruitment but others had come from Aragon, Castile, Portugal, England, Germany, Italy, Dalmatia and Morea. The Rule mentions ten Templar provinces. These were Jerusalem, Tripoli and Antioch in the East, and also France, England, Poitou, Aragon, Portugal, Apulia and Hungary. Local preceptories or commanderies in these provinces would act as a recruitment point for the order and also as a departure point for journeys to the East.

Once a man had decided he wanted to join the Templars there was a procedure to follow. This is preserved in the Rule as a separate (and evidently well-thumbed) section. The Rule itself had to be read out to the recruit. The section on reception is thought to date from around 1260 although the procedure it describes is not thought to have been greatly different in the past. The receptor was usually the local commander or sometimes a senior official such as a Visitor. The recruit was left in no doubt over the hardships he would face as a Templar. Once the brothers of the house had come together in chapter the question was put to them regarding whether anyone knew of good reason why the postulant should not be allowed to join. Overall, this question was posed three times throughout the entire procedure. All being well, the recruit was taken to a different room where the graveness of his commitment was explained to him in the sense that he would be willingly suffering all for God for the rest of his life. He was also asked if he had a woman in his life and whether or not he had made any vows to other orders, or owed any debt. He was asked if he was in good health. He then returned to the chapter where he knelt before the receptor with his hands joined and spoke the following words: 'Sire, I am come before God and before you and before the brothers, and ask and request you for love of God and Our Lady, to welcome me into your company and the favours of the house, as one who wishes to be a serf and slave of the house for ever'.

The receptor then told him that he was not to expect a life of luxury within the order, but that he could get sent to any of its outposts. If the recruit wished to serve in the East, he might be sent to the West. If he wanted to go to Acre, he could end up in Tripoli or Antioch. If he wished to sleep he could be could be woken or vice-versa. Sergeants were reminded that they could be given some of the 'basest' tasks of the order involving working at the oven, the mill, the kitchens or with the camels or in the pigsty. If the entrant was still prepared to accept these conditions, he was reminded again of the three reasons for joining. The entrant then left the room and the receptor once again posed the question if anyone knew of a reason why he could not join. When he came back the entrant had to swear on the Gospels and was warned throughout the process of the dire consequences of lying. Then there came the vows of obedience, chastity and poverty:

> 'Now, good brother, now hear well what we will say to you: do you promise to God and Our Lady that henceforth all the days of your life you will be obedient to the Master of the Temple and whatever commander will be over you?' And he should say 'Yes, sire, if it please God.'
>
> 'Do you also promise to God and to Lady St Mary that henceforth all the days of your life you will live chastely in your body?' And he should say 'Yes, sire, if it please God.'
>
> 'Do you also promise to God and to Our Lady St Mary that you, all the remaining days of your life, will live without property?' And he should say 'Yes, sire, if it please God.'

This was followed by a promise to conquer and defend Jerusalem:

> 'Do you also promise to God and to Lady St Mary that you, all the remaining days of your life, will help to conquer, with the strength and power that God has given you, the Holy Land of Jerusalem; and that which Christians hold you will help keep and save within your power?' And he should say 'Yes, sire, if it please God.'

The new brother also promised never to leave the order. The mantle was then placed around the entrant's neck and the laces fastened. A chaplain said a psalm and a prayer and the brothers said the paternoster. The person making the entrant into a brother, says the Rule, should 'raise him up and kiss him on the mouth'. The chaplain should do so also. The postulant then listened carefully to the receptor who explained the offences which could lead to expulsion from the house or to the loss of the habit and other penances. There can be no doubt that anyone joining the Templars knew of the sort of commitment expected of them. Some abandoned great wealth to join, others acquired a much sought after stability and elevated status. But the main thing was the work itself. There was fighting and campaigning to be done. How then, did he put into practice the core role for which he had been chosen? How did the Knight Templar actually campaign?

Chapter 29

The Hierarchical Statutes

We have seen how the Latin, or Primitive Rule of the Templars touched upon some aspects of the military life of the order, but it was not until the production of the Hierarchical Statutes (sometime after 1165) that specific military matters were given a kind of legislative framework within the order. Much campaign experience had been gained by the brothers by this time and it is not clear whether the methods written down around this time were the result of long held practice or were entirely innovative. It is certain that the military professionalism of the Templars attracted the praise of the French king as early as the late 1140s (p. 31) and it is most likely that what was being written down in the time of Grand Master Bertrand of Blancfort (1156–69), the man whose guiding hand is thought to have been behind the Hierarchical Statutes, was a regulation of what had come to be thought of as best practice.

The Rule, as it survives, is evidence of an evolution over 150 years of Templar history. The three manuscripts most commonly referred to are those from Paris, Rome and Dijon. The Parisian and Roman ones date from the turn of the thirteenth and fourteenth centuries and are nearly identical. The one from Dijon contains just the Primitive Rule and the Hierarchical Statutes and dates from the early thirteenth century. Another French Rule also exists and there are several Latin manuscripts of the Primitive Rule. The original Rule was soon translated from the Latin into French, probably under the Grand Master Robert of Craon (1136–49). It was clear that the Rule would be used by Frankish men whose knowledge of Latin was minimal.

The full Rule consists of seven main parts: the Primitive Rule (translated from the Latin but with some differences), the Hierarchical Statutes, Penances, Conventual Life, the Holding of Ordinary Chapters, Further Details on Penances, and Reception into the order. Clause numbers mentioned here refer to the scholar Judith Upton-Ward's translation of the French text of the Rule. In clause 326 under Conventual Life lies a distinction between the *retrais* and the Rule and a hint as to the military significance of the former. The *retrais* (of which an incomplete version also exists in Barcelona) are distinct from the Primitive Rule in that they consist of the Hierarchical Statutes and the section governing Conventual Life. As the French verb 'retraire' (to take out, or withdraw) might indicate, these were areas of particularly sensitive Templar activity and it is thought their distribution was limited to high ranking officials within the order. Clause 326 states that no brother, unless he is a bailli (an appointed administrative official), should have the *retrais* or the Rule without the convent's permission. There had been a time once, says the author of the clause, when the texts had been found by squires who had disclosed their contents to secular men. When we look at the Hierarchical Statutes, it is little wonder that the order should wish for its contents not to fall into the hands of the enemy.

The Hierarchical Statutes begin at Clause 77 with the *retrais* of the Master. After this comes a list of ranks of officials within the order. However, as a document which seems to pre-date the fall of Jerusalem in 1187, the list represents a moment in the evolution of the order rather than the definitive and lasting structure. For example, the Hierarchical Statutes include the office of the Commander of the City of Jerusalem, a role which became obsolete in 1187. Also, the office of Seneschal was dropped at the end of the twelfth century and a rather confusingly titled 'Grand Commander' took on part of the role. The confusion arises because when a Master died, it was a different 'Grand Commander' who took over the running of the order and organised the election of the next Master. Moreover, there were officials in the order at the time, such as Geoffrey Fulcher, who held titles which do not appear in the Hierarchical Statutes perhaps indicating that it was not as comprehensive as it might appear. Fulcher appears as 'procurator' or 'preceptor' in the 1160s and as 'Commander of the Order Overseas' in the 1170s. This notwithstanding, the Hierarchical Statutes do indeed present a unique window into the military life of the Templars from which we might draw some useful conclusions about how their warfare was organised and waged.

The *retrais* of the Master lists his entourage and equipment and outlines the rules governing his activities within the order. The Master should have four horses and one Chaplain brother, one clerk with three horses, one sergeant brother with two horses, one gentleman valet with one horse to carry his shield and his lance. He should also have a Saracen scribe (to be an interpreter) and a turcopole.

The Master was also entitled to two foot soldiers (whose equipment is not specified), a cook and a Turcoman (a fine riding horse which was to be kept in the caravan during peace time but allowed in the 'string' of other horses during wartime campaigning). Two pack animals were allowed for the Master which was raised to four when he was either crossing the River Jordan or travelling the dangerous pass on the Dog River between the mountains and the sea near Beirut where the road was virtually impassable.

In his service, the Master was to have two trusty knight brothers as companions, who should have the same barley ration as the Master himself. Should either of them succumb in battle the Master may take what he pleases of the man's equipment, returning the remainder to the Marshal in the caravan. But the Master's giving of arms as gifts was somewhat restricted. Such items could be given away with the exception of swords, lances and coats of mail.

TABLE 1:
Hierarchical Statutes (c.1165–c.1187) – Personal Retinues Taken From Each *Retrais*
(Numbers in parenthesis indicate numbers of horses)

Master

Horses	Chaplain	Clerk	Sergeant	Valet	Farrier	Saracen	Scribe	Turcopole	Cook	Infantry	Turcoman	Pack Animals	Tents
4	1	1(3)	1(2)	1(1)	1	1	1	1	1	2	1	2–4	1 round

Plus two knight brothers in accompaniment. When under arms in the field, can take six, eight or up to ten knight brothers.

Seneschal

Horses	Sergeant	Squire	Deacon Scribe	Saracen Scribe	Turcopole	Infantry	Tents
4	1(2)	2	1	1(1)		2	1 round

Plus one knight brother in accompaniment (with four horses and two squires).

Marshal

Horses	Sergeant	Squire	Turcopole	Turcoman	Tents
4	1(1)	2	1(1)	1	1 pavilion (four flaps, three poles, two pegs), 1 tent for squires and equipment.

Commander of the Land of Jerusalem and of the Kingdom

Horses	Sergeant	Squire	Deacon Scribe	Turcopole	Saracen Scribe	Infantry	Tents
4	1(1)	2	1	1(1)	1(1)	2	1 pavilion (four flaps, three poles, two pegs), 1 tent for squires and equipment.

Should also be accompanied by the Draper. Could also purchase pack animals including camels.

Commander of the City of Jerusalem

Horses	Sergeant	Squire	Turcopole	Turcoman	Saracen Scribe	Tents
4	1(2)	2	1(1)	1	1(1)	1 round

Turcoman may be replaced by a fine roncin (workhorse). Commander also has the Commander of Knights beneath him in Jerusalem. Also, ten knight brothers.

Commanders of the Lands of Tripoli and Antioch

Horses	Chaplain/Chapel	Sergeant	Deacon	Turcopole	Saracen Scribe	Infantry	Tents
4	1 (Antioch only)	1(2)	1(1)	1(1)	1(1)	1	1 round

Plus one knight in accompaniment who held position high enough to allow him to travel from one land to another.

Draper

Horses	Squire	Pack Animal	Custodian	Tents
4	2		1	1 pavilion (four flaps, three poles, two pegs), 2 round for squires and Tailors

For the Drapers of Tripoli and Antioch the pavilion was not permitted.

Knight Brothers, Commanders of the Houses

Horses	Squire
4	2

Knight Brothers*

Horses	Squire	Tent
3	1	1

A fourth horse and a second squire (if the knight has them) are at the discretion of the Master.

Sergeant Brothers (At Arms, Without Office)

Horses
1

All sergeant brothers were equipped identically to knights except their mailcoats were sleeveless, their hoes feetless and the head covering was a *chapeau de fer* and they were not allowed the knights' equestrian equipment, tent or cauldron. They wore black surcoats with a red cross on back and front and black or brown mantles. Unarmed craftsmen sergeants were given Turkish arms when the need arose.

Turcopolier

Horses	Turcoman	Pack Animals	Tent	Cauldron
4	1	Unspecified	1	1

Under-Marshal

Horses	Pack Animals	Tent
2	Unspecified	1

Standard Bearer (Confanonier)

Horses	Pack Animals	Tent
2	Unspecified	1

Also in charge of the officers of the grain store and its sentries who each had one horse.

Sergeant Brothers, Commanders of the Houses

Horses	Squire
1	1

Could have up to two squires. One from another brother on payment and one from the Standard Bearer if it pleased him.

Caselier Brothers

Horses	Squire
2	1

* For military equipment, see Table 2.

On the matter of receiving horses from the West, the *retrais* are specific. In clause 84, such horses are to be placed in the Marshal's caravan and the Marshal is to do nothing with them until they are seen by the Master. The Master may take some himself and may keep one or two of these new mounts in the caravan to give to worthy secular friends of the order. He may also give horses to any brother of his choice. Moreover, the Master had the power to demand a horse from any brother but could offer up to one hundred besants in compensation for it if the horse had been looked after well.

The Master's strategic role in warfare is mentioned in clause 85. He may not give away or sell land or take castles in the marcher areas without the permission of the Chapter. This rule highlights the importance given to the Chapter in military decision making and the equal importance of what went on in the borderlands of Outremer. The concept of 'mission creep', as modern military commentators might term it, is also covered here. The Master cannot 'relax or widen the scope of any order made by him or by the convent, except with his and the convent's consent'. Likewise, the starting of a war, or the making of a truce on Templar lands or within a Templar castle cannot be done without the consent of the convent. But it would seem that the rules do allow for a quick reaction when a truce is broken. In such cases, the Master can extend a truce 'with the advice of the brothers who are in that country'. Clauses 92 and 93 also require the consent of the chapter for sending a worthy brother overseas to carry out the work of the house, or to send an ill brother. The pressure to retain numbers in the East must have been very great. The order's Marshal, the Commander of the Land, the Draper, the Commander of Acre and three or four other worthy men were called to deliberate on such matters as sending brothers overseas and a formal list of candidates was expected to be produced and presented to the Master.

When in the field the Master had a gravitational effect on other Templars who joined him. The Rule says (clause 95) that any brother who meets up with the Master when he is riding, or joins him on his way, was not to leave him without permission. Moreover, in times of war the Master's entourage was swollen in numbers once more. Clause 98 states that when under arms the Master may take six or eight or up to ten knight brothers with him. All the brothers were to obey the Master and yet the Master says the Rule, should obey his house.

The *retrais* of the Seneschal – the next rank listed – also includes an allowance of men and horses. He may have four mounts and a palfrey in place of a mule. For company he can take two squires and one knight brother. He could also have a sergeant brother with two horses. He can also have a deacon scribe 'to say his hours' and a mounted turcopole plus a Saracen scribe with his own horse. Furthermore, he could take two infantrymen with him and must also carry the same seal as the Master. The Seneschal carried the renowned Templar piebald banner. He also carried a round tent like the Master and deputised for him in his absence. 'All the equipment of the lands and houses, and all the houses and food' came under the command of the Seneschal, says clause 99. Moreover, he had a strategic capability in that he was able to move people and equipment around when in lands without the Master, thus making 'one house help another'.

The Marshal of the Convent of the Temple is the next officer considered. 'He should have four horses and two squires and in place of a mule he may have one fine Turcoman'. He should also have a sergeant brother with one horse and a turcopole with one horse. Furthermore, the Marshal took with him a pavilion tent which he could place in the commanders' baggage train. It had four flaps and three poles and two pegs and a tent for his squires and equipment. Apart from this, he was to have the same equipment as the knight brothers. The baggage train would also contain the Marshal's barley and cauldron. The Marshal's military power was extensive. He had command of all the arms of the house, says clause 102. These included those which had been bought for the brothers as gifts, alms or come as booty. Spoils of war which were treated as arms or were auctioned also came to the Marshal, including saddled horses (clause 116). So it was too with the equipment of brothers who had died, with the notable exception of crossbows (which went to the Commander of the Land) and the Turkish arms which the commanders bought to give to the craftsmen sergeant brothers. These latter brothers, distinct from the sergeant-at-arms, were generally the unarmed class of sergeants who were pressed into service when given such weaponry. It was also the Marshal who gave the brothers their orders and deployed them. At the raising of the war-cry (clause 103) the commanders of the Temple's houses should gather their horses, assemble, and then join the Marshal's squadron. As with the Master, they were not to leave it without permission. The sergeant brothers at this stage were to join with the Turcopolier and were not to leave him. Whilst under arms, all were under the command of the Marshal.

Clauses 104 to 106 of the Hierarchical Statutes cover the relationship between the Marshal of the Convent and the Commanders and Marshals of the lands of Tripoli and Antioch, a relationship which seemed to rest on permission for the marshalcy being both given and accepted for the Marshal of the Convent to have any primacy in those lands.

The next office considered was the Commander of the Land of Jerusalem and of the Kingdom. Like the Seneschal, he should have four horses and in place of a mule may have a palfrey. Two squires and one sergeant brother with two horses were permitted also, and a deacon scribe. One mounted turcopole was to go with the Commander and also one Saracen scribe. He was also to have two infantrymen like the Seneschal and one tent for his squires and a pavilion tent like that of the Marshal. He should also be accompanied by the Draper of the order. The Commander of the Land was the treasurer of the convent, who working closely with the Master kept meticulous lists of the contents of the treasury. He was also to work closely with the Draper for whom he should 'furnish the drapery with everything that is necessary, and may take what he wishes with the advice of the Draper; and the Draper must obey him.' The Commander of the Land had wide-ranging power. Within the Kingdom of Jerusalem, all the houses and casals (villages dependent upon a castle or other larger house) of the Templars were under him (clause 118). He could also claim expenses providing he informed the Master and gained his consent (clause 119).

The Commander of the Land of Jerusalem also had a role to play in the management of the spoils of war. Whereas the Marshal had command of all arms gained in such a way, the Commander of the Land of Jerusalem had command of all the animals with packsaddles, all the slaves and all the livestock the houses of the kingdom gained through warfare (clause 116). Also, the Commander could call upon the Marshal if his own horses became tired and worn out and he could borrow some horses and rest his own in the caravan, so long as he retrieved them later (clause 117). The Commander of the Land of Jerusalem also had control of the sharing-out of the brothers amongst the houses of the kingdom. To do this he needed the cooperation of the Marshal, who although he technically outranked the Commander of the Land, was obliged to keep to the exact numbers specified (clause 119).

The vitally important port of Acre was of special significance to the Templars. It had a Commander of the Shipyard, who although only a sergeant, held a very important post. However, all the Templars' ships at Acre came under the command of the Commander of the Land, as did their cargo, unless it was specifically addressed to the Master or another brother. So too did the Commander of the Shipyard and the brothers who worked alongside him (clause 119).

Within the City of Jerusalem itself the Templars had a Commander of the City of Jerusalem up to 1187. According to the *retrais*, his role seems to have evolved from the principal role of the first Templars of the days of Hugh of Payns. He was to have ten knight brothers under his command (clause 121) to lead and guard the pilgrims who came to the River Jordan and he should take with him a round tent and carry the piebald banner. The Commander of the City of Jerusalem also had an obligation to supply an unspecified number of pack animals whose role it was to carry pilgrims from the Jordan if necessary. Should he discover a nobleman in need he was to 'take him to his tent and serve him with the alms of the order', hence the need for a round tent which must also be provisioned with food. These same ten knights were also to guard the True Cross when it was transported by horse (clause 122). Lost to the Muslims at the Battle of Hattin in 1187, this revered fragment was to be guarded by day and night by these men. They were to camp as near as they could to the True Cross with two knights appointed as night-watchmen and when that camp was set 'everyone should lodge with the convent'.

The resources allotted to the Commander of the City of Jerusalem in the *retrais* were as follows: he should have four horses and in place of a mule could have a Turcoman or a fine roncin (workhorse). He could have two squires and a sergeant brother with two horses, a Saracen Scribe with one horse and a mounted turcopole. He should also have the Commander of Knights under him when in Jerusalem itself, otherwise this office came under the Commander of the Land.

There were a number of peculiarities of the office of Commander of the City of Jerusalem which marked it out as a very important position with the potential for its holder to create power and wealth within his own patrimony. If the spoils war were gained by the order, their rightful custodian would be the Commander of the Land, but should these be gained beyond the River Jordan says clause 123, the Commander of the City of Jerusalem should have half, but nothing 'this side of the river'. This clause perhaps allows for the Commander of the City to lend the Templars' military muscle to support acquisitive crusader activity beyond the borders of Jerusalem. It may be significant that the next clause (clause 124) says that all the secular knights who are in Jerusalem and who are associated with the house should lodge near him and ride under the Commander of the City's banner. All the brothers in Jerusalem and all those who came and went whilst the Marshal was absent, were under the Commander of the City's authority.

The Hierarchical Statutes then move onto the role of the Commanders of the Lands of Tripoli and Antioch for whom the *retrais* speak as one. They were to have four horses and in place of a mule may have a palfrey. They should have a sergeant brother with two horses and a deacon with one horse. In addition he should also have a turcopole with one horse, a Saracen scribe with one horse and an infantryman. The commanders of the Lands of Tripoli and Antioch were to carry the piebald banner and were to have one knight as companion, being able to elevate him in rank to a position where he could travel from one land to another. These officials were powerful within their own lands and could have the same rations of barley as the Master and in his absence could hold chapter. But they also had an important logistical role. It was their responsibility to provision their castles with leather, wheat, wine, iron, steel and sergeants to guard the gates. All other provisions within castles were to be the responsibility of the castellans, who could ask for practical or financial assistance to the Commanders who must then oblige. Should there be no Marshal in the land the commander must take care of provisioning the equipment to the brothers and could also issue the instructions of the house. The Commanders also had the power to appoint the Marshal in their lands and also the drapers and the castellans, with the consent of the chapter. But there were areas where the Commanders of these lands must defer to the Master. These areas were mainly logistical, although clause 129 does insert a line saying that the Commanders could not give orders to any man without the Master's permission. The Commanders did not have the power to increase or decrease the ration of barley or to put the brothers' horses out to stud unless under instructions from the Master and the chapter, should the Master be in the land. If the Master was not there, 'they could do so with the advice of the brothers of the convent' but this did not include the fourth horse which was at the discretion of the brothers 'to put to stud or to keep on half rations'.

The one discernible difference between the Commanders of the Lands of Tripoli and Antioch in the *retrais* was that if the commander of the Land of Antioch was to venture into the land of Armenia he was allowed to take a Chaplain and a Chapel. Because in Christian Armenia the rite was different from that of the Latin, the chapel would have contained vessels and vestments and probably a portable altar necessary for the celebration of mass.

The Draper of the Convent is the next official to be listed. His role was more important than the position in the list might indicate. He was to accompany the Commander of the Land of Jerusalem. Both these officials benefitted if a new brother donated gold or silver to the house, with ten besants of the gift going to the Drapery and the remainder to the Commander of the Land. The Draper had four horses, two squires and a man in charge of the pack animals which were needed to carry all his tailoring equipment and the pavilion tent he took with him (similar to the Marshal's pavilion). For the Drapers of Tripoli and Antioch the pavilion tent was not permitted. Two further tents were required for the squires and the tailors. The Draper's duty was to distribute on demand clothes and bed linen to the brothers (with the exception of woollen blankets). Decent standards of dress were the business of the Draper. The Drapers could order a brother to dress properly and this order must be obeyed, for the *retrais* of the Draper states that 'after the Master and the Marshal, the Draper is superior to all other brothers'. The Draper kept his eye on imbalances in clothing distribution. Brothers with an excess of anything were forced to put material back where it belonged.

Although it was possible for sergeant brothers to become commanders of houses, the first listing in the Hierarchical Statutes were for knight brothers in such a role. The Knight Commanders of the Houses were to have four horses and two squires each. Sergeant Brother Commanders of the Houses listed later in the document could have just one horse and could have a sergeant from another brother acting as a squire. They could also have a squire given by the Standard Bearer. Two of the knights' horses were to have the same rations as the Master and the other two the same as the convent, whereas the sergeant's rations were the same as the convent. The Knight Commanders of the Houses were allowed to retain one more horse than a regular knight brother. The *retrais* concentrate mainly on outlining the gift-giving restrictions of the office as well as outlining the legal or judgemental limitations of the role. Also, the Knight Commander of the House could only repair his houses and not build a new one without the permission of the Master or the Commander of the Land. But again, the vital subject of horses is touched upon. The Knight Commander of the House could give any fine foals or other mounts to brothers under his command. They in turn could give a mule or money to caselier brothers (who looked after the casals or small farms of the order). From the villeins of these farms the caselier brothers could purchase foals and pack animals for raising. There follows a brief entry concerning the *retrais* of the Commander of the Knights. His entitlements are not listed, but clause 137 does state that his office should be under the command of the Commander of the Land during both war and peace, in the absence of the Marshal.

Clauses 138 to 147 of the Hierarchical Statutes provide a wealth of information contained within the *retrais* of the Knight Brothers and the Sergeant Brothers of the Convent. Each Knight Brother should have three horses and one squire. A fourth horse and squire were at the discretion of the Master. The horses were to have a communal ration of barley. The *retrais* then lists in detail the weaponry and equipment of the Knight Brothers and Sergeant Brothers (see Table 2).

TABLE 2: Weapons, Armour, Clothing and Equipment of the Knight Brothers of the Convent, c.1165–c.1187, From the Hierarchical Statutes

Arms and Armour

One hauberk (coat of mail with integral coif and mail covering for the hands – not to be repaired without permission – clause 324 of the Rule)

Iron chausses (mail covering for the legs)

Helmet (probably conical or domed shape) or *chapeau de fer* (a wide-brimmed helmet to protect from blows from above. Not to be repaired or thrown according to clause 324 of the Rule)

Sword (not to be repaired without permission – clause 324 of the Rule)

Shield

Lance (not to be thrown without permission – clause 324 of the Rule)

Turkish mace

Surcoat, completely white (possibly the white capae or monastic style tunic, although a mantle is mentioned separately)

Haubergeon (padded garment usually worn beneath mail as a shock absorber)

Mail shoes

Three knives

Dagger

Breadknife

Pocket knife

Caparison (a fabric covering laid over the horse)

Clothing and Equipment

Two shirts

Two pairs of breeches

Two pairs of hose

Small belt to tie over the shirt

Jerkin with tails back and front

Fur jacket

Two white mantles (one with fur to be given back to the Draper in summertime and the other without)

Hooded cope, or cloak

Tunic (worn over the shirt)

Leather belt

Three pieces of bed linen (a bag filled with straw to act as a mattress, a light blanket and sheet)

A white, black or striped rug to cover his bed or coat of mail when he rides out

One small bag to keep his nightshirt in

One small bag to keep his surcoat and haubergeon in

Either a leather or wire mesh bag to place his hauberk in (clause 322 of the Rule states the wire bag was not to be carried by the straps without permission but to be carried in the hands by the knight or the sergeant)

Two cloths (one for eating and one to wash his head)

Another rug to sift barley on

Another blanket for his horse (but not if he has the rug for the barley sifting)

Cooking cauldron

Measuring bowl (for the barley)

Axe and grinder (but only with permission and not to be taken out of the land without the Master's permission)

Three saddle bags (two for the squires)

Two cups

Two flasks

A strap

Two girdles (one with a buckle and one without)

Bowl of horn and a spoon

One cloth cap

One felt hat

One tent and one tent peg

The list of weapons and equipment is certainly impressive. It was written at a time in the development of Western medieval armour when full plate armour had yet to be introduced. As a consequence, the Knight Templar of c.1165–c.1187 represented (as did his secular colleagues) the heaviest cavalryman of the medieval age. His mail armour, which covered him from head to foot would have weighed more than the later medieval plate armour which contrary to popular belief, was lighter than mail and spread the load more evenly. But it is not entirely clear what the Knight Templar actually looked like when he thundered onto the battlefield, although a good idea can be gained from the Hierarchical Statutes and later descriptions. Pope Gregory IX, writing in 1240 allowed the Templars to wear a white super-tunic with a cross on the breast over their armour in place of the old cappa. By this time the knight's helmets had evolved from the conical helm through the enclosed helm to the first forms of the Great Helm familiar at the end of our period around the turn of the thirteenth and fourteenth centuries.

Likewise, shields were in a process of evolution throughout the period of the Templars' existence. At the start of our period in the early twelfth century the knights' shield was similar if not identical in shape to the famous 'Norman' or kite-shaped shields of the Bayeux Tapestry. By the middle of the century, the length of these shields had shortened and the shape had become more triangular, with the top of the shield being no longer curved, but flat. By the mid-thirteenth century this type of shield is in good evidence on one of the illustrations of two knights Templar on horseback by Matthew Paris (see Fig. 4), which has the shields painted in the distinctive black and white markings of the order.

Fig. 4. Two Templar knights as depicted in Matthew Paris's thirteenth-century Chronica Majora.

The arms and armour allotted to the sergeants were only a little less impressive than that of the knights. Their surcoats were to be completely black with a red cross on both the back and front. They were also allowed a black or brown mantle. Only the horses' equipment, the tent and the cauldron were not allowed to them. There were, however, some differences in armour. The sergeants' mailcoats were to be sleeveless and their mail hose to be without feet. Also, their head protection was to consist of the *chapeau de fer* only. The sergeant could only have one horse. However, there were five types of sergeant brothers who held certain offices who could have two horses, unless they were moved to the office of Commander of a House, in which case their second horse went back to the Marshal. These were the Under-Marshal, the Standard Bearer, the Cook Brother of the Convent, the Farrier of the Convent and the Commander of the Shipyard at Acre. Each of these could have one squire as well. Their second horse was lent to them by the Master.

Clauses 144 to 147 of the Hierarchical Statutes deal with various aspects of the brothers' behaviour, not all of them overtly military, but some which continue to highlight military matters. The first of these clauses states that 'no brother may shorten his stirrup leathers, nor his girth, nor his sword belt, nor his breech-girdle without permission, but he may adjust his buckle without permission'. The implication here is that a brother cannot make himself ready for battle without permission. Nor could any brother bathe, let blood, take medicine, go into town or ride a horse at the gallop without permission. The latter measure, repeated elsewhere in the Rule would seem to be motivated by the desire to conserve the horses' energy. Clause 145 highlights the few things for which a brother could leave the table at meal times, a solemn time of the day. Only if the warcry was raised, or there was a fire, or the horses were unsettled, could a brother leave the table and then he could return to it when his work was done. The same clause also mentions that when camped on campaign the Templars were not to go to the lodging of a secular or religious person unless they were camped 'rope to rope' with the Hospitallers, indicating a closeness of cooperation between the military orders.

The Hierarchical Statutes (clauses 148 to 168) next give consideration to the arrangements made for camping, how to form a line of march and how to 'go in a squadron' (see below pp. 161–80). But the role of officials within the order is taken up again from clause 169 to 197. It starts with the *retrais* of the Turcopolier. This brother could have four horses and a Turcoman in place of a mule if he wished. He could also have the same rations as the convent, a small tent, a cauldron and some pack animals. The *retrais* imply that the Turcopolier was in charge, amongst other things, of reconnaissance. He would work closely with the Marshal when an alarm was raised and in the first instance would be responsible for sending one or two of his turcopoles to where the alarm was. He would inform the Marshal of their findings. The Turcopolier might go with his scouts and could be given five, six, eight or up to ten of them. He would be in sole charge of them unless a Commander of Knights with a piebald banner was in the company. An example of Templars and turcopoles being employed on a reconnaissance mission comes from the author of the *Itinerarium* who states that King Richard I sent out the Templars and the turcopoles to reconnoitre the countryside. They discovered twenty Saracens who were reaping barley in the fields and captured them all and sent them to Ascalon.

There is then an enigmatic entry in the *retrais* stating that when the squadrons of the convent are lined up, the Turcopolier should 'keep his men in the squadron and be like the others, and behave in such a way as to carry the banner, as is given above for the Marshal. Nor should he charge or attack unless the Master or Marshal orders him to.'

When they were under arms, all the sergeant brothers were under the command of the Turcopolier, but this was not the case in peacetime. However, the turcopoles themselves were always under his command during both war and peace. There were some sergeant brothers who would not fall under the command of the Turcopolier, provided that they did not find themselves in his squadron. These were the Under-Marshal, the Standard Bearer, the Master's sergeant brother and those sergeants of the Marshal and of the Commander of the Land.

Next, we have the *retrais* of the Under-Marshal, who was a sergeant brother. He was to have two horses and a tent and the same rations as the convent and a collection of pack animals to carry the tent. He was responsible for distributing and repairing the smaller items of equipment. One gets the impression from the *retrais* that this role was an extremely busy one during the frequent periods of conflict. The Under-Marshal would distribute old saddles and saddle pads, rugs, barrels, fishing nets, lances, swords, *chapeaux de fer*, old Turkish arms and crossbows (those which belonged to the marshalcy and not the Commander of the Land). The mention of a responsibility for repairing equipment stems from the fact that the Under-Marshal was also in charge of the craftsmen brothers of the marshalcy. He could further extend his power over men of equal rank by assuming command over the Standard Bearer if the Marshal was absent. He could also take uncommitted squires from the caravan, provided they did not constitute its garrison and give them to other brothers, but in particular to the Standard Bearer should he have need of them. This made sense in that the Standard Bearer was the official in charge of the squires. The Standard Bearer, also a sergeant, was allotted two horses, pack animals and a tent and the same rations as the convent. As part of his duties of overseeing the squires, he was also responsible for seeing they were paid when they had served their term. He could hold chapter when he pleased and punish wrong-doers. The Standard Bearer was also in charge of the officers who were in charge of the grain store and the sentries. Each of these were given one horse. The last overtly military official listed in the Hierarchical Statutes (notwithstanding the *retrais* of the Infirmarer Brothers) is that of the Caselier Brothers, responsible for the casals or villages of the order. They were allotted two horses and one squire and the same ration of barley as the Master and could keep one girth for the horses they rode.

Before we look at how the brothers of the convent went off to war, we will evaluate the type of warfare which they mainly fought. Frequently on the march or encamped in the field, the Templars were also masters of the strategic art of raiding.

Chapter 30

Strategic Raiding, Camping and Marching

from the River Jordan to Damascus the land remains uncultivated like a desert because the Saracens are in fear of the castle of Safad, from which the knights of the Temple make important sorties as far as Damascus causing destruction and havoc. There they have achieved many miraculous victories over the enemies of the faith which it would not be easy to describe without making this into a large book . . .

Anonymous author of *De Constructione castri Saphet* (c.1260–6)

When James of Molay (c.1293–1314), the last Templar Grand Master, replied to Pope Clement V's enquiry as to the usefulness of the idea of amalgamating the military orders, he outlined one of the functions of his own order by saying 'there was never any lull in the chevauchées or other military operations against the Saracens'. He went on to construct various arguments largely against the proposals, but here in this one line we have what is probably not an exaggeration of a role performed by the Templars countless times throughout their existence.

The chevauchée at its basic level was a widely adopted strategy of landscape reduction performed by mounted bands of men who burnt and destroyed crops and settlements thus rendering them useless to the enemy. It was employed from ancient times through the Dark Ages and was particularly popular with the armies of the English during the Hundred Years War (1337–1453). It is no surprise to find the military orders using the method to their advantage. On the other hand, it was widely adopted by the Turks, Mamelukes and others in response to the crusader presence in the Levant. The reasons for anyone adopting the strategy could be many. One historian of thirteenth-century military history has identified five chief reasons, these being reprisals against enemy activity; the maintenance or exaction of tribute; the acquisition of supplies whilst on campaign; a means to damage enemy moral and attacks upon symbolic non-military targets. The advantage of conducting such activities were that they did not require a great deal of man or horse power. This was not the activity required of a vast feudal host for example, although detachments from such a host would employ the measure. Because of this, with their constant availability, small numbers and excellent equestrian skills, the Templars and Hospitallers were perfectly suited to this kind of warfare. One fine example of the Templars adopting the acquisitive approach was during the Fifth Crusade (1217–21) outside Damietta in Egypt. Oliver of Paderborn reports that the Templars conducted their own raid in search of supplies, independent of the main crusading force. The impression given is that the exploit was accomplished with a minimum of fuss: 'Then the Templars, with their own special following, advanced in a swift march to a town on the sea coast, which is called Broil, and brought back many spoils – about one hundred camels, the same number of captives, horses, mules, oxen, and asses and goats, clothing and much household furniture, returning unharmed after two days.'

The fact that due to lack of water some of the animals perished is perhaps not as important as the ease with which the Templars took them in the first place. This particular expedition would have had the agreement of the Marshal or Master at the time, but when raids were launched without such permission, trouble would surely follow. Clause 610 of the Rule recalls the actions of Brother Jacques (James) Ravane, the Commander of the Palace of Acre who took it upon himself to go with knights, turcopoles and sergeants on a raid to Casal Robert (a Hospitaller possession) and was caught by the Saracens and defeated and even had some of his men captured. He had done this without permission and as a consequence lost his habit and was put in irons. As we have seen, a much larger opportunistic raid took place in 1261 when the Templar Marshal Stephen of Saissy was caught in the Jaulan region and suffered a similar punishment and the ire of his Grand Master (see p. 111). The Templars sometimes accompanied the freshly arrived crusaders on raids. Such was the case in 1271 When the future Edward I of England launched a raid on the village of St George of La Baene near Acre. Here, some of his men perished through eating honey from bees which was described as either gone off, or too rich. However, another joint raid later that year saw a failed attempt at taking the fortification at Qaqun, but a successful capture of 12,000 animals.

Because the strategy was so often adopted, it might have seemed to be the bread and butter of the warfare of the age. Few bothered even to record it in detail. This paucity of evidence is made worse by the loss of the Templar archives on Cyprus to the Ottomans in 1571, which might have revealed more episodes. Examples of the measure being adopted as part of a retaliation for damage done to the order, however, are still there. The Civil War in Tripoli (1277–82) is characterised by such cyclic raiding. Examples also include an incident in 1227 when some warriors from Aleppo had seized and killed a Templar knight. The order's response was to kill a number of the enemy and capture booty on a raid, which they were forced by the Aleppan government to return. Perhaps the best example of the practice is the 1242 punitive raid by the Templars on Nablus in the wake of a Muslim crack-down on Christian pilgrims (see p. 98).

To raid in order to exact tribute or to make sure that such tribute was kept up must have been a constant feature of the Templar work out of Tortosa where in the mountains beyond sat the Assassins. However, sometimes the Templars were part of a force which would hope to persuade the enemy to release Christian prisoners as well. One such example comes from 1264 when both the Templars and Hospitallers accompanied a secular force in a raid out of Jaffa to persuade the Muslims to release John of Jaffa's castellan Gerard of Picquigny. Despite reducing the countryside around Ascalon to a smouldering wasteland, the castellan was not released, however.

To raid in order to acquire supplies was the mainstay of the work. The military orders and secular forces alike would have carried out such raids on a regular basis. The Templars for example, accompanied the Hospitallers and Oliver of Termes in 1264 on a raid which destroyed Bethsan and three surrounding villages from which much booty and prisoners resulted.

The Templars were so often in the field that is not surprising their Rule has a provision for how they should conduct themselves when camping and marching. The Anonymous Pilgrim (writing between 1167 and 1187) said of the order 'These Templars live under a strict religious rule, obeying humbly, having no private property, eating sparingly, dressing meanly, and dwelling in tents.' The military orders' ability to be readily available was their great advantage over the slow to recruit feudal hosts of the time (who could take several weeks to muster). Staying for lengthy periods in the field was part of this preparedness. The Templar Marshal's order to make camp was hailed, like other instructions, in French. 'Herbergés vos, seigniors frères, de par Dieu!' was the cry. In modern English, this would be roughly 'Make camp, Lord Brothers, on behalf of God'. It is contained in a section of the Rule (clauses 148 to 155) entitled 'How the Brothers Should Make Camp'. The rules were clear and the procedure must surely have been well rehearsed. Not until this cry had been heard and the Marshal had pitched his tent, was any brother allowed to pitch his. If anyone did so, the Marshal could give his tent away.

It was the Confanonier (Standard Bearer) who oversaw the setting of the camp and got the squires to organise and feed the horses. The Confanonier had his own place in camp alongside the crier of orders and the officer in charge of the grain store (Granatier). It was from here that orders were transmitted including the alarm signal. Staying within earshot of the camp's alarm was paramount. Brothers could not go out foraging or seeking firewood beyond this range unless the order was given. The food the brothers could look for beyond the camp was limited. Green vegetables, fish, birds and wild animals were permitted but only if they were retrieved by means other than hunting which was prohibited.

The focal centre of the camp was the Chapel tent, in which each brother was to claim his place alongside another. The Master, Marshal, mess tent commander and the Commander of the Land were allowed to pitch their tents close to the chapel. Clause 148 contains some ambiguous wording regarding the arrangement. The brothers 'should pitch their tents round the Chapel and outside the ropes, each one coming in his troop [troops, or *routes*, seem to be the smallest organisational unit]. And those who are outside should pitch their tents outside and place their equipment inside; and each brother may select an area for all his following'. The 'ropes' are usually taken to be the Chapel tent's guy ropes, but such ropes do not extend very far at all on medieval tents. It is possible that the Rule is referring to a roped-off area at the centre of the camp within which the Chapel and the tents of some key personnel form the centre. One interpretation of this clause is that the brothers pitched their tents outside this roped off area, and then placed the equipment of their immediate entourage either inside their own tents or inside the roped off area. Clause 155 demands that if the alarm is raised in the camp, 'those that are near the shout should leave that area with their shields and lances, and the other brothers should go to the Chapel to hear the orders that are issued'. This further emphasises the importance of the Chapel core area as a rallying point and source of equipment.

Within the camp was a Commander of the Victuals. Gifts of food coming into the camp were under his control. No brother should have food on him or in his tent without permission of the commander. The Commander of the Victuals would call the rations. When he did so he was to inform the Master's sergeant so that the Master could have the best. The remainder was shared as fairly as possible amongst the brothers with no one brother getting two pieces of meat from the same part of an animal. There was also a leniency towards the sick in the infirmary who would be given more food and the best meat. 'And when the healthy have two pieces of meat, the sick should have three or more' says the Rule. There was also a pecking order in the consumption of rations. The meat for two brothers (a pairing system is very evident in this part of the Rule dealing with active service) 'should be such that what is left by two brothers may sustain two paupers' (clause 153). It is not clear exactly how much meat this was, but the Rule says 'from two brothers' servings those of three turcopoles may be made up; and from two turcopoles' those of three sergeants'. Also, when the brothers were not fasting five measures of wine were shared between the brothers and three between the turcopoles. Oil was rationed in the same measures.

The section of the Rule dealing with Conventual Life (clauses 279 to 385) contains further details of camp life when the Templars were on campaign. Life here was supposed to reflect Templar life when not on campaign as much as possible, but there are some references to camp life which serve to further explain the clauses we encounter between 148 and 155 but with some repetitive material and a notable contradiction. The clause which mentions again the reaction expected on hearing the raising of the camp alarm inside the camp (clause 380) says that those who are camped in and are moving away from the area where the alarm is raised with their shields and lances 'should not go far from the camp until there has been another order'. This order would come from the Chapel, as explained in clause 155. Only if the alarm is raised *outside* the camp however, were those nearest to it expected to go and deal with it, which they should do so without permission, whatever the reason. However, clause 155 had stated that if the alarm had been raised outside the camp the brothers should not leave without permission 'not even for a lion or a wild beast'. It is not clear why there is this contradiction in a response to an outside attack on the camp in the Rule.

What is known however, is that the Templars and crusaders in general did have their camps attacked by their enemies. On 31 July 1219 during the Fifth Crusade according to Oliver of Paderborn it was Templar camp discipline which repelled the Egyptians. Here, a force of Muslim infantry and cavalry had infiltrated the crusader camp and the Templars repelled the attack after permission to charge was given (see p. 88). Oliver may even have witnessed the charge himself. They were supported in this effort by both secular knights and the Teutonic Knights.

The section of the Rule on Conventual Life also states that the commander in charge of food in the camp 'should be one of the old men of the house, and such who fears God and loves his soul'. It also goes on to say that brothers should not erect three tents or more together without permission, implying an importance attached to spacing them out. Two together, were however, permitted. Brothers were forbidden to take things from each other's campsite areas without permission and if one brother's horse wandered into another brother's area, he was to take it back (clause 316).

In a section outlining the distribution of rations (clause 368) it is apparent that the brothers queued for their food. Sharing of food between messes was also permitted (clause 370). This latter clause goes on to say that rations were never generous enough for men to fill their stomachs and also warns that rations could of course be reduced. When being served meat or cheese (clause 371) the brothers were to be sure to cut the food so that the remaining piece was of sufficient quality and completeness to serve to a pauper. The sharing of food is outlined again in clause 373: 'And each brother may give some of the food in front of him, as far as he can stretch his arm, but no farther; and always he who has the best should invite the one who has the worst.'

There is also some instruction on horse management. No brother could lend his horse to anyone, either a brother or someone else 'to go far away for pleasure' without permission. This applied to other animals as well. Grooming was obviously encouraged and sometimes the brothers were given permission to do this at night (clause 378), although when they did so the horse blanket was not to be kept on the horse. The horses' diet was carefully monitored (clauses 319 and 379). No brother was to give greater rations to any of his horses so that the other horses suffered. Seeking to obtain barley without permission was forbidden, except the ration that was given at the grain store. When brothers gave their horses half-rations, as sometimes might have to be the case, this was to be in measures of ten and those in the caravan were always to receive such measures, as were the horses of the craftsmen brothers. Horses eating straw were not to be given grass by the brothers without permission. The preservation of horses' energy seems to be the focus of this clause, since it states that brothers should not place harness or ropes on a horse which might make them amble. Moreover, in a sentence which perhaps illustrates that the famous Templar seal depiction of two knights riding one horse was more symbolic than actual, the Rule states 'And two brothers should not ride on one horse'.

There would clearly come a time when the Templar camp needed to be struck and the brothers returned to their houses. This was to be done with a minimum of fuss and none was to mount or load his equipment without permission, except for certain items. To organise this, the Marshal had to liaise with the Commander of the Land, for it was only he who knew the numbers required in the houses of the land at that time. It might be the case that a brother could find himself in one place before a campaign and then after the camp was struck, be sent to another. The Rule also specifies that at the striking of the camp no equipment was to be left without permission.

Fig. 5. Knights move out on campaign. From a fresco at the Templars' chapel at Cressac-sur-Charente, France, thought to show the campaigns of 1163 in which Nur ed-Din was defeated. Both figures may be Templars, with crosses on their surcoats, though neither have a black and white shield.

When the Templars were on campaign if they weren't at camp or actually fighting, then they were most likely marching. A whole section is given over to 'How the Brothers Form the Line of March' (clauses 156 to 160). As the Templar camp prepared to move out and form a line of march there were a few things which the brothers were allowed to place on their horses before receiving the Marshal's order to move. These included tent pegs, empty flasks, the camping axe, the camping rope (possibly the same rope as that which cordoned off the central area) and fishing net.

It was a time of strict adherence to protocol and if any brother wished to speak to the Marshal he should go to him on foot.

When the order was given to mount, the brothers were to go at a walk or amble with their immediate entourage, keeping their squires behind them until they positioned themselves in the column. At this point, the squires were sent in front of the brothers with all the equipment. Although the Rule does not specify, it seems most likely the brothers formed up behind individual commanders of knights. When on the march, the Standard Bearer or Confanonier was to go in front of the banner and was to have a squire or sentry carry it. The Rule also states that when marching at night time, silence was to be kept throughout until prime the next morning (around 6am). This demonstrates what must have been a high degree of capability for the Templars. To march in silence at night would have involved overcoming problems of communication, visibility and the management in darkness of the alarm system if something went wrong. The fact that the Rule makes a provision for it, implies that it was done fairly frequently. Both the Templars and the Hospitallers not only knew of the dangers of night marches, but knew that secular forces were ill equipped to deal with them. This is borne out by the anonymous account of the re-building in 1240 of the Templar castle at Safad (see p. 199) which states that before the decision was taken to rebuild the castle, the barons and nobles in the army of Count Theobald IV of Champagne discussed how their huge army should proceed from Jaffa. On the eve of 12 November 1239, some nobles 'spurned the advice of the Templars and Hospitallers and other religious and noble men of the land. Confident in their own strength they left the army under cover of night . . . they suffered an ignominious defeat, several being killed or captured'. Quite what the military orders' objections were is not clear but they may have thought that their own training and discipline may not have been matched by the secular forces.

During the daytime march, it might be the case that a brother wished to speak to another. If he wanted to do this he was to position himself so that the equipment of both the brothers was still in front of them for ease of access, before returning to his place where his troop or entourage were walking. If a brother wished to ride alongside the column for 'his own purposes', then he was to come and go downwind for fear of kicking up the desert dust into the faces of his fellow brothers. Generally, riding beside the line of march was discouraged.

The matter of the horses' constant need for water is also addressed, but this was never allowed at the expense of the physical cohesion of the column. Should they pass by running water in peaceful territory then they were allowed to water their horses, but again not to 'endanger the line of march'. Those who were on reconnaissance (presumably the turcopoles, although the Rule is not specific) who passed by water were not to water their horses there without permission from the Standard Bearer who was with them. If the Standard Bearer watered his own horses there, then this was taken as a sign of permission being given. This hot and hostile landscape meant that marching armies were often to be found at watering places. Here, they could be vulnerable unless certain measures were taken.

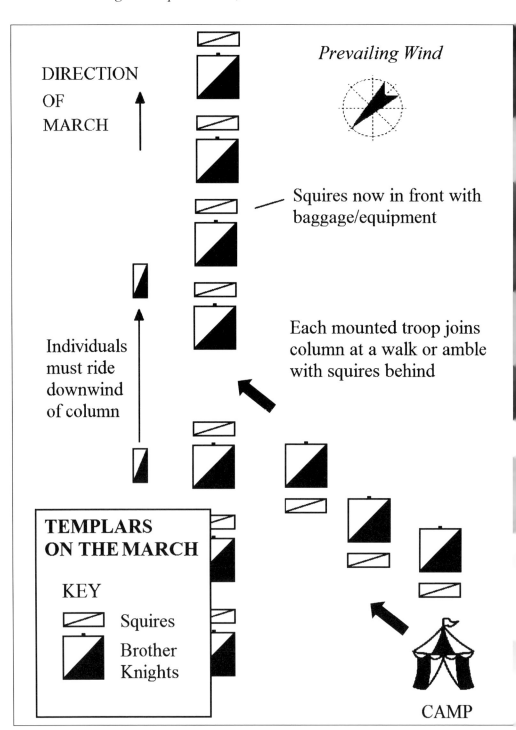

Fig. 6. Templars on the march.

Should the alarm be raised during the march the reaction was similar to the same scenario within the camp. The brothers nearest the shout were to take up their shields and lances and calmly await the Marshal's orders whilst the others went towards the Marshal to receive their orders. At all times on the march and also when lying in ambush, guarding pasture, or on reconnaissance, the brothers were not to remove the bridle or saddle of their horses, or even feed them without permission. Nor were they to arm or disarm without permission.

The organisational skills and disciplines required during the gap in time between camping and fighting were obviously important. The Templars' perfection of such matters clearly gained them a fine reputation. On the Second Crusade, although Everard des Barres's response (of grouping the crusaders into units of fifty each under a Templar leader answerable to his own commander) is not a specific arrangement encountered in the Rule, it is clear that imposing a disciplined leadership structure on a shaken army comprising various elements of differing morale and capabilities, was enough to rescue a perilous situation.

What happened when a column was attacked is perhaps best illustrated by the events of the Third Crusade between 1189 and 1192 (pp. 80–3). The military orders were often used to form either the van or the rear guards of Richard I's marching armies to counter Turkish attacks. The *Itinerarium* records the Templars in the van and the Hospitallers at the rear during the coastal march from Caifas. It also records that after being harassed by Turks 'who constantly remained on their flank' King Richard decided that he himself would lead the vanguard and place the Templars in the rear specifically to counter the Turkish flanking attacks. But the dangers of occupying such a position within a crusading army were evident. When travelling through difficult mountainous terrain instead of a preferred coastal path which was blocked by foliage, the *Itinerarium* records that the companies 'kept closer together' and that the Templars were once again in the rear guard. The Templars apparently lost many horses that day as the Turks had charged them from behind, probably taking advantage of a lack of cohesion which the Templars could do little about. It was however, a position which the Templars were usually comfortable with. Again, in the aftermath of the Battle of Arsuf, on 9 September 1191 the Templars found themselves fending off Turkish flanking attacks which were said to come to little or nothing. Nor was this role confined to the Third Crusade. In 1203 on a raid into Galilee the Templars constituted the advanced guard and the Hospitallers the rear. In 1249 when Saint Louis was marching up the Nile his force was fronted by a Templar contingent which successfully saw off an ambush on its advanced guard which resulted in the destruction of half of the attackers (p. 104). In fact, it was the familiarity the Templars and Hospitallers had gained in performing these roles of rear and advance guards in crusader armies which led James of Molay to argue against the proposed amalgamation of the military orders in a letter to Pope Clement V written between 1306 and 1307. He was referring to secular crusading armies headed by noblemen when he wrote:

it has always been the custom of the religious military orders that one precedes, filling the role of vanguard, while the other forms the rearguard. In this way they cover and envelop the strangers like a mother her child. This is a good thing, since they know the ways of the Saracens and the Saracens recognise them, and whoever has conducted a cavalry operation without them has fared badly . . . Now, if the two orders were united, others would have to form the vanguard or the rearguard.

There are frequent references to the order's baggage train in the Rule. It is not certain exactly how the baggage train was organised, but clause 176 does mention that the main caravan and horse caravan were separate. The house's baggage train is also mentioned as a separate entity in clause 178 where the Standard Bearer plays a specific role in organising non-combatant group movements when on the march. Here, it is said that if the brothers send their horses and squires to the baggage train or to pasture the Standard Bearer should lead them out and back in a troop with a piebald banner at its head.

So, discipline, cohesion and clear organisation on the march were clearly a part of the Knights Templars' approach to warfare. But what of their organisation and performance on the battlefield? This section of the Rule is perhaps the most sensitive and revealing account of how the Templars plied their trade. Between clauses 161 and 168 are contained the instructions for the secret of Templar success on the field. 'How the Brothers Should Go in a Squadron' and 'When the Marshal takes up the Banner to Charge' are sections of the Rule whose contents – if revealed to the wider world – would be far more damaging than any esoteric secret. We will examine these next.

Chapter 31

Battlefield Tactics

When the Lord's Cross proceeds to battle, these two [orders] escort it, one on each side: the Templars on the Right and the Hospitallers on the left. The Templars are excellent knights wearing white mantles with a red cross. Their bicoloured standard which is called the 'baucant' [*sic*] goes before them into battle. They go into battle in order and without making a noise, they are first to desire engagement and more vigorous than others; they are the first to go and the last to return, and they wait for their Master's command before acting. When they make the decision that it would be profitable to fight and the trumpet sounds to give the order to advance, they piously sing this psalm of David: 'Not to us, Lord, not to us but to your name give the glory', couch their lances and charge into the enemy. As one person they strongly seek out the units and wings of the battle, they never dare to give way, they either completely break up the enemy or they die. In returning from the battle they are the last and they go behind the rest of the crowd, looking after all the rest and protecting them.

Anonymous Pilgrim, c.1167–c.1187

The pitched battle is not as common a thing in medieval history as strategic campaigning, raiding and siege warfare. This is because fighting a battle is a very risky business. In fact, there were some leaders in Western Christendom during the crusading era whose military policies were based on battle evasion, preferring to win a war with strategic manoeuvring and political coercion. The reason for all this caution was that the death of key personnel could have a profound effect on the outcome of any campaign and in some cases on the future of kingdoms. Replacing lost men of the equivalent high fighting calibre of the fallen was also difficult. Templars (in theory) had a constant flow of recruits of high quality. Each man was dedicated to his role and prepared to die for his faith. If he did die, he would be replaced. This much was known by the Turks and other enemies of the crusaders.

It would be misleading however, to say that pitched battles were very rare. They might occur for a number of reasons. An attack on a marching column was a particular favourite strategy of the Turks, which could lead to a battle in the right circumstances (such as at Hattin and Arsuf). Battles could be fought against siege armies to relieve a besieged force within a stronghold. Elsewhere, ambushes may be set (such as at Montgisard). For most of the time, the Templars would find themselves conducting chevauchées, garrisoning their fortresses, escorting pilgrims or political dignitaries through the hostile landscape, or guarding pasture or secular crusaders on campaign. At times of war, however, they needed to be prepared for the pitched battle when it came, and it was here that the Knights Templar were often so impressive as to sometimes surprise both their enemies and their own allies on the field of battle with tactics which are often misinterpreted as reckless or irresponsible.

The Eastern Franks' approach to warfare in the Latin East was different from warfare in the West. Geography, politics and a simple lack of numbers had led the Franks of Outremer to adopt a more battle-seeking and aggressive response than was usual in the West, despite the obvious dangers. This had meant a change in the army cohesion when on the march. The 'Fighting March' was often adopted whereby an army would proceed with its cavalry in the middle, defended by a ring of infantry with missile capability to try to keep the enemy at bay. This can be seen at Hattin in 1187 (where it was not enough to avoid disaster) and at Arsuf (1191) where under Richard I the result was different. Arab observers of the latter encounter describe the crusader army as already being in formation. The key to success would seem to have been a density of formation. In 1170 when the Templars accompanied King Amalric's army to Daron (p. 52), their successful repulse of the enemy attacks was due, says William of Tyre, to the fact they had huddled together more than was usual. This meant the Saracens were unable to break them apart.

There was also a move towards a more compact and massed cavalry charge than was normally the case. Western Franks were no stranger to the cavalry charge and used it as effectively as they could at a small unit level with individual leaders taking their conrois (a unit of up to around twenty closely affiliated men) into the charge. But to organise a mass cavalry charge at a level above this is extremely difficult. Arsuf is a fine example of it all going well, but here the army was in the hands of one of the great generals of the age. It would seem that what the military orders (and the Templars in particular) brought to the fields of Outremer was the discipline and organisation to achieve the move on a regular basis. The Templars would all try to move as one when on the offensive, keeping cohesion at all times.

Let us first examine what the Rule says about forming up in squadron, or 'en eschielles'. This unit is the larger unit of the Templar army, the smaller being the troops, or *routes*, which may only have contained up to ten or twelve men, but were the equivalent of the secular conrois, albeit much smaller.

It was the Marshal's job to call the brothers to arms. On the raising of the 'war-cry', the Commanders of the Houses gathered their horses and went to join the Marshal's squadron. When the convent was lined up in squadrons the Turcopolier was to keep his men in his squadron and behave like the others 'in such a way as to carry the banner'. He was not to charge or attack unless expressly permitted by the Marshal or the Master. Lines of communication on the battlefield between the Marshal and the Turcopolier were clearly important.

The Rule states what was expected of the sergeants. The armoured sergeants were to behave exactly as the knight brothers in battle. This meant an unwavering commitment to the attack. However, the other class of sergeants (those who were pressed into service from the craftsmen ranks with Turkish arms) were permitted to move to the rear if wounded or overwhelmed. This instruction compares markedly with clause 167 which deals with brother knights in the heat of battle. Here, it is stated that no brother should leave his squadron because of cuts or wounds without permission, although if he was so badly hurt that he could not obtain the permission himself, he could send another to get it. The Rule also shows that there were occasions when brothers might be placed to command the sergeants-at-arms. Under these circumstances the knights were to stay with the sergeants and not leave them. If the Marshal or the knight's squadrons charged then these brothers leading the sergeants were to line-up the sergeants' units in close ranks behind the knights to provide rear support and assistance during battle.

Once these squadrons were set, no brother was to move from one to another (clause 161). The brothers were to place their squires with lances in front of them and those with horses behind, giving the impression of an infantry screen and a rear support probably providing replacement mounts. Another interpretation of the squires with lances at the front has been postulated. It may be that these men were to hand the knights their lances before the onset of the charge. Cohesion once again was paramount: 'no brother should turn his horse's head towards the back to fight or shout, or for anything else, while they are in a squadron'. However, horses – no matter how well trained – could be difficult to handle. The Rule mentions restive or jibbing horses as a problem for the brothers and also mentions bucking or throwing animals (clause 154). It was the duty of the Marshal to replace such horses if he could, such was the importance of the horse to the tactical cohesion of the squadron. It was better to permit a brother to go without his horse than to suffer a bad one. Brothers were permitted to leave the squadron temporarily to check on the soundness of their mount and sort out their horse's saddle adjustments. They could take their lances and shields with them, but must return to the squadron immediately in silence. If they elected to wear their coifs (a mailed hood) during such a move, they must leave them on. But charging or leaving the ranks of the squadron without permission was strictly forbidden. The only exception to not leaving the squadron was when a brother saw a Christian in trouble 'in peril of death' at the hands of a Turk. Here, the brother could step out of formation and deal with the Turk, but again must return to his squadron in silence. There is however, a later example in the section of the Rule on Further Details on Penances which outlines the dangers of charging without permission and the specific punishment given out. Clause 614 explains that the convent was once lodged in Jaffa. The Turks had set two ambushes at Fontaine Barbe. Here is what happened:

the Turcopolier came out first, and brother Margot was delivered to all ten brothers who were to guard him; and the Turcopolier went forward between the two ambushes; and it seemed to the brothers who were guarding him that they [the enemy] wanted to attack the Turcopolier, and of the ten brothers who guarded him four brothers left without the permission of the commander – and one had no chapeau de fer – and they charged the ambushers. And two of these brothers lost two horses; and then the others who were left charged, with the permission of the commander, and defeated the ambushes, and the Turcopolier charged afterwards and defeated the others.

Although the outcome at Fontaine Barbe had eventually been favourable to the Templars, the Chapter had much to say about it:

Brother Margot did not make peace with those who had charged without permission and he told the Marshal before all the brothers, and the brothers [who had charged without permission] rose and pleaded for mercy; and for those two brothers who had not lost anything, it was decided that they could forfeit the habit, and for those two who lost their horses it was judged that they could not keep their habits. But because the thing turned out well, and the Turcopolier would have been at risk if that charge had not been made, those who lost their horses were allowed to keep their habits for the love of God, and the other two were put on two days [fasting] . . .

The role of the Standard Bearer (Confanonier) during battle is outlined by the Rule. It gives us an idea of the physical arrangement on the field. The Standard Bearer was to form the squires into a squadron whilst a turcopole held the banner. When the Marshal and the brothers charged, the squires who lead the knights' replacement destriers (warhorses) were to charge behind them providing them with re-mounts (a very difficult thing to do in the heat of battle), whilst other squires were to take the riding mules and palfreys to the Standard Bearer and remain with him. The Standard Bearer was to have a banner furled around his lance and when the Marshal charged he was to go after the action in an orderly fashion at a walk or an amble.

The Bauceant, Baucant or Piebald Banner

The Templar banner was called the Baucant, the name being derived from the Low Latin for piebald. It is depicted in black and white sections. The name was often corrupted to Beau Séant or similar. James of Vitry said that its two-tone appearance meant that 'they [the Templars] are fair and kindly towards their friends, but black and terrible to their enemies'. However, the true meaning of the standard is not really known. The triumph of light over darkness or purity over evil are just as convincing arguments. Contemporary illustrations vary and some show the top half black and the bottom half white or vice versa (Fig. 7. a, b, c).

The depictions in Matthew Paris's *Chronica Majora* show a black top half, whilst that in the church at San Bevignate shows a white top half adorned with a cross. This latter standard may be that of the Master whilst those of the *Chronica Majora* could be squadron standards. A secondary gonfalon, or banner, (Fig. 7, d), is postulated depending on whether we think the medieval illustrations are depicting Templars or just general secular crusaders or even St George. This appears as a three-tailed banner adorned with a red cross.

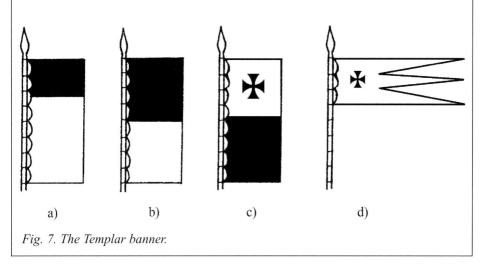

a)   b)   c)   d)

Fig. 7. The Templar banner.

The Rule contains a number of clauses under a section entitled 'When the Marshal takes up the banner to charge'. Unleashing the power of a well ordered medieval cavalry charge was no easy undertaking. The concepts of timing, distance and unit cohesion were of greater importance than sheer weight of numbers. In fact, Saint Bernard of Clairvaux had written that the Templars 'charge their adversaries as though they consider enemies to be sheep, not fearing a bit the savagery of the Barbarians or the size of their army, even if they themselves are a mere handful in number'. The Anonymous Pilgrim noted how the Templar units sought out the enemy 'as one person' implying a robust cohesion. It was vital though, to actually make contact with the enemy. The Turks were adept at melting away from a cavalry charge thus leaving their enemy overstretched. They did this by opening up their ranks and allowing the energy of the charge to dissipate, followed by a pre-arranged signal at which they rallied and poured missile fire into the disordered foe. This was noted by Fidenzio of Padua a Franciscan friar writing in the second half of the thirteenth century, but it was a tactic widely employed before this time. For Fidenzio the Westerners' main problem immediately after their charge was not knowing how to gather themselves again. The tactic was deployed against the crusaders at the retreat from Fariskur in 1219 and again at the Battle of Mansourah in 1250 and in both cases the Franks were swamped. However, as we have seen at Montgisard in

1177 the issue of a continuing momentum brought about by swiftness and surprise impressed Saladin. Ralph of Diss recorded that the Templars 'incessantly knocked down, scattered, struck and crushed' (see pp. 59–60 for account of the battle), implying a weighty forward momentum.

It is not surprising therefore that there are numerous references in the Rule to the decision to charge being made by the Marshal and not by individual unit leaders. Once the Marshal had decided to charge, he took the piebald standard from the Under-Marshal and appointed a guard of five, six or up to ten knights whose job it was to stay with the banner and protect it whilst other brothers would 'attack in front and behind, to left and right, and wherever they think they can torment their enemies in such a way that, if the banner needs them they may help it, and the banner help them . . .'. The emphasis was on a maximisation of protection for the banner and those around it. The Commander of Knights in charge of the group of brothers around the Marshal was to carry a furled banner on his lance. He was to keep as close to the Marshal as possible so that if the Marshal's banner should fall or be torn 'or any misadventure befall it, which God forbid, he can unfurl his banner'. The Marshal's Commander of Knights would also lead the attack in the event of the Marshal being wounded or incapacitated. It was however, forbidden to charge with or lower the banner for any reason, whether you were the Marshal or the Commander of Knights. Elsewhere in the Rule (clause 241), those commanders who lowered the banner in order to strike ran the risk (if harm came of it) of losing the habit and being clapped in irons never to command or carry the banner again. The risk is described in the section on Further Penances which states (clause 611) that if a banner is lowered 'those who are far off do not know why it is lowered, for good or ill, for a Turk could more easily take or seize it when it is lowered than when it is aloft; and men who lose their banner are very afraid, and may suffer a very great defeat'. An example of such misdemeanour is given in clause 640. At 'Atlit (Château Pèlerin) a certain brother Baudoin de Borages held the rank of Commander of Knights. A force of Turks rushed the castle when he was outside of it. Baudoin's scouts told him to turn back because the Turks were too numerous. Baudoin did not turn back and got caught up with the Turks as far as Mirla (between 'Atlit and Caesarea) where he was surrounded. In desperation he lowered the banner in order to charge and managed to reach the shore with two brothers although the others with him were killed or captured and all the equipment taken. Baudoin however, went overseas to forget about what he had done. One of the other two remaining brothers did the same whilst the last remaining brother stayed behind 'and never again did he have authority in the Temple: thus it was'.

The importance of banners as rallying points is emphasised in the Rule. Like the Marshal's squadron, each squadron of knights had its own commander with a furled banner and up to ten brothers to guard him and the banner. The rules were the same for the commanders in these squadrons as they were for the Marshal. The commanders could not charge or leave the squadron without permission from the Master 'or of the one who is in his place'. The punishment for doing so could result

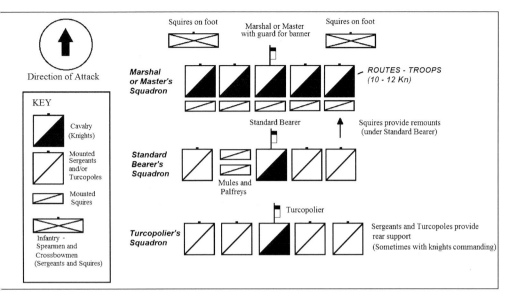

Fig. 8. The Templar cavalry charge.

in the loss of the habit. The Rule clearly acknowledges the fog of war in the midst of a battle. Should a brother have travelled too far from the banner and found himself with enemy forces between him and his banner (or simply be unable to find it), he was to go to the first Christian banner he found. If that banner was that of the Hospitallers, the knight was to tell the Hospital that he could not find his banner and then remain silent until he is able to re-join his banner.

The Rule approaches the difficult subject of defeat. It is here where the dedication of the Knight Templar displays itself in contrast to the secular warriors of the day. In the event of a battlefield defeat no brother was to leave the field to return to the garrison 'while there is still a piebald banner raised aloft'. Expulsion was the punishment. This was repeated later in the Rule (clauses 232 and 241–2). Leaving your banner 'for fear of the Saracens' was one of the nine sins for which expulsion was the result, ranking alongside desertion to the Saracens, leaving a fortification by anything other than the prescribed gate, and disclosing the affairs of the Chapter to any brother who was not there or to anyone else. Even if the last Templar banner fell and the brother saw 'that there is no longer any recourse' he was to go to the nearest Christian or Hospital banner and only when these fell, could he leave to join the garrison.

The impression given by the Rule of a well-trained heavy cavalry army is overwhelming, as is the propensity for the adoption of the offensive and the necessity to stay to the last. Command rules were clear. Fighting instructions are also unambiguous. The support of the squires, turcopoles and sergeants was organised in such a way as to resupply the energy of the attack. It was the function of the

Fig. 9. A charging knight from a fresco at the Templars' chapel at Cressac-sur-Charente, France, thought to show the campaigns of 1163 in which Nur ed-Din was defeated. It is not clear if the figure is a brother knight (his shield decoration is suspiciously elaborate), but the couched lance fighting style is typical of that employed by the Templars at the charge.

sergeants to keep the enemy at bay whilst the knights re-formed. Even infantry screening and support is hinted at in the Rule and there is mention of crossbow provision although the nature of its deployment is not known. That the knights fought on horseback is hardly in doubt, but it was possible for the brothers to dismount to fight. This concept is one that was sometimes derided in medieval knightly circles as being unbecoming for such a social rank. Eleventh century Franks and Normans alike frowned upon such a deployment, but during the twelfth century in northern Europe where a strong infantry tradition (such as that in Anglo-Saxon England and Scandinavia) was influencing mounted tactics, we see more of this dismounted tactic being used to the point where the Anglo-Norman kings and their commanders were using it extensively to provide a defensive option on the battlefield. However, the Templars' experience of fighting dismounted was not altogether a happy one. During the Third Crusade in 1191 King Richard's crusading army was out foraging and the Templars had been deployed to protect the squires and men-at-arms in the fields. Four thousand Turks are reported in the *Itinerarium* as descending in ambush on the Templars and compressing them into a constricted position. The Templar response was to dismount and stand with their backs to their comrades' backs and face outwards towards the onslaught. It was a clearly defensive response and despite their efforts the order lost three brothers almost immediately. 'Helmets rang and sparks flew as striking swords collided' says the colourful account. The Templars resolutely threw the Turks back. The Turks eventually broke through the Templars who were only relieved by the charging Andrew of Chavigny and his mounted knights.

As for the Templars' cavalry charge in action, the Battle of Montgisard in 1177 (pp. 57–60) perhaps provides the order's finest hour in this respect. However, we have also seen from examples in the Rule such as the incident at Fontaine Barbe (pp. 173–4) that the Templars' smaller scale actions also involved the cavalry charge. It is likely that the order's reputation was built upon countless repetitions of such actions on a small scale. The tactic clearly has its weaknesses, especially if the enemy evaded the oncoming Templar units, but we must spare a thought for the great courage it took for the brothers of the military orders to undertake such a thing.

The Rule concentrates on the arrangements for the cavalry charge for a reason. It was something which required instruction. By association, it must have required a degree of training to perfect. The lack of instruction in the Rule for the more simplified infantry roles is not surprising. Spearmen and bowmen require less complicated training. But here we have an issue which has troubled the historians of the Templars. If the section of the Rule which outlines the squadron organisation and cavalry charge arrangements reads like a military manual, then it differs from other manuals of the medieval era such as the much-copied Late Roman manual *De Re Militari* of Vegetius, the Byzantine Emperor Maurice's *Strategicon* and other Byzantine manuals such as Leo VI's *Taktika* and the *Praecepta Militaria* of Nikephoras Phocas. The difference is that unlike the others, the Rule is silent on the vital subject of training.

On the matter of the deployment of crossbowmen in the Templar army the evidence is poor. However, it is clear that this tactical option was employed and that the Templars thought it to be very important. The castle at Safad for example, had a garrison which consisted of around 300 crossbowmen. They are thought to have served for pay. In fact, a letter of 1218 written by Pope Honorius III specifically mentioned the military orders spending a great deal of money maintaining crossbowmen. But the fact that crossbowmen were not the responsibility of the marshalcy and were instead entrusted to the Commanders of the Lands, would indicate that their social value was obviously less than that of the brother knights. It would seem the Templars did not just purchase the services of crossbowmen as mercenaries but also carried the weapons themselves. They are most likely to have been widely used amongst the sergeants, but the Latin Rule mentions in a section which bans the Templars from hunting, that all brothers were not to go in the woods with a longbow or crossbow to hunt or to accompany anyone who was hunting unless 'out of love to save him from faithless pagans'. This would indicate that the Templars were more than familiar with having the weapon around them. Moreover, the banning of betting 'on the draw of a crossbow' (p. 182) would further confirm this. There is also evidence of the sharing of the use of bowmen between both the Hospital and the Temple. Recorded in Ibn 'Abd al-Zahir's *Life of Baibars*, in 1266 the Muslims defeated fifty Frankish archers and crossbowmen who were on their way from the castle at Chastel Blanc (Templar) to that at Crac des Chevaliers (Hospitaller) implying an arrangement between the two chief military orders.

Archery in general was considered a rather unknightly thing. But this social stigma does not preclude the employment of the weapon by the Templars. However, the method of their tactical military deployment is unclear. The anonymous account of the rebuilding of the castle at Safad (around 1240) mentions that in the landscape around this new castle lay 260 casals or villages in which were stationed 'upwards of ten thousand men with bows and arrows'. According to the widely travelled Muslim intellectual al-Idrisi (1100–1165) who lived in Palermo, there were archery grounds outside the Temple Mount which went as far as the area of Gethsemane. Quite who practiced there, if any one at all, is not known. However, the very mention of such a provision raises another question about the Templar war machine and that is the subject of how the Templars approached their training.

Chapter 32

Training

There are very few specific instructions of the training of the Templar in the Rule. What is clear however, is that these knights were already highly trained in the art of warfare having literally had it bred into them from an early age in their secular lives. For example, the clause of the Latin Rule which advises against the giving of children into the order, states that 'For he who wishes to give his child eternally to the order of knighthood should bring him up until such time as he is able to bear arms with vigour'. Although no age is specified, it is clear that the expectation was that the young men should possess the fighting skills common amongst the men of their social background. Given the complexities of what the Rule required of the Templars in the field in terms of discipline, formation keeping and skills with arms, it is perhaps surprising that there is no evidence for drills or regular practice. In secular society, knightly training came in the form of group exercises such as hunting, where horsemanship, cohesion, communication and the acquisition of a target were practiced. The tournament was also popular, although in some cases it was dangerous to the point where medieval monarchs sought to severely restrict or ban it outright. There are references to Templars and tournaments, but these would tend to support the notion of prohibition. Matthew Paris mentions that a Templar serving as an almoner, was one of a group of people sent by the English King Henry III (1216–72) to stop a proposed tournament at Northampton and an actual tournament at York in the 1240s.

Permission was sometimes given for the Templars to joust but they were forbidden to throw their lances in case someone got injured. The giving of permission for such jousting is important as it allows us to argue for some sort of training. Clauses 95 and 128 both mention that nobody was to give permission to race horses or joust where the Master was present without his permission. The implication is that such permission could indeed be given as must frequently have been the case. Because the dangerous undertaking of training was heavily regulated by the Templars, this does not mean it was banned outright. In fact, far from it. Clause 315 explains what a Templar could and couldn't do when he wanted to hone his horse riding skills. Whilst there is an emphasis on the preservation of the horses' energy and general welfare, the implied desire to practice is unmistakable:

No brother should run his horse over a complete course without permission. If he does not carry a crossbow and wishes to ride a horse on the course, he may run his horse over one course or two or three without permission if he wishes. No brother may impetuously race his horse against another person over half a course without permission. No brother should run his horse over a complete course, nor carry arms in hose without permission; but he may over half a course. When brothers go with the intention of running a course, they should pull on their boots. When brothers joust, they should not throw lances, for it is forbidden because of the injury which could arise . . .

So, horse racing and jousting, two key skills, were practiced under certain conditions by the Templars. But the Rule does not explain how or where these things were done. The racing is perhaps clearer than the jousting. The French word 'bouhorder' ('to tilt') implies a known medieval training exercise whereby each cavalryman travelled past the other separated by a fence called a 'bohorde'. The participants passed each other on the left hand side, shield to shield. The employment of blunted implements made for a safer exercise. It is not clear if this was the exact arrangement for the joust or how often it was practiced but it is still clearly there in the Rule. As to where such training took place the evidence is silent. Some have speculated that a large fifteen acre area of land belonging to the Templars across the River Thames on the south side opposite the New Temple in London (known as Fickettscroft) may well have been used by the Templars in London as a training area, but what actually went on here is not known.

Sometimes the Rule gives a clue as to the possibility of frequent military training, although it is enigmatic. For example, clause 317, which states that the brothers were forbidden to bet 'on the draw of a crossbow' implies that this had been a common practice in the secular world. Wagers could however, be placed on 'an arrow without iron' perhaps indicating that target practice was somehow linked to recreation.

When we get a mention of something in the Rule which seems to pertain to the subject of training, it is often restrictive in nature. Clause 257 states that if a brother should try out his arms and equipment and harm should come of it, he could lose the habit. Clause 607 gives an example of a brother who tried out his sword at Montpelier and broke it. He subsequently had to go to the Holy Land and plead for mercy over what he had done.

The enigma of the Templar training issue still persists. It is however, worth considering one obvious aspect of it. The horses the knights rode were trained animals. It is inconceivable they were anything else. They had to be accustomed to the sounds and smells of battle and be taught to overcome fear when approaching enemy lines. But even at the level of simply being ridden by a human being, a horse needs to have established in its mind how to interpret the riders' signals and lead off from another leg when the instruction is given to change direction. Such a change usually takes place when the horse is at a phase in its travel once known as 'unsupported transit', that is when all four feet are off the ground at once. The rider signals to the horse with subtle indications from his spurs behind the girth on the opposite side of the intended directional change. The horse will then plant his rear legs on the ground in the reverse order from the one he is currently using, thus allowing him to lead off with the other leg and change direction. If it goes wrong and the front legs hit the ground first instead, the result is a disunited and very uncomfortable change. Whilst it is probable these animals were already trained before they were handed to brother knights and sergeants it remains likely that the Templars found some time in their busy schedule to practise with their mounts. In fact, as experienced horsemen, they must have been anxious to do just that.

Chapter 33

Penances and Life in the Convent

Discipline was there for good reason. There were numerous punishments for a variety of infringements ranging from minor penances to outright expulsion from the order. The Temple needed to ensure that brothers understood the need for good behaviour. Originally, there were nine infringements for which a brother could be expelled. These were entering the house through simony (the selling of Church offices); disclosing the affairs of Chapter; killing or causing to be killed a Christian man or woman; theft; leaving a castle or fortification by means other than the gate; conspiracy; going to the Saracens; heresy and finally, leaving the banner and fleeing for fear of the Saracens. Five of these are overtly military in nature. The section of the Rule dealing with penances is roughly contemporary with the Hierarchical Statutes (1165–87) and included a further thirty-one things for which the habit might be lost. Later in the Rule, around the time of the great upheaval caused by the Mongol invasions, a section on Further Penances was written, this time with some useful examples given to illustrate the points made in the earlier section.

Keeping quiet about what you heard in Chapter was an obvious requirement. Military plans and methods will surely have been discussed. The next point, the killing of a Christian person, might find a brother cast into the prison at 'Atlit (Château Pèlerin) after c.1219. Also, in the section on Further Penances, it is explained that the leaving of a castle or fortification by any other way than the prescribed gate could single a brother out as a thief. The Rule is very concerned about theft and is careful to describe what can and cannot be taken out of the house. Arms and armour were forbidden to be removed, or anything appertaining to them. On the matter of going to the Saracens, it is reported that one Brother Roger the German had been taken at Gaza and that the Muslims made him 'swear the oath' (to the prophet). On his release, he was expelled.

As well as expulsion, a brother could also lose his habit. On the battlefield, charging without permission was one these (see p. 174). Generally, insubordination was another. One Templar from Tortosa, says clause 588, was given an order by his commander to which he responded by saying 'perhaps I will do it'. The brother was made to plea for mercy in front of other brothers and said that he would carry out the command after all. However, the brothers (who usually had the discretion as to whether an offender could keep the habit) could not prevent him from losing it because he 'had not consented to the order at the first word'. Another habit-losing offence with a military connotation was the killing or wounding of an equine animal or mule through a brother's own fault, to which was added the unauthorised giving away of a four legged animal excepting a cat or dog. Again, the brothers would hold the discretionary position on this. The misuse or loss of military equipment is an oft-repeated theme throughout the Rule. At Casal Brahim says clause 605, some brothers walked out for pleasure and one of them threw his mace at a bird on the bank of the river. The mace fell into the water and was lost. On this occasion the brothers allowed him to keep the habit 'for love of God'.

As one might expect, the rules governing daily life were very strict. The Rule sets out how the brothers ate, awoke and went to bed. In the section on Conventual Life the issues of inter personal relationships between brothers, religious offices, fasting and discipline whilst on campaign are addressed. The Templar day was a monastic one and was firmly based on the Rule of St Benedict (see Table 3 below). If the Templar house had a chapel the brothers would hear the divine office, or 'hours' each day. These took place at the first, third, sixth and ninth hour. When on campaign it might not be possible to hear the hours in this way, but the brothers were to try to observe as close a monastic day as possible when in the field and might replace the hours with repetitions of the Lord's Prayer.

The day began at around 4am with Matins after which the brothers attended to their horses and returned to bed. Prime, Terce and Sext followed which took the day to noon. The first meal of the day would be eaten in silence whilst a clerk read aloud from a Holy Scripture. There were then two or three hours in which the Templars could go about their duties before approximately 2.30pm to 3.00pm when Nones was observed. Vespers came at around 6pm followed by Compline after which silence was observed until after Prime the next day. What is apparent from the Rule however, is how much of the time spent outside of the hearing of the 'hours' (when orders were issued) was spent in the crucial areas of military preparation and maintenance. The Rule implies that this was to keep the Devil from finding work for lazy brothers, but the practicalities of having enough campaign equipment such as tent pegs and posts is obvious.

On campaign, daily life was obviously effected by the requirements of the military objectives and the need to react quickly to circumstance. This is why the Rule concentrates on the dividing up of rations, what to do on the raising of the camp alarm and how to behave when the brothers were housed in accommodation other than their camp. For example, if brothers were housed in any farm, the commander of the house or castle under whose command the farm falls was bound to provide the things the brothers needed for their existence there.

On the matter of what a Templar ate and drank, the Hierarchical Statutes have something to say. Bread, of course, featured. Each brother was to say one paternoster before he cut his bread. Beef and Mutton are also mentioned, and the brothers who ate one but not the other might be separately accommodated at the table. Pigsties and henhouses in the commanderies and other properties would provide supplementary foods as well as the gardens of the houses. But it was not always meat at the table.

TABLE 3: The Templars' Day From the Rule (After Nicholson)

At night	Matins in Chapel– Brothers pray and then go and check their horses and equipment and liaise with their squires. They return to sleep until daybreak
c.6am	Prime. Mass (or after Sext)
c.9am	Terce
c.12 noon	Sext. After which the repair of armour and equipment and the making of tent pegs was undertaken, plus other practical field equipment preparations. Mass would then be heard (if not earlier). Followed by lunch where the knights eat at the first sitting and the sergeants at the second. The clerk reads aloud while they eat. Then they go to the Chapel and give thanks and then go to their posts
c.3pm	Nones. Vespers for the dead. Vigils for the dead
Dusk	Vespers followed by supper. Then Compline followed by a drink. Then check upon horses and equipment once again
Dark	Bed.

Two cooked dishes were to be consumed on days when meat was not served, but if these dishes were based on cheese or fish they should have only one dish. Fresh or salted fish was usual on Sundays, Tuesdays or Thursdays. On Fridays, a cooked dish was eaten along with green vegetables or 'something else to be eaten with bread'. Whilst listening to the clerk reading the lesson, brothers were permitted to share their food with those around them 'but only as far as he can stretch out his arm'. Wine was also consumed, and the Catalan Rule has a peculiarity concerning drunkenness (clause 34) not present in the other examples, in which it states that a persistently drunk brother would be asked to leave for another order or give up wine for the rest of his life.

At the Infirmary table, the Infirmarer brother prepared food for the sick. Here, the allowances were more tailored to the needs of the sick and were often more generous. 'The Infirmarer brother' says clause 195, 'should have as much food prepared for the brothers who lie in the infirmary as each asks for, if he can find it in the house or for sale in the town, and syrup if they ask for it'. It was either the Commander of the Land or the Master's obligation to provide for the provision of a visiting doctor for the sick of the Temple's houses.

Much of this produce was provided locally, either grown or bought at market. But it was not always possible to supply an active military force with everything it needed from just one local vicinity. The whole question of how the Templars were supplied with men, food and raw materials, how they were financed, and from what sort of distance, is considered next.

Chapter 34

Logistics, Supply and Shipping

Undertaking a crusading expedition was a hugely expensive affair. But despite specific taxation exercises such as King Henry II of England's Saladin Tithe of 1188 which was raised in response to the fall of Jerusalem, reactive financing was not the main drain on the coffers of the West. Outremer needed maintenance. The Templar commitment to this problem was huge. One can only imagine the cost of maintaining fortified sites from great castles such as 'Atlit (Château Pèlerin) to minor towers and fortified posts and toll collecting outposts along countless pilgrim and other routes. At their peak the Templars maintained fifty-three of these, which required provisioning and garrisoning. Then there was the problem of the supply of men from the West, their arms, armour and clothing, the cash needed to support them and their food, their horses and their horses' food and equipment. Matters were made harder as the thirteenth century drew on. The decreasing size of Outremer meant less revenue for the secular lords who frequently faced financial ruin in the face of high costs. The simple maintenance of a knight and his equipment had soared since the twelfth century, to give just one example of an economic challenge. The price of a horse tripled between 1140 and 1180 and by the 1220s it had doubled again. It would increasingly fall to the military orders to provide for the defence of the Holy Land.

As well as their fortifications, the Templars had to maintain their smaller houses of which there were 970 by the beginning of the fourteenth century. They also had at various times significant buildings in major cities such as Jerusalem, Caesarea, Acre, Tyre, Gibelet (Jubail), Tripoli, Tortosa, Antioch and across a semi-autonomous area north of Antioch running from Port Bonnel inland to Baghras, Darbsak and the other marcher castles of the north. There was always pressure on Templar houses in the West to provide for the order, but during the early thirteenth century this pressure increased. The general strain on the West as a whole led some to question what was seen as a waste of resources. One such dissenting voice was that of Matthew Paris, the English Chronicler from St Albans. To Matthew, the income of the West was somehow being 'plunged . . . into the abyss of the lower world'. But Paris's assessment, like others of a similar mind, was an unfair one. If the Crusader States were to survive, the money and resources had to be found.

The Templars obtained their income in a number of ways. In the Holy Land their right to keep their military spoils was one of these ways and must have been substantial given that we are missing the record of countless small scale military actions. Also, there was the tribute money from the Assassins and ransom money too. In the West there were the generous donations of land and money to the order and the rewards given by leaders such as Louis VII after the Second Crusade. Cash injections were always welcomed. There were also important concessions made which allowed the order to capitalise on trading activity. As early as 1139 Eleanor of Aquitaine had granted various privileges to the Templars at the burgeoning port of La Rochelle in which Templar buildings were to be held free from custom. She also granted freedom to her vassals to make any donation to the order and gave the Templars the right to transport anything of their own throughout her land thus providing the foundation for the famous Templar mercantile presence at the French port.

11. The Templars' wealth relied in part on favours from powerful sympathisers. In 1139 Eleanor of Aquitaine declared the Templar buildings in the port of La Rochelle were to be 'entirely free and quit of all custom . . .'. Eleanor also allowed the Templars to transport anything by land or water freely. The port became a focus of Templar mercantile activity.

Land was important in that it provided an income. This income could be further enhanced if the right could be gained to chop down forests (a procedure known as assarting) to enhance agricultural productivity. The Templar commandery at Garway in Herefordshire (England) evolved from a privilege granted by King Henry II (1154–89) which allowed the assarting of 2,000 acres of woodland at Archenfield.

Similarly, the landscape around Temple Brewer in Lincolnshire and Temple Newsham in Yorkshire was greatly exploited by the order. In the West, concessions made by kings which allowed the Templars the right to hold their own markets and fairs were of financial importance to the order. King Stephen of England (1135–54) granted such a right in Witham in Essex. His wife, Matilda of Boulogne, had also granted the manor of Cressing in Essex to the Templars, one of their earliest English estates where some substantial thirteenth-century Templar barns still exist. Annual fairs were also held by the Templars in Baldock in Hertfordshire and Wetherby in Yorkshire. In the case of the former, it was King John who in 1199 granted a weekly market at Baldock on Wednesdays and an annual fair of four days' duration.

The Templars gained most of their income through the acquisition of land and property but are perhaps most famous for making money out of an early form of banking. They took to money lending quite early on in Aragon (1130s) and with the huge loan made to Louis VII in the 1140s. The order's subsequent financial activities are the subject of much literature. They even developed a form of credit note whereby money deposited in one Templar commandery could be withdrawn at

12. St Michael's Church, Garway, Herefordshire, England.

13. Foundations of the circular nave of the Templar church, Garway.

14. A well-preserved Templar coffin lid at the Sanctuary Rail, Garway.

15. A purported twelfth-century wooden chest, attributed to the time of the Templars at Garway church. The land around the Garway commandery was an important source of income for the Templars. The right to assart (to chop down forests and pull the trees out by their roots) 2,000 acres of woodland was granted to the order by Henry II (1154–89) thus allowing for cultivation.

another upon production of the note. Such a system would have led to attentive record keeping. The order was not averse to making money out of loans either. In 1274 they were repaid with interest by Edward I of England for their loan to him (p. 112). There are countless examples of Templar financial transactions, some of which seem to be perfectly straightforward business, others more murky and dark in their motives perhaps giving rise to Westerners' consternation at the order making deals with the Muslims. But the basic mechanism which allowed money to flow to the East was the payment of responsions from the commanderies of the West. This required that the houses sent one-third of their income in cash. The payments appear to have been made mainly in the summer and winter, perhaps in tandem with the pilgrim passages to the East. There were also short-term taxations on the houses levied by the Grand Master for specific projects, such as those introduced in Cyprus by James of Molay for his naval activities after the fall of Acre. However, for the most part, the main goal of all this financial activity was the maintenance of men, horses and other equipment in the fields of the Holy Land.

Estimation of the numbers of men the Templars had in the field is always fraught with difficulty due to the paucity of the evidence but it is suggested that the Templars at the eve of Hattin (1187) had in the region of around 600 knights in the East and approximately 2,000 sergeants. Referring perhaps to just the Kingdom of Jerusalem, William of Tyre mentions 300 knights and in the *Itinerary* of Benjamin of Tudela 300 knights are said to have been stationed at the Temple of Solomon (c.1169–71).

What is significant is the cost of replacing these knights. Templar battles were very costly in terms of loss of knights. At Harim in 1164 sixty were killed. In 1187 at the Springs of Cresson and Hattin, 290 perished. At Darbsak in 1237 they lost around 100 knights. At La Forbie in 1244 according to one account, just 33 survived from 300. At Mansourah in 1250, the Grand Master reported to Joinville that 280 men at arms succumbed, 'plus all of his horsemen'. It has been calculated that by 1267 the cost of maintaining a knight for the defence of Acre for a year was 90 livres tournois. An estimate of the average income of the French Monarchy at the time of Louis IX's crusade of 1248 has been given at 250,000 livres tournois. If 267 brothers perished at La Forbie, for example (assuming this number represents just knights and not brother sergeants as well, which it may not), the replacement value equates to roughly 10 per cent of the French royal income for one year.

It was noted by Imad-ad-Din that a Frankish knight was particularly vulnerable without his horse. The Templars put great efforts into the supply and maintenance of their horses. Clause 606 of the Rule even states that some outsiders might send their sick horses to the Templars for treatment. The need to constantly import horses was always acute given the losses accrued in campaigning and through natural attrition and disease (the average life span of horse being only twenty years). It was an offence for example for a Templar to kill, lose or wound an equine animal for which the Rule stated (clause 596) that 'the habit is at the discretion of the brothers', just one step away from expulsion. An example of the value of the horse to the Templars comes during the second crusade in Asia Minor (1147–8) when all around them were losing their horses and consuming them to survive Odo of Deuil reported that the Templars had kept their horses even though they were starving. The Rule is particularly attentive to the matter of horses for war, for riding and pack animals in general. Specifically, clauses 84 and 107 imply that some deliveries of horses were expected to come from the West in which case they should be kept in the Marshal's caravan. Also, clause 115 provides the power to Templar commanders to purchase pack animals, camels and 'any other animals that he needs for his work'. Similarly, clause 135 allows for the purchase of foals and pack animals from the villeins of the casals. Templar knights were to check on their horses regularly. In fact, attending to any emergencies with their horses was one of the few reasons a Templar could leave the dining table (clause 145).

Again, numbers of horses are difficult to estimate, but in the 1160s John of Würzburg who was visiting Jerusalem commented that the Templars had space for 2,000 horses or 1,500 camels. In the 1170s, Theoderich, a German pilgrim claimed the fabled Solomon's Stables at Temple Mount could take an impressive, though probably exaggerated 10,000 horses. It is roughly the case that if the horse allowances outlined in the Hierarchical Statutes are followed then the Templars at around the time those Statutes were written (1165–87) would have needed to maintain around 4,000 horses for effective campaigning not including pack animals. The hay and grain alone for these animals would amount to 100,000lb a day not to mention the 24,000 gallons of water needed. The Commander of the Vault's duties (as mentioned in clause 84) involved the storage of the wheat for the horses and this was clearly no small undertaking. In clause 609 of the Rule in the section on Further Penances there is a sad story of what could happen if the Commander of the Vault got it all wrong. On one occasion, says the Rule, the Commander of the Vault purchased a ship laden with wheat. He was told by the brother in the granary that the wheat should not be put in there as had been the instruction. This was because the wheat was wet from the sea voyage and the brother did not wish to take responsibility for it if it were stored in such condition. Instead, argued the brother, the wheat should be spread on the drying terrace. The Commander overrode the brother and the wheat was stored in the granary, only for it to be brought out one day and found to be largely spoilt. The Commander of the Vault lost his habit for knowingly allowing the harm to be done.

Much of the transportation of wheat, horses, men and equipment was by sea. It was a perilous business. Once the horses were put in the hold of a ship the strakes around the door had to be caulked to make the seal watertight since much of it would be submerged during the journey. The horses came from far away. Spain (particularly Aragon) and Apulia were popular sources, although Apulian trade was effected by a dispute between the Templars and Frederick II from around the 1220s. Registers from Messina (Sicily) show Templar horses and mules passing through en route to the East. France was obviously another source of animals as were England and Ireland. Two orders made by Edward I of England at Berwick in 1296 are known which grant permission for the export of horses, worsted cloth and cash to the Templars of Dover. The Templars appear to have adopted both a policy of specific chartering of vessels and of building their own. The Hierarchical Statutes (1165–87) clearly show a Templar Commander of the Shipyard at Acre and refer to 'all the ships which belong to the house at Acre . . .'. However, not until 1207 at Constantinople do specific references appear to Templar ships. In 1242 a prominent sea-faring Venetian observed shipwrights on the Dalmatian coast building a ship for the Temple in dry dock at Zara. In February 1300 the Templars specifically chartered a ship from the Genoese named Sanctus Johannes at the port of Famagusta from where it could put in at Tortosa, Tripoli, Tyre and Acre.

Between a period from 1216 to 1233 the Templar fleet seems either to expand or be more active on the seas. A developing problem at the key port of Marseille made worse by restrictions in access to the Adriatic coast around this time, perhaps highlights this increase in maritime activity. Here, in 1216 the two main military orders were granted the right to keep their ships in the port and carry pilgrims and merchants with very little restriction but it became clear to the consuls of Marseille that their own captains were being undercut along a coastline which stretched from Collioure in the west to Monaco in the east. So in 1233 the orders were restricted to two each of their ships sailing at Easter and August each year (one from each order on each occasion). Interestingly, the agreement, written up in the Acre residence of Lord Odo of Montbéliard (Constable of the Kingdom of Jerusalem 1218–44) mentions that the number of pilgrims these ships were permitted to take was up to a maximum of 1,500 'and any number of merchants' giving a clear indication not only of the capacity of the vessels of this time, but of the income the Templars might expect from their cargo.

It was not just horses, wheat, pilgrims and merchants the Templars transported across the sea. There is evidence of a number of commodities being shipped out including the export of iron. In 1162 the Templars made a contract with a commercial operator from Venice, the Mairano Brothers whose ship carried a sizable amount of iron for the order, an arrangement apparently carried out through an agent. It is perhaps indicative of the order manufacturing its own weaponry and armour through its large body of craftsmen sergeants. Clause 109 of the Rule mentions that steel and Burgundy Wire were imported, but fell outside the responsibility of the Marshal and Commander of the Land. This may have been because supply was erratic and the provision of such material could not be guaranteed but it also implies that swords and mailcoats (hauberks) were being made in the East.

There is also evidence of the Templar involvement (along with the other military orders) in lucrative industries such as glass manufacturing. A glass factory has been excavated at Somelaria next to a Templar courtyard estate and is believed to have been controlled by the order. Here, many blue-green glass beakers were made whose remains are to be found scattered around the castles and towns of Outremer.

For all we have said about the Templars' impressive military machine in the field, backed up by an extraordinary logistical and economic network, it is clear that the Templars in the Holy Land, like the other military orders, needed some sort of physical protection in a hostile landscape. Throughout the whole crusading era the acquisition of strongholds was an important factor in the prosecution of the war. The modern day ruins of the castles and fortifications of the military orders in Outremer stand as grim testimony as to how these places were so vital to the defence of the Holy Land.

Part 4

Castles and Fortifications

Chapter 35

The Role of the Templar Castles

When I came to your land and inquired to whom the castles belonged, I sometimes received the reply: 'This belongs to the Temple'; elsewhere I was told: 'It is the Hospital's'.

These words were allegedly spoken by King Thoros of Armenia to King Amalric of Jerusalem in the 1160s. Whether they were intended as an exaggeration is unclear. However, the physical evidence would seem to prove him right. By 1150 the Templars were established in marcher castles in the Amanus Mountains and also in the Kingdom of Jerusalem at Gaza. These were strategic deployments designed to defend marcher areas or to intimidate and limit the effectiveness of nearby enemy citadels. In the early years, as a complement to their role of protecting pilgrims with escorts the Templars built fortifications and towers along the many pilgrim routes. Le Destroit (Districtum) and Le Saffran (Shafar'am) are two examples. Le Destroit was built above a pass on a coastal road near 'Atlit and was later superseded in the area by the huge thirteenth century castle of Château Pèlerin. Le Saffran was on a pilgrim route leading from Acre to Nazareth. On the road to Jerusalem from the coast several towers were built. Casal des Pleins (Yazur), Toron des Chevaliers (Latrun) and Castellum Arnaldi (Yalu) are examples. Toron Des Chevaliers was later enhanced by Count Rodrigo Gonzalez of Toledo to fit in with a wider strategic plan (p. 24). Casal des Pleins was restored by King Richard I during the Third Crusade according the *Itinerarium* 'for the sake of pilgrims journeying by that route'. On the eastern side of Jerusalem protecting pilgrims on their way to sites on the Jordan were towers at Cisterna Rubea (Maldoim) and also one probably at Bait Jubr at-Tahtani.

Some castles and fortifications were to do with the protection of the pilgrim routes, but it is also clear that strategic thinking had a part to play. The protection of the passes in the Amanus March is an obvious example. However, it was not just mountain passes over which a castle could exert a sphere of influence. The short lived Templar castle at Jacob's Ford (see pp. 207–8) had begun to be built, much to Saladin's chagrin, to control ingress into the kingdom via that very ford. Similarly, the positioning of Safad and Beaufort (which the order controlled from 1260–8) controlled the hinterland of this region thus limiting the effects of any thrust from Damascus and providing a pool of resources for a potential strike in the other direction. The anonymous account written between 1260 and 1266, of the rebuilding of Safad by the Templars mentioned that Benedict the Bishop of Marseille was told by Damascenes on a visit to Damascus that they had heard of its rebuilding, and that if this were true 'it would mean the closing of the gates of Damascus'.

Some smaller fortifications served as little more than fortified toll collecting points along strategic roads. A kilometre south of Sari Seki, just north of Alexandretta (Iskenderum), was such a post known as the 'pillar of Jonah' overlooking the road to the Cilician plain. For the most part though, Templar castles operated a mixed role. Those situated in the open country could act as a base for reconnaissance and could combine that function with the regional administration of the order itself, such as occurred at the larger castles of Safad and 'Atlit (Château Pèlerin). Castles will also have been used as refuge points and storage places for taxations and foodstuffs. In the major cities and ports, the Templars had numerous houses and fortifications, not least of which was the highly impressive castle at Tortosa which served as the nerve centre for a vast regional patrimony. In 1152 the town had been burnt and all but destroyed by a Saracen raid, but the local diocesan gave the Templars enhanced rights within the city and required them to build a castle there. This complemented their inland fortifications at Chastel Blanc (Safita) and Arima to the south.

One of the great eyewitness accounts of a Templar castle being built belongs to Oliver of Paderborn, who took part in the Fifth Crusade (1217–21). The coastal road from Acre and Haifa had been protected by the Templar fortification of Le Destroit at the base of Mount Carmel. However, Oliver of Paderborn describes how during the Fifth Crusade a new castle was built on a nearby promontory on an altogether larger scale as its predecessor. As early as 1220 when incomplete, it was able to see off an attack by the ruler of Damascus, al-Mu'azzam. This new castle, built at 'Atlit, due to the huge amount of pilgrims who worked on it alongside Walter of Avesnes, the Templars, Hospitallers and Teutonic Knights was also known by the popular name of 'Pilgrims' Castle' (Château Pèlerin). The castle was protected on three sides (north, west and south) by the sea. For six weeks, the Templars dug across the promontory and uncovered an old wall, some ancient coins and 'generous fresh springs'. Here is how Oliver describes the form of the castle:

> Two towers were constructed in front of the castle from squared and hewn stones of such great size that one is almost too heavy for a two oxen cart. Each tower is 100 feet long and 74 wide and its thickness contains two vaulted halls. Its height is considerable, exceeding the height of the promontory. Between the two towers a new, high wall has been built with bulwarks, and by wonderful ingenuity armed knights can go up and down on the inside. Also another wall at a small distance from the towers extends from one shore of the sea to another, enclosing a well of fresh water.

Thus, says Oliver, the Templars were able to move away from the sin and vice of the city of Acre, some 20 miles away. They 'would stay in the garrison of this castle until

16. Château Pèlerin, or the 'Pilgrims' Castle', at 'Atlit, modern Israel.

17. and 18. All Hallows by the Tower, London, England (left) and the stone altar in All Hollows' Crypt Chapel (above). The altar is from Château Pèlerin, built by crusaders and Templars around 1218 at 'Atlit. A cross can be seen on the frontal. The altar was seized by Miss Frances E. Newton from the castle in 1930 and eventually given to All Hallows in 1945. Several English Templar trials took place at the church.

the walls of Jerusalem have been rebuilt'. He also says that the new castle dominated its territory, so that between Acre and Jerusalem the enemy was forced to abandon their cultivated land.

It is worth looking at what contemporaries thought a large Templar castle could do. Safad was acquired once again by the order in 1240 having been lost to Saladin in 1188. The anonymous author of *De Constructione castri Saphet* describes the expectations of this grand project which gives a vital outline of how a castle of this size could exert an influence over a wide landscape. He says that when the Bishop of Marseille left Damascus and came to Safad he met with a castellan known as Brother Rainhard of Caro. They spent the night amidst the rubble of the former castle and the bishop asked the castellan why the Saracens at Damascus were so afraid of it. The answer he received was soon related back to the baronial army and the General Chapter of the Temple:

> he discovered that the presence of the castle would constitute a secure defence as far as Acre to shield the Christians against the Saracens. It would be a formidable strong base offering ease and opportunities for launching attacks and forays into Saracen territory as far as Damascus. Furthermore, the building of the castle would entail a great loss of revenue for the sultan, of huge aid and service in men and goods of those who would henceforth be under the jurisdiction of the said castle. He [the sultan] would also lose in his own territory his villages and agricultural produce, pastures and other customary services because his men would not dare cultivate the land through fear of the said castle, thus turning his land into a desert waste. Moreover, he would have to spend enormous sums and maintain a large paid army to protect Damascus and its environs.

When it was built, says the author of the *De Constructione*, the castle was stocked with a huge number of 'crossbows, quarrels, machines and other arms', but it required huge sums to maintain:

> They [the Templars] said that in the first two and half years, in addition to the revenues and income of the castle of Safad itself, the house of the Temple spent eleven hundred thousand Saracen bezants on its construction, and approximately forty thousand Saracen bezants in each successive year. Food is provided for more than 1,700 people on a daily basis, for 2,200 in time of war. For everyday purposes the castle needs a garrison of 50 knights, 30 sergeant brothers with arms and horses, 50 turcopoles with horses and arms, 300 crossbowmen, 820 people for labour and other tasks, [and] 400 slaves. There are the payments made to mercenary soldiers and hired persons [this appears to be separate from the crossbowmen, who were also stipendary] as well as the provision of horses, equipment, arms and other essentials – a sum not easy to calculate.

From these descriptions it is easy to see why the chronicler Ibn al-Furat, writing in the following century recalled that Safad was referred to as 'an obstruction in the throat of Syria'. The numbers mentioned in the garrison would appear to have been accurately recorded. A group of brothers later testifying at the Trial of the Templars in Paris recalled the fact that eighty brothers had been executed when the castle finally fell in 1266. This would equate with the fifty knights and thirty sergeants mentioned in the account. But despite its ultimate sad fate the impact of the castle was clear. This was why it had to be eliminated. The author of the *De Constructione* knew that it had foiled attacks on Acre from Saracens, Bedouins, Turks and Turcomans alike. Prophetically, the author said that the only way the enemy could attack now was in 'enormous numbers'. As it turned out, Safad was so strong that in 1266 Baibars tried in vain three times to take it and only succeeded when he employed a form of psychological warfare by offering its large Syrian Christian contingent safe passage and playing that group off against the smaller Templar group, who were ultimately betrayed and when the gates were opened, executed. In all, 917 defenders and two friars were killed.

The ways in which castles were surrendered differed from case to case. For example, Gaza was surrendered after the Battle of Hattin in exchange for the release of the Templar Grand Master. It was forbidden to surrender a castle without permission. We do not know the nature of the arrangement which cost the Templars who surrendered the cave fortress of Akaf their lives in around 1166. A more celebrated surrender, made harder by a lack of communication between garrison, Commander of the Land and a distant Master, was that of Baghras (Gaston) in 1268. This story is captured in clause 180 of the Catalan version of the Rule. Baibars had moved against Antioch and taken it in just two days. This had not been predicted by the Grand Master Thomas Bérard who had told the nervous Commander of the Land he would send men to Baghras for its garrison which lacked in men and equipment. Matters were made worse when one brother Gins de Belin stole away to the sultan with the keys to the castle, telling him the brothers wished to abandon it. The commander and the brothers, after some prevarication and wishing to stay to defend their castle, decided instead to leave it and destroy everything in it. They would go to La Roche Guillaume and restore the castle there instead. On their leaving however, they did not destroy everything at Baghras in its entirety. On hearing of the fall of Antioch, the Grand Master and the convent, who knew of the predicament of the Baghras garrison, made the decision to allow an abandonment of it. But the garrison had already gone before that permission was granted. There was much argument as to whether the fleeing brothers should be expelled from the house, with one Templar camp arguing strictly that they should and the other that they should not because the Master and the convent were going to allow it anyway.

> And their decision was that, according to the establishments of the Temple, the Commander and all the brothers who agreed to abandon the castle of Gaston without permission and without the castle being besieged or attacked,

or not knowing if it would be . . . abandoned it, would have been expelled from the house if the Master and the convent had not decided to send a message to the Commander and the brothers of the land of Antioch that, since the town [Antioch] was taken, they should abandon Gaston . . . But for love of God and pity, and because it is a new thing, and because the Master and the convent wanted it to be abandoned, we agree that they should not be expelled from the house. But because they did not destroy everything that was in the castle, we agree that they should be on two days [fasting punishment] . . . And when the Master had their reply he informed the convent of it, and together all the convent held with what they had declared; thus was the fault of Gaston judged.

There is some evidence that the Templars used castles as prisons for offenders within the order. Clause 554 of the Rule has Brother Paris along with two others murdering some Christian merchants. The case was brought before the convent and they were sentenced to expulsion and a flogging around Antioch, Tripoli, Tyre and Acre and then placed in perpetual imprisonment at Château Pèlerin where they died. Similarly, says the clause, the same thing happened to another brother at Acre. Clause 593 also has a brother who pulled the hair of another brother being clapped in irons and sent to Château Pèlerin. Desertion or defection was something which the Templars also had to deal with. Clause 603 mentions the case of Brother George the Mason who left Acre to join with the Muslims. The Master had sent brothers after George. They found him wearing 'the clothing of a secular man under his own clothing'. He too was found guilty and sent to Château Pèlerin where he also died in prison.

Clearly, the fortifications of the Templars were diverse in nature, ranging from a mere toll point or tower along a pilgrim road to the multi-functional fortresses of Château Pèlerin, Safad and regional centres such as Tortosa. The next section provides an outline of the history of those which are known.

Chapter 36

Templar Fortifications in Outremer

Templar fortifications in the Latin East seem to have suffered a more destructive history than the buildings of other military orders since the fall of Acre in 1291. The known fortifications at Tripoli, Gibelet, Tyre, Caifas, Gaza and Jaffa have provided little physical evidence. The reason for this unhappy circumstance is not known although subsequent usage as stone quarries for later building work and earthquakes are as likely a reason as any specific targeting by later Muslim rulers. Tortosa still incorporates substantial structures (see colour Plate 17) as does the magnificent Château Pèlerin, despite Mameluke destruction.

The following section summarises the fortifications of the order in Outremer. There have been multiple names given to these places over the centuries. Some are French, some Latin, some Spanish, some Arabic and some Hebrew or Anglicised versions of any of these. Where it is possible to be clear, the names listed first in each case are those by which a site is most popularly known, at least in most modern English language texts.

1. Acre, Akko
Captured by crusaders in 1104 and surrendered to Saladin shortly after the Hattin disaster in 1187. Just two years later King Guy commenced a two year siege which was greatly enhanced by the arrival of King Richard I of England and King Philip II Augustus of France. The city fell to the crusaders again in 1191 and for a hundred years served as the capital of the Kingdom of Jerusalem until in 1291 the Mameluke siege finally expelled the Franks from Outremer. Throughout the thirteenth century, however, Acre was perhaps the most fortified of all cities in Outremer and its great Templar palace was not fully dismantled until 1752.

2. Akaf, Fortified Cave
This natural cave-fortress in Transjordan was besieged by Nur ed-Din's troops under Shirkuh in 1166. On his way to relieve the fortress, held by the Templars, King Amalric I came across twelve Templars heading back across the Jordan. They told him they had surrendered the place to the enemy. Each Templar was hanged by the king for surrendering the place without his permission.

Map 9 – Templar castles and fortifications in Outremer.

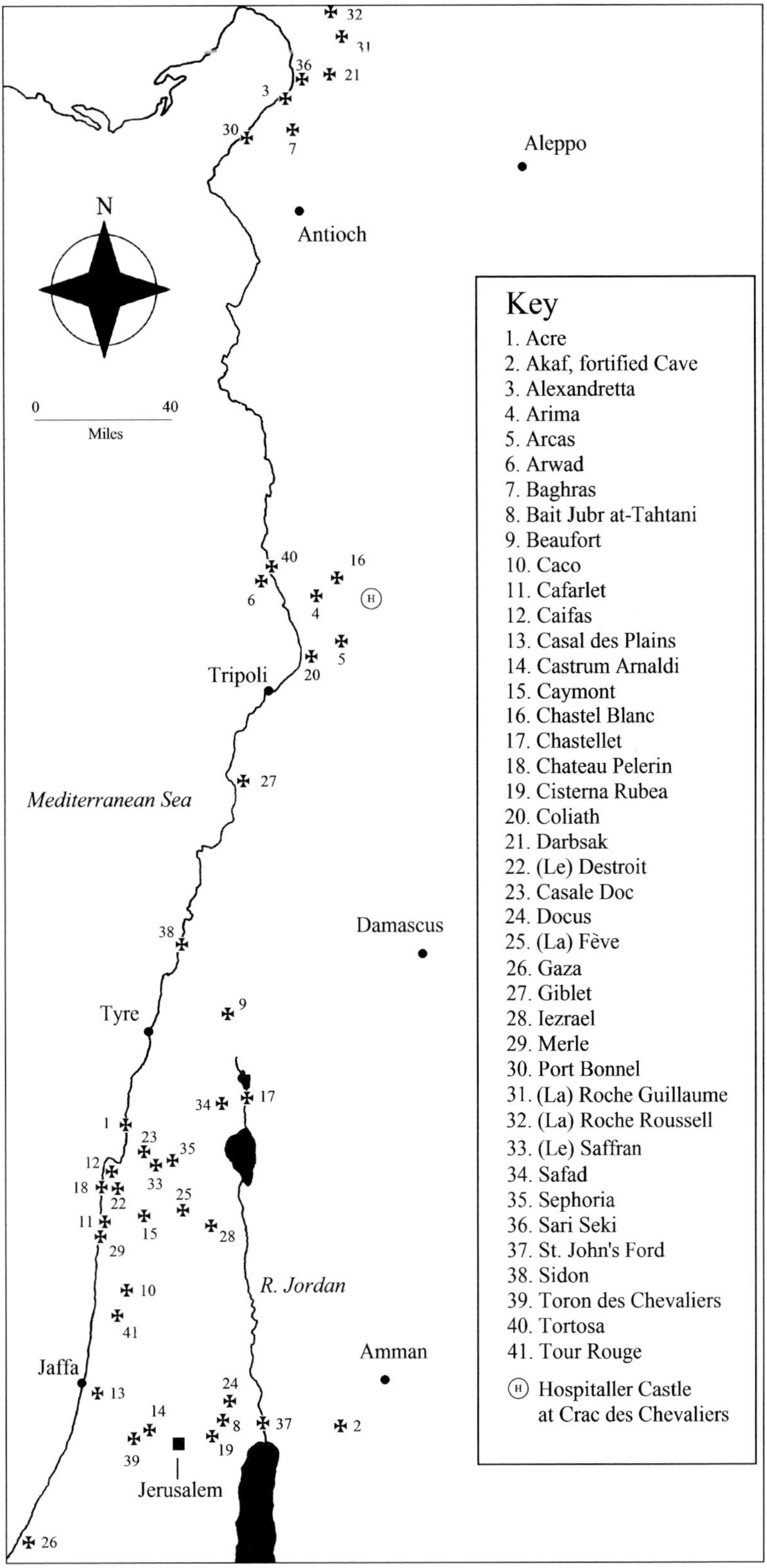

N

0   40
Miles

Aleppo

Antioch

Tripoli

Mediterranean Sea

Damascus

Tyre

R. Jordan

Amman

Jaffa

Jerusalem

Key
1. Acre
2. Akaf, fortified Cave
3. Alexandretta
4. Arima
5. Arcas
6. Arwad
7. Baghras
8. Bait Jubr at-Tahtani
9. Beaufort
10. Caco
11. Cafarlet
12. Caifas
13. Casal des Plains
14. Castrum Arnaldi
15. Caymont
16. Chastel Blanc
17. Chastellet
18. Chateau Pelerin
19. Cisterna Rubea
20. Coliath
21. Darbsak
22. (Le) Destroit
23. Casale Doc
24. Docus
25. (La) Fève
26. Gaza
27. Giblet
28. Iezrael
29. Merle
30. Port Bonnel
31. (La) Roche Guillaume
32. (La) Roche Roussell
33. (Le) Saffran
34. Safad
35. Sephoria
36. Sari Seki
37. St. John's Ford
38. Sidon
39. Toron des Chevaliers
40. Tortosa
41. Tour Rouge

ⓗ Hospitaller Castle
at Crac des Chevaliers

3. Alexandretta, Alessandria, Iskenderun, Isso

A small fortress at the sea port in the modern day Hatay province in southern Turkey (now Iskenderun). Captured by the crusaders in 1097 and given to the Templars in 1155, the fort was lost in 1188 and recovered in 1211 and lost once again to Baibars in 1268.

4. Arima, al-'Arimah, al-Ariymah, Araima, Aryma,

Formerly a Byzantine fortress Arima was in part rebuilt by the Franks. It was seized from Raymond II of Tripoli by his rival Bertrand of Toulouse in 1148 and then dismantled by Nur ed-Din. It was rebuilt and may have passed into Templar hands before being taken again in 1167 and dismantled once more by Nur ed-Din. Sacked yet again in 1171 suggesting it had once again fallen into Christian hands, it was acquired by the Templars towards the end of the twelfth century. The castle was built high up on a rocky ridge and was in visual contact with Chastel-Blanc and the plain of Akkar to the South.

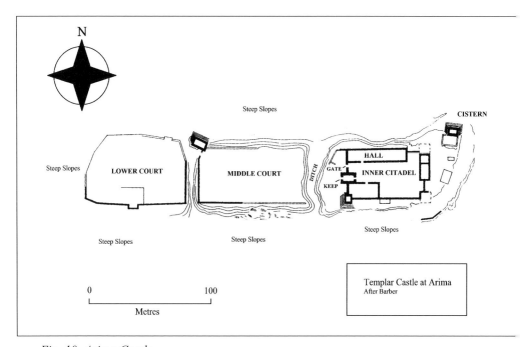

Fig. 10. Arima Castle.

5. Arcas

This fortified town passed to the Templars sometime before 1266 when its garrison abandoned it after the fall of neighbouring fortifications. Originally taken in 1109 by William-Jordan, Count of Cerdagne it was recaptured by the Muslims in 1138 and again in 1171. A year earlier it had been given to the Hospitallers. The fortification was lost again in 1188, but may have been recovered in 1192. After its abandonment in 1266, the fortification was dismantled.

6. Arwad, Ru'ad
See 40.

7. Baghras, Castrum des Bachelers, Gastin, Gaston, Gastun
Originally captured by Bohemond of Antioch in 1099 Baghras was granted to the
Templars around 1137 and named Gaston. Historically, there had been an Umayyad
fortification here and it was later known as Pagrae, built by the Byzantine Emperor
Nicephorus II Phocas (963–9) to dominate the Amanian Gate which provided access
between southern Asia Minor and Cilicia. Heavily re-built by the Templars in around
1153 the castle was so strategically important that it changed hands between
Byzantine, Armenian, Templar and secular Frankish leaders a number of times. The
Templars held it from 1153 to 1169 and regained it from the Armenians in 1175. It
fell to Saladin from the Templars in 1188. Imad ad-Din described it then as 'rising
on an impregnable rock, its foundations touching the sky'. It was dismantled by
Saladin in 1191 but was quickly taken by Leo the Roupenid Prince of Lesser
Armenia (Cilicia). In Armenian hands until 1216 when it was grudgingly restored to
the Templars, the castle withstood a siege from the Muslim forces of Aleppo in 1237
and was not finally abandoned until May 1268, when its understrength garrison
faced the prospect of a triumphant Mameluke army which had just taken Antioch.

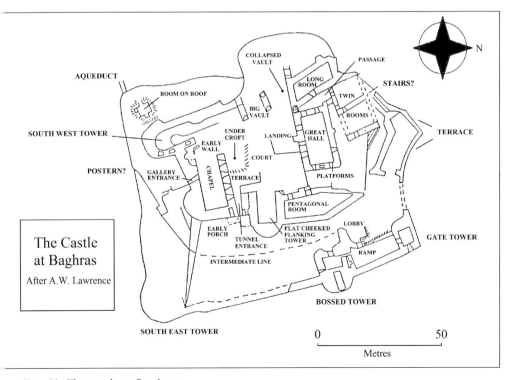

Fig. 11. The castle at Baghras.

8. Bait Jubr at-Tahtani

Situated on the road to Jericho as it emerges from the Wadi Qilt onto the plain of the Jordan, this rectangular structure has no literary evidence to link it to the Templars. However, it is similar in form to the tower at Cisterna Rubea (Maldoim) and is generally thought to be Templar. Only the barrel-vaulted ground floor survives.

9. Beaufort, Belfort, Qal'at al-Shaqif

Set on a rocky outcrop high above the River Litani in southern Lebanon, this fortification was captured by Fulk, King of Jerusalem (1131–43) in 1139 and was much rebuilt. It had been known in Arabic as Qal'at al-Shaqif, the 'fortification of the High-Rock'. The king handed much property and power in the area to the lords of Sidon and their names seem to be associated with Beaufort throughout its history. It was one of the last castles to fall to Saladin after Hattin, not falling until 1190. In 1219 the castle was dismantled but was recovered again by treaty in 1240 and then sold to the Templars in 1260 by Julian of Sidon, after which its defences were augmented. It finally fell to Sultan Baibars in April 1268 who employed twenty-six siege engines against it and repaired the damage he had done, placing a garrison within its walls.

10. Caco, Qaqun

Built in 1123 in the Lordship of Caesarea as a tower keep and associated with the Hospitallers by 1131, the Templars may have gained this castle in the 1180s. It may have been this garrison which was annihilated along with that of Castrum Fabae (La Fève) at the Springs of Cresson in 1187, but little is known about this fortification. Recovered in 1192 but lost in 1265 and refortified by the Mamelukes in 1267.

11. Cafarlet, Capharleth, Habonim, Kafarletum, Kafr Lam

Situated on a sandstone ridge on the Mediterranean coast just 5 miles south of 'Atlit in modern Israel, and probably later a dependency of Château Pèlerin, Cafarlet was a small trapezoidal shaped fortified town with a heritage stretching back to the Umayyad period many centuries earlier. It was purchased from the lords of Caesarea in 1213 by the Hospitallers who by 1255 had sold it to the Templars for the sum of 16,000 besants. The Templars held it until it was captured by the Mamelukes in 1265. Much of its crusader period activity seems to have taken place outside its walls, with the interior being partially neglected.

12. Caifas (St Margaret's Castle) Haifa

According to Theoderich, a German pilgrim writing in the mid to late twelfth century the Templars built this castle on top of Mount Carmel at Caifas which was used by mariners as a landmark. Its exact location is disputed but it is thought to be on the site of the Stella Maris Monastery although there is little physical evidence to support it.

13. Casal des Plains, Casellum Balneorum/Casellum de Templo (Azor/Yazur)

This two storey keep with barrel-vaulting surviving at ground floor level dates to the early twelfth century. Just 3½ miles east of Jaffa, the place was lost to the Fatimids as early as 1102 but soon regained. It was lost again in 1187, after which Saladin dismantled it in 1191 following his own defeat at Arsuf. In October the same year King Richard I of England occupied the site during his advance on Jerusalem and it was re-fortified by the Templars. It was destroyed again by Saladin in 1192 before being restored to the crusaders as part of Saladin's treaty with King Richard. It was restored once again at the beginning of the thirteenth century and probably lost in the 1240s.

14. *Castrum Arnaldi, Castellum Arnaldi, Chastel Arnaud, Chastel Arnoul, Chastel Ernant, Yalo*

Situated on the road from Jaffa to Jerusalem a few miles to the north-east of Latrun, the castle had been an early royal castle destroyed by a Fatimid Egyptian raiding party during construction in 1106. Placed on a hill which is an extension of the Deir Ayyub-Latrun to protect the pilgrim route, the castle was completed by the Patriarch of Jerusalem in around 1133. It was in Templar hands by 1179 and perhaps even before this. It was lost following Hattin in 1187 and dismantled by Saladin after his own defeat to Richard at Arsuf in 1191.

15. *Caymont, al Qaymun, Caimum, Mons Cain, Yoqne'am*

Possibly a royal castle assigned to a lordship before 1187, Caymont fell to Saladin after Hattin. Balain of Ibelin received it back from Saladin in 1192. In 1262 the Templars appear to have won it after a dispute with the Hospitallers. By 1283 it was in the hands of the Mamelukes.

16. *Chastel Blanc, Safita*

An impressive keep (25m high) still survives here 380m above sea level. Situated in line of sight of the Templar stronghold at Tortosa and the Hospitaller castle at Crac des Chevaliers, this was a commanding position. An earlier fortification was replaced by the Templars in around 1171. Saladin did not manage to take it in 1188 when he came through the region, an indication of its strength. The castle was surrounded by two enceintes which were preserved in the concentric pattern of the later village buildings. In 1202 the castle was badly damaged by an earthquake after which it was rebuilt and further strengthened by Louis IX in 1251. Surrendered to Baibars after a brief siege in 1271.

17. *Chastellet, Jacob's Ford, Le Chastellet, Le Chastelez, Vadum Jacob*

Situated to the west of the Jordan overlooking an important ford, the Templars began to build this castle in 1178–9 despite Saladin's expectations to the contrary. The offer of 60,000 dinars to cease building fell on deaf ears and so Saladin successfully stormed the castle and slew the Templar garrison (see above, pp. 65–8). The Muslims then began dismantling the site until a plague forced them to abandon it. Historians and archaeologists are left with a rare snap-shot in time as there was no further development of the site. Tools, equipment, unfinished dressed stone blocks and other paraphernalia of the twelfth-century building trade were left lying about. Further discoveries of five battle-damaged human skeletons and equid remains have also been made (pp. 67–8).

18. Château Pèlerin, 'Atlit, Castellum Peregrinorum, or 'Pilgrims' Castle'

Built by the Templars with assistance from the Teutonic Knights and the Hospitallers, Walter of Avesnes and the crusaders of the Fifth Crusade in 1217–18, this castle was one of the largest of the crusader castles including an outer village or faubourg. It replaced the tower of Destroit which protected the pilgrim route, but was actually an entire centre of administration for the Templars. Built on a promontory with the sea on three sides, it withstood a siege in 1220 even when incomplete, and further resisted Frederick II's forces in 1229. The castle was never taken. It was the last place to be abandoned in 1291 when the Franks vacated the mainland and departed for Cyprus.

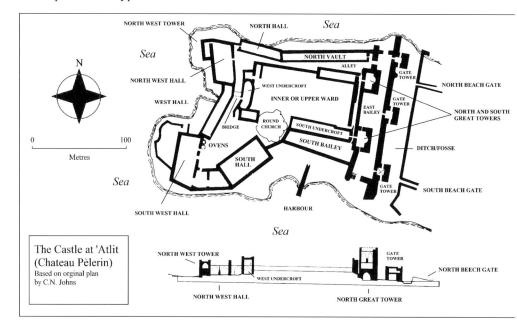

Fig. 12. The castle at 'Atlit (Château Pèlerin).

19. Cisterna Rubea, Castrum Dumi, Le Rouge Cisterne, Maldoim, Turris Rubea, Qal'at ad-Dam

Situated opposite the site of the Inn of the Good Samaritan on the pilgrim route to the place of the baptism of Christ. Probably a Templar foundation until it was lost after Hattin. It consists of a barrel-vaulted small keep. Similar to that at Bait Jubr at-Tahtani.

20. Coliath, La Colée, Qalaat
Located in the plain north of Tripoli the castle was given to the Hospitallers by Count Pons of Tripoli in 1127. They held on to it except for a brief period in the 1140s when it was in the hands of the Assassins. It was sacked by al-Malik al-Adil in 1207–8 and was still in ruins in 1212. Sometime later, it appears to have been in Templar hands (at least by 1243) before being finally lost to Baibars in 1266. The castle is a classic Rectangular structure with corner towers and additional towers at the mid-wall position.

21. Darbsak, Darbsaq, Trapesac
Guarding the northern approaches of the Belen Pass, this was a Templar castle which operated in conjunction with its southern neighbour at Baghras and was one of the early Templar marcher castles. It was briefly occupied by the rebel Armenian Mleh between 1171 and 1175 and later fell to Saladin on 16 September 1188. It was returned once again to the Templars and withstood an Armenian siege in 1205 but was once again taken by the Muslims. In 1237 the Templars tried to retake the castle but suffered heavy losses in their defeat (p. 96). The Mongols gifted Darbsak to the Armenians in 1261 and it was surrendered to the Mamelukes in 1268.

22. (Le) Destroit, Districtum, Petra Incisa
Ultimately replaced by the colossal Château Pèlerin this relatively small tower sits on the sandstone ridge overlooking the coastal road from Acre to Jaffa at a point where it travels through a narrow strait, or defile (destroit). Its stables were cut into the rock, hence the alternative name 'Petra Incisa'. After the completion of Château Pèlerin the fortress was dismantled lest it fall into the hands of the enemy and provide a base for a counter-castle operations.

23. Casale Doc, Khirbat Da'uk
Situated about 2 miles north of the Templar Mill at Doc, these remains are poorly documented but consist of a rectangular courtyard building (70m by 40m) incorporating three long barrel vaults. In 1235 the Templars of the mill at Doc were engaged in a quarrel with the Hospitallers who owned a mill upstream called Recordane. By holding back the water, the Templars who were downstream of Recordane could flood the wheel chambers of the Hospitaller mill. By the same token, the Hospitallers could hold back water from their upstream position and prevent enough reaching Doc. The dispute was settled with mutual promises on each side until it broke out again in earnest in 1262 when the Hospitallers diverted some of the river to their sugar plantation fields.

24. Docus, Castellum Abrahami, Duk, Jabal Quruntul
In the mountainside at the place where Jesus fasted and was tempted by the Devil, there are a series of caves which the German pilgrim Theoderich recalled were used by the Templars to store food and arms. He believed the place to be virtually

impregnable but after its loss in 1187 it was never recovered. A separate ruined medieval structure may have been the castle of Docus.

25. (La) Fève, Castrum Fabe

Theoderich described this place as 'a castle of no small size' in 1169. Sometime before this the Templars had built the castle here on the Campus Fabae or 'plain of the Broad Bean'. They had placed it near a water source alongside the road from Acre to Beit She'an. For this reason its use as an assembly point in the wars of 1183 when Guy of Lusignan stayed there should not surprise. It was also strategically important, overlooking the Jezreel valley. Its Templar garrison was annihilated at the Battle of the Springs of Cresson on 1 May 1187 in a prelude to the Hattin disaster on 4 July. Little remains today, but Imad ad-Din stated that the castle, which he calls al Fula was 'the best castle and most fortified, the fullest of men and munitions and the best provided'. Theoderich even mentions that it had a mechanised antilliyah well (a wheel driven mechanism with water jars attached to ropes). It was dismantled after Hattin at which time its garrison was around forty brethren.

26. Gaza, Gadres

At the time of the First Crusade this was a Fatimid garrison town, but it was refortified between 1149 and 1150 by Baldwin III and handed to the Templars as part of a strategic campaign against Fatimid Ascalon. It soon proved worthy by repulsing an attack. Its surrender in 1187 was only due to the orders of the Grand Master who was subsequently released as a result. Although it was torn down by Saladin in 1191 it was captured once again by Richard I in 1192 and restored and given again to the Templars. However, by the terms of the Treaty of Jaffa later that year it was dismantled once more.

27. Giblet, Gibelet, Jubail

On the site of ancient Byblos, this was a sturdy central keep with an external enclosure, much of which still survives. Little is known of the Templar association with this castle and fortified town. Initially captured by Raymond de Saint-Gilles in 1104, the actual fortification was added later. Although it fell to Saladin in 1187 it was so well built that attempts to dismantle it were abandoned. It was recaptured in 1197 and remained in Frankish possession until 1289.

28. Iezrael, Petit Gerin, Tel Yizra'el

Situated around 14 miles north-west of Beit She'an, this is a fortified settlement with some remains of a church and a castle, although little is known of it. Held by the Templars in the 1180s until 1187.

29. Merle, Merla Templi, Tel Dor

Built in the first half of the twelfth century and assigned to the Templars before 1187 when it was lost. Restored to the Templars at the beginning of the thirteenth century, little else is known about it and few remains survive. Probably dependent upon Château Pèlerin in the thirteenth century and abandoned along with it. Like Château Pèlerin, although on a vastly reduced scale, it was defended on three sides by the sea.

30. Port Bonnel (Arsouz)

A vitally important port held by the Templars from around the same time as the fortifications in the nearby Amanus March in the late 1130s. A fortification overlooked the port. It was lost to Saladin in 1188 and abandoned by Muslim forces on the approach of the German crusaders in 1190. It was soon occupied by the Armenians on and off for a few years. The Templars regained it once again between 1211 and 1213. It was only abandoned after the fall of Antioch in 1268.

31. (La) Roche Guillaume and 32. (La) Roche de Roussell, Çalan Kalesi, Chilvan

The exact identity and location of both these sites is disputed. They may even be identical. However, La Roche de Roussell, or Roissol, is sometimes identified with remains on the Nur Daglari overlooking the Hajar Shuglan Pass, about 11 miles north from the Belen Pass. High upon a plateau at 1,200m above sea level are the remains of a castle with an upper and lower bailey with a ruined chapel evident in the upper bailey. Some say that this (Çalan Kalesi) is La Roche de Roussell and that La Roche Guillaume is a separate fortification situated further south at an unknown site, although others have La Roche de Roussell even further south than Port Bonnel and La Roche Guillaume at Çalan Kalesi. La Roche de Roussell was abandoned after the fall of Antioch in 1268 whereas La Roche Guillaume appears not have been abandoned until 1299, long after the siege of Acre in 1291.

33. (Le) Saffran, Cafram, Castrum Zafetanum, Sapharanum, Shefar'am

Only tentatively identified as the remains within an Ottoman castle built in 1761. The medieval castle was mentioned in the twelfth century by Theoderich as being built by the Templars here and was described as 'very strong'.

34. Safad, Safed, Saphet, Zefat

This was a key Templar castle with a story told in two halves. Situated about 10 miles west of the Jordan to the north of the Sea of Galilee, Safad was built by Hugh of Saint-Omer in 1102. In around 1140 it was further fortified and was then purchased by the Templars in 1167 or 1168. When Saladin destroyed the castle at Jacob's Ford (Chastellet) in 1179, the outer area of Safad was also badly damaged, but the castle remained. It fell on 6 December 1188 after a heavy attack and was later dismantled. It was recovered by treaty in 1240 which was when its remarkable second life began (pp. 199–2). Heavily refortified and garrisoned with up to 2,200 men in wartime, the castle proved a thorn in the side of its enemies and Templar raids took place as far as Damascus. But on 23 July 1266 the castle fell to the trickery of the besieging Baibars who up until then had been unable to successfully overcome its defences.

35. Saphoria, Le Sephorie

The citadel here was fortified soon after the First Crusade. It was the starting point for the fateful Hattin campaign in 1187 and was lost thereafter. It returned to crusader hands in 1229. At some stage before 1251 it was assigned to the Templars, but was lost in 1263.

36. Sari Seki

Not to be confused with the toll post known as the 'pillar of Jonah' established by the Templars less than a mile to the south, the Templar fortification at Sari Seki is thought to have been built to protect the Nur Daglari pass, a small pass through the Amanus Mountains. Throughout the early twelfth century (1135–50) it was variously controlled by Armenians and Byzantines but when Antioch (c.1154) gained control over the regional fortifications here, Sari Seki was handed back to the Templars. It did not fall until 1266 when its garrison was massacred.

37. St John's Ford

Situated at the site on the Jordan where pilgrims would bathe in the baptismal waters near to the Dead Sea, there was a Templar fortification here in the twelfth century. It is mentioned by Theoderich as 'a strong castle of the Templars'. It was lost after 1187.

38. Sidon

This crucial port was captured by Baldwin I in 1110 after a long siege. It stayed in Frankish hands until 1187 when Saladin took it, but its walls were not destroyed until 1190. Half of the town and its revenues were granted to Reynald of Sidon, although James of Vitry records it as still largely a Muslim town in 1217. By November 1227 after a fresh influx of crusaders the town was back under the control of the Westerners and work began on the great sea castle (see image 13 in the plate section), situated on an island at the entrance to the northern bay. The town was briefly taken by Damascus in 1249 to 1250 but returned to Frankish rule. In 1253 Louis IX strengthened the defences after another raid. In 1260 however, the entire lordship was sold to the Templars who moved from other accommodation to the sea castle which they held until 1291.

39. Toron des Chevaliers, al-Atrun, Latrun, Toron de los Caballeros, Toron Militum

Built on a low hill at the point where the road from Jaffa to Jerusalem was met by one from Ascalon. The original tower was hugely expanded and equipped by Count Rodrigo Gonzalez of Toledo whilst he was in the Holy Land on crusade and assigned to the Templars between 1137 and 1141. It fell to Saladin in 1187. In December 1191 and again in the following summer Richard I camped here. The Templars regained it in 1229 but lost it once more in 1244 in the wake of the disaster at La Forbie.

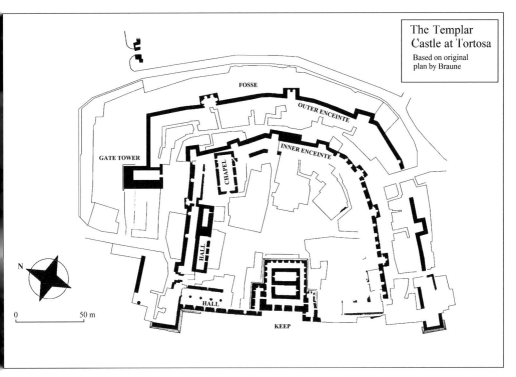

Fig. 13. The Templar castle at Tortosa.

40. Tortosa, Tartous, Tartus and Arwad, Tortouse, Ru'ad.

Another vital coastal city in Syria, Tortosa was captured during the First Crusade and recaptured once more by Raymond de Saint-Gilles in 1102. Important for pilgrims as the place where St Peter's first mass was heard and where a painting of the Virgin attributed to St Luke was supposed to have been kept, the town was attacked in a Muslim raid of 1152 headed by Nur ed-Din, after which the Templars were granted land by William, the Bishop of Tortosa on which they were expected to build a new castle. The previous castle had been held by Raynouard of Maraclea but he gave it up after the devastation, probably lacking the money to meet with the new plans. The area covered by the concession to the Templars was substantial. 'From the entrance to the port to the house of William of Tiberias and reaching on all sides to the gate of St. Helen'. A 35m square keep formed the centrepiece with two flanking towers on its seaward side. A postern gate at this side allowed for shipping to resupply the castle. Two vast ring walls enclosed the site on its landward side and incorporated eleven towers by 1212. The Templars had gained so many concessions in this area that in conjunction with their regional network of castles they ruled virtually independently. Saladin had briefly occupied Tortosa in July 1188 but could not take the keep and the Templars regained control. Tortosa did not fall until 3 August 1291.

The island of Arwad (Ru'ad) just 2 miles offshore of Tortosa had been garrisoned by the last Grand Master James of Molay in 1301. It held out until 1302. When it fell, its garrison consisted of 120 brothers and 500 Syrian or Maronite archers, representing a serious attempt by the Templars to regain a foothold on the mainland (p. 217). It is not known to what extent the Templars rebuilt the island's defences when they were planning their amphibious assaults to regain Outremer.

41. Tour Rouge, Burj al-Ahmar, Red Tower

Situated in the Plain of Sharon and probably first built in the early twelfth century, it is recorded as belonging to the Abbey of St Mary Latina by 1158. It was leased to the Hospitallers between 1187 and 1191 and then was in the hands of the Templars in 1236 and returned to the Hospitallers in 1248. Destroyed by the Mamelukes in 1265.

Part 5

After Acre

Chapter 37

Military Activity and the Plans
for a New Crusade

James of Molay, our last Grand Master, inherited a greater collection of problems than any of his forebears. He was, like many before him, a career Templar. Little is known of his activities before he rose to lead the order. After his arrest in 1307 he stated that he had been a Templar for forty-two years. He was a Burgundian who had joined the order in Beaune in 1265 at a time when Outremer was shrinking in the face of the rising Mameluke threat. His receptors had been the Masters in England and France. He had certainly been in Nicosia in 1291 but it is not known for sure if he stood shoulder to shoulder with the defenders of Acre.

There had been recrimination and criticism of the military orders in the wake of the fall of Acre in 1291. Some councils convened by Pope Nicholas IV (1288–92) had ruminated that if the military orders and the people in general had not squabbled, Acre may have been saved. In May 1308 when William of Plaisians addressed the Pope at a consistory (which also heard French Templar confessions) he did so with the words 'it is said that because of their [the military orders] weakness and their agreements with the sultan the Holy Land was lost'. But William was, along with others such as William of Nogaret and various other advisors of the French King Philip IV, a highly partisan figure.

There was however, plenty of military activity after Acre's fall. Because of the nature of the loss of an entire land base and the crusader retreat to Cyprus, it naturally followed that naval activity would feature in the warfare of the period. Between 1291 and 1307 the Templars combined with the Cypriots to assist in trying to enforce a ban on maritime trade with Egypt and to generally guard Cyprus by sea. But progress was slow and resources hard to come by. In 1292 Pope Nicholas IV had written to the Templars and the Hospitallers to encourage their naval intervention in support of the Kingdom of Armenia. But the orders' efforts were made less effective by the ongoing war between Venice and Genoa who controlled most of the shipping in the region and indeed supplied the Temple with galleys. By 1300 the Cypriots, Templars and Hospitallars could only count sixteen galleys between them. This fleet however, sailed from Famagusta and raided the coasts of Egypt, Palestine and Syria attacking Rosetta, Alexandria, Acre, Tortosa and Maraclea.

It is possible that some Templars still stationed in Cilicia fought alongside the

Armenians and Mongols against the Mamelukes at the Battle of Homs in 1299, but it was James of Molay's expedition to the Templar outpost of Arwad (Ru'ad), the island 2 miles off the coast of Tortosa which stands out as the main Templar military effort of this period. This came at a time of heightened anticipation of an alliance with the Mongols, for which the naval raiding expedition in the summer of 1300 may have been a preliminary. In November of 1300 Amaury of Lusignan (who had equipped the fleet of the summer) combined with the Masters of the Temple and the Hospital and sailed to Arwad (Ru'ad) with a force of about 600 knights, half of which were from the military orders. The garrisoning of this waterless island made good strategic sense provided the Mongols would support a thrust against the Mameluke-held coastal cities from the East at the same time. But they did not come in good time. Amaury and the Hospitallers withdrew to Cyprus in 1301 leaving the Templars behind, who enhanced their presence on the island still anticipating (as Molay told James II of Aragon in a letter) a Mongol alliance. The garrison was a strong one at 120 knights, 500 archers and 400 servants under the order's Marshal Bartholomew. But without a naval shield to protect them they were isolated. In 1302 the Mamelukes sent a fleet of sixteen galleys from Tripoli to besiege the island and by October the garrison surrendered having fought hard. The Templar of Tyre says that mounted charges had hurled the enemy back to the sea shore, but that ultimately the knights had to retire leaving the work of their Syrian archers unexploited. The men were killed or sold into captivity. King Henry II of Cyprus organised a fleet which arrived far too late to save the force. In Molay's eyes, the disaster appears to have been a demonstration of the weakness of the plan in terms of numbers.

If the Holy Land were ever to be won again, the military orders were to be at the heart of the operation. Since the 1260s there had been a sense of impending doom amongst the rulers of what remained of Outremer. Charters of the later thirteenth century involving the sale or alienation of real estate would often contain the phrase 'if the kingdom is not lost'. It had long been the case that as the secular nobility had struggled to garrison castles and wage a consistent war with the infidel, the military orders had gained in land ownership as the lords retreated to Cyprus and sold their property. The Templars, Hospitallers and to a lesser extent the Teutonic Knights had been the main beneficiaries of this and it was their field forces, their castle garrisons, their leadership and increasingly their naval capabilities which were the glue which held Outremer together. As early as 1244 at La Forbie, for example (pp. 100–2), the combined military orders accounted for over half of the knighthood of around 2,000 men on the field.

There were many who came up with a plan, not least of which were the Masters of the Temple and Hospital themselves. But everyone who did so knew that the military orders would have to feature as a key component of any campaign. However, in 1292 Raymon Lull (d. c.1315), a Christian philosopher and zealous promotor of the conversion of Muslims, saw a re-conquest of the Holy Land as a combined land and sea operation in which Saracen coastal settlements were first to be destroyed, followed by a land war led by a Western king and the Masters of the three main military orders. Through Lesser Armenia the land army would march on to Jerusalem and the Knights Templar would go on and conquer 'Berbary' in North Africa. The Hospitallers would conquer Turkey and the Teutonic Knights would ally with the Armenian king and take the port of Laodicea. Although they were central in his plans, Lull was keen to keep the military orders apart.

Less keen to separate the orders was Charles II of Anjou. In fact, he proposed the by now widely discussed idea of an amalgamation of the orders. He too had a crusading plan divided into two stages with a land push led by the military orders. But both he and the French King Philip IV saw this being led by a single chief at the head of merged new order. It should be the son of a king or someone of high lineage it was argued, something which no Grand Master of the Templars had been to date. Some even promoted the idea that the head of the merged order could one day be the new King of Jerusalem and that Philip IV had planned his own son to be such. In June 1306, James of Molay and Fulk of Villaret (1305–17), the Masters of the Temple and Hospital were summoned by Pope Clement V (1305–14) to Poitiers to consider both the idea of a merger of their orders and plans for a new crusade. In the months that followed they replied to the Pope. In his treatise on the subject of a merger, Molay argued that it would be a dishonourable scandal and that the mutual rivalry between the two orders had been a sort of competitive drive which made both orders all the better for it. The concern was that a merger would ignite friction and not quell it. The rivalry he said had strengthened Christendom against the Saracens 'since any good foray of arms against the Saracens by the Hospitallers was matched or bettered by the Templars and vice-versa'. If one order had good knights renowned for fighting, the other strove to better them and hence there was great expenditure (and debt) accrued for the betterment of Christendom, argued James. The rivalry had even positively affected logistics: 'if the Templars transported to Outremer a large number of brothers, horses and other animals, the Hospitallers did not rest until they had done as much or more'. Apart from recognising a reduction in expenses which a merger might bring about, James of Molay had little else positive (from a military point of view) to say about the matter.

However, on the idea of regaining the Holy Land, Molay revealed his military mind. His letter to the Pope of 1306–7 was unequivocal. There had been an ongoing debate over whether a preliminary parvum passagium ('little passage') should precede a larger expedition. Possibly based on his own recent experiences James of Molay denounced a small scale expedition saying it would lead to the loss of all those involved. They had no strongholds at all in the Holy Land where they could hope to re-group if faced with adversity. Moreover, a small force would simply be swamped by numbers. In particular, Molay brought up the topic of a small scale force being sent to Armenia. Here, attrition would be the problem: 'the land itself is so unhealthy and harsh that it would be a miracle if a force of 4,000 strong, healthy knights could muster 500 survivors at the end of the year'. He went on to point out that Armenian cowardice and a reluctance to share their strongholds with the Franks would hamper the operation.

Molay was convinced that a large 'all-embracing' expedition was the only way to recover the Holy Land. For such a 'passagium generale' ('large passage'), the kings of France, England, Germany, Sicily, Aragon and Spain [*sic*] should all be consulted along with others with a view to providing a force. The Italian merchant maritime cities of Genoa and Venice would supply the shipping, for which only large vessels and not galleys were to be considered. The sultan he said, feared the Franks more than he did the Mongols, so large numbers were important. In fact, Molay had heard that the sultan would recoil from around 15,000 Franks. So Molay proposed that the crusading force should have 12–15,000 armed horsemen and 5,000 foot soldiers. He proposed that 2,000 of the force should be crossbowmen. Molay's army was to be a combined-arms mobile army. The force would gather in Cyprus and Molay told the Pope that he would not share with him in writing the place for its landing in the Holy Land but he would advise him of this in secret. As a preliminary measure ten galleys were to be sent to the defence of Cyprus and to police the illegal supply by Christians of provisions to the Saracens, which according to Molay was especially prevalent amongst the Genoese, Venetians and Pisans in the form of weaponry. The job of captaining this small fleet should not fall to a member of a military order since the conflict with the Italian naval states may result in complications for the Templars. Instead, it should be a man called Rogeron, the son of the late admiral Roger of Loria (d.1305).

Fulk of Villaret put forward two Hospitaller plans. The first was in three stages. He first proposed a maritime blockade of Egypt and an initial landing in the Holy Land of a fleet of fifty to sixty galleys capable of carrying forty to fifty horses as an advanced force. Then, the passagium generale would follow a year later. His other plan was more specifically a Hospitaller affair involving preliminary crusader activity for a five year period designed to protect Cyprus and Armenia and to police the illegal provision of goods to the Saracens, including the trade of white slaves to the Egyptians (who would thus swell the ranks of the Mameluke army). Of the plans of both the Templar and Hospital Masters this last plan of Fulk's was the only one which was in some way put into practice. Fulk's preliminary Crusade did go ahead and resulted in the conquering of Rhodes by the Hospitallers. But by this time the Templars were facing their final ignominy just three years after Philip IV's dawn arrests of 1307.

The Pope dissolved the Templars at the Council of Vienne (1311–12) in the bull *Vox in excelso*. Another papal bull *Ad Providam* of 1312 effectively handed most Templar assets to the Hospitallers. In March 1314 James of Molay and Geoffrey of Charney, the Templar Preceptor of Normandy perished in the fires lit for them on a small island in the Seine between the King's Gardens and the Convent of St Augustine. Defiant to the last, James of Molay had mounted a scaffold before Notre Dame and publically retracted Templar confessions, accusing his accusers of lies and deception. It was a dramatic moment in the history of the Western world. The warrior monks of the Order of the Temple would no longer fight to protect the pilgrims and religious sites of the East. The crusader states had gone, and with their fall the very reason for the existence of the Templars had gone too. Molay became the subject of legend: at his death he had uttered a curse against the French king and the Pope, both of whom died within a year of him. Another legend grew amongst the French that Molay had in fact commanded a wing of the Mongol army and briefly taken Jerusalem in 1300. The legend was purported as fact in the 1800s and demonstrates that the last Grand Master of the Templars was felt to embody the same warrior zeal and Christian commitment as his predecessors. The world however, was changing in the West. Within fourteen years of the demise of the Templars, the French Capetian dynasty was finished. In France and England the Houses of Valois and Plantagenet would slug it out in a hundred-year battle over the control of the throne of France.

19. Detail of a miniature of the burning of the Grand Master of the Templars and another Templar. From the Chroniques de France ou de St Denis, BL Royal MS 20 C vii f. 48r. c.1380–1420.

Conclusion

The views of the enemy are often revealing. The military orders were both feared and respected in the Muslim world. Ibn al-Athir, when writing of Saladin's motives after the capture in 1188 of two prominent Hospitallers wrote that 'it was his custom to massacre the Templars and Hospitallers because of the violent hatred which they bore against the Muslims and because of their bravery'. Saladin knew that these warriors would be prepared to pay the ultimate price for their commitment to their cause. He knew they were dangerous as well. He had seen the Templars scatter his army at Montgisard in 1177 and he had also won victories over them at Jacob's Ford and Hattin. Muslim writers continued to be impressed in the thirteenth century. Ibn Wasil, wrote of the Mamelukes who faced down King Louis IX's French armies and referred to the Mamelukes of Malik al-Salih as the most brave and fierce warriors. 'They fought furiously' he said. 'It was they who flung themselves into the pursuit of the enemy: they were Islam's Templars'. For such a lasting impression to have been made, the Templars must have been an ever-present force to their Muslim enemies.

It is easy to misunderstand the sacrifices made by the Templars over the 200 years of their existence. Some might dismiss their passion as misguided religious zeal. This is an unfair assessment. The Templar leadership was drawn from a rank of society trained and experienced in fighting. These men were for the most part devoted warrior monks and when James of Vitry wrote of them that 'on Christ's behalf they exposed their bodies to death precious in the sight of the Lord' he was referring to their willingness to become martyrs. But this is not to say the Templars were in any way suicidal in their approach.

The fate of many of the Templar Grand Masters should at least give a clue as to their commitment. Bernard of Tremelay had died during the siege of Ascalon leading his men into a slaughter in 1153. Both Bertrand of Blancfort and Odo of Saint-Amand had spent two years in captivity when they were seized by Nur ed-Din in 1157. Odo came out battling and triumphed against Saladin in the Battle of Montgisard years later. As for the much derided Gerard of Rideford, whose involvement in the disaster at Hattin usually condemns him to a legacy of recklessness, the obvious bravery is still there for all to see. He battled and fought his way through his career, surviving until he was killed doing what Templars do best – fighting for Christianity beneath the walls of the captured city of Acre. Another Grand Master, William of Chartres had died whilst on active campaign during the Fifth Crusade in Egypt. His immediate successor Peter of Montaigu had waded through the Egyptian mud in the immediate aftermath of the disaster, fighting along the way. Armand of Périgord fought in the bloodbath at La Forbie in 1244, a battle from which he even fails to emerge. William of Sonnac's heroism against all odds during the Seventh Crusade in Egypt, already blinded in one eye, saw him perish amidst the flames of an Egyptian attack at a barricade in front of Mansourah. William had been the model Templar. He had counselled against the rashness of Count Robert of Artois and yet as a matter of honour to his order had thrust himself into the fray as all Templars did. It cost him life. William of Beaujeu had also hurled himself into the enemy at the final stand at Acre in 1291. Another much derided Grand Master, accused of pride and of politicking when there was desperate defending of Outremer to be done, William of Beaujeu cannot be reasonably accused of lacking in bravery.

As for the 'rank and file' Templars, the story is one of obvious sacrifice. The Templars' casualty list was disproportionately huge. Frequently their numbers – although replaced – were wiped out in single actions. At Hattin (1187), La Forbie (1244) and Mansourah (1250) the losses were several hundred each time. Smaller scale chevauchées, if they went wrong, might also result in ten or twenty brothers falling. These men were not reckless. They had been the first into the fray and the last to leave it, because their order told them this is how they should behave for the love of God and for the protection of other Christians. There must be countless unrecorded deaths and sacrifices.

The depth of the Templars' military contribution to the Crusades as a whole cannot be underestimated. They had shown themselves to be trusted advisors to kings when those kings came east on crusade. Their organisational skills were much admired by King Louis VII during the Second Crusade and kings and popes continued to come to Grand Masters for military advice right to the end. The royal armies which came to the Holy Land were 'cloaked' by the military orders who provided a front and rear protection and who were flexible enough to swap these roles with one another when the need arose.

Constantly in the saddle and quick to muster, the Templars refined and adapted a version of Eastern Frankish tactics concentrating on the organised massed cavalry charge. They also raided and punished their enemies across Outremer, accruing wealth in the process. From the great crusader castles such as 'Atlit (Château Pèlerin), Tortosa and Safad they sortied countless times. Such strongholds provided the core of the defence of the Holy Land during the era and the Templars and Hospitallers were by the end, the key providers of that defence and were clearly the only hope of any re-conquest. The Templars' vast logistical network was also pressed into service on numerous occasions, sometimes even overstretched. And by the end of the thirteenth century, perhaps through necessity the order had begun to make more use of a naval arm in its operations.

In battle and on campaign the discipline of the Templars is clear. The rules surrounding camping and marching and how to respond to the alarm were all clearly set out. The Templars possessed an ability to withstand provocation, to form up and time their fearsome cavalry charges to the Marshal or Master's order, and to remain committed to the offensive in a cohesive formation whenever possible.

The Templars never forgot their core role of the protection of pilgrims. Some 120 years after their establishment, their attack on Nablus came in the wake of attacks on Christian pilgrims. Moreover, it was always a hostile landscape for the Christians. The basic work of escort duties such as that provided to James of Vitry in the early thirteenth century who recalls travelling from Chastel Blanc to Tortosa must have consumed much Templar time. In some ways the Templars were a victim of their own success. After the fall of Acre in 1291 the problem for the order was that they had been so closely associated with the military aspects of crusading in the Holy Land that they were unable to escape criticism for military failures, despite all their sacrifices. For the Hospitallars there was another outlet. Their altruistic work meant that they could continue to do good elsewhere. But for the Templars this was not the case. Until they could set foot in the Holy Land again, they were without a fundamental cause, despite James of Molay's' earnest activities. And yet the Templars had helped in prolonging the life of Outremer when secular lords had squabbled and divided the land. It might be true that Templar politics were often partisan, especially during the civil war in Tripoli (1277–82) but it is also true that some commentators such as Richard of Poitiers (d. c.1174) in his *Chronica (XXVI)* were saying as early as the mid twelfth century that had it not been for the Templars, the Franks would have already lost Jerusalem and Palestine.

But perhaps the last word should go to a man of the Champagne area of France, a region so closely associated with the early history of the Templars. Guiot of Provins was a poet with more than a hint of satirical humour about his work. In his *La Bible Guiot* (not the Holy Bible, but a satirical volume), written between 1203 and 1208, this man, who eventually joined a Cluniac religious house, wrote of the different religious orders around at the time. Perhaps his words are a case of the truth arising from playful language. Here it seems, is the very essence of a Knight Templar:

> The Templars are greatly honoured in Syria; the Turks fear them terribly; they defend the castles, the ramparts; in battle they never flee. But this is exactly what upsets me. If I belonged to this order I know very well that I should flee. I would not wait to be struck, for I am not fond of such things. They fight too bravely. I have no desire to be killed: I would rather pass for a coward and remain alive than experience the most glorious death in the world. I would readily go to sing the hours with them; that would not bother me at all. I would be very exact in the service, but not at the hour of battle; there I should be completely wanting.

Long before the politically motivated accusations of heresy against the Templars were drawn up, or of numerous other scandalous activities, none of which were associated with the battlefields of Outremer, Guiot of Provins clearly knew what it took to become a Templar. It is perhaps worth contemplating that if all Christian warriors during the Crusades fought in the same way as the Templars, the history of Outremer might have been different. Faith of course, was a vital requirement for a Templar, and discipline was another. Nobody however, could match the courage and fearlessness of the 'Poor Knights of Christ of the Temple which is in Jerusalem'.

Bibliography

SOME USEFUL GENERAL WORKS

Addison, C.G. (1842), *The History of the Knights Templars, the Temple Church and the Temple*, London, Longman, Brown, Green and Longmans. Published long ago and written in a style no longer fashionable, this still provides a comprehensive overview of the history of the Templars despite some 'legends' being purported as fact.

Barber, M. (1994), *The New Knighthood*, Cambridge, Cambridge University Press. The classic modern work.

Barber, M. and Bate, K. (eds) (2002), *The Templars. Selected Sources translated and annotated by Malcolm Barber and Keith Bate*, Manchester, Manchester University Press. Essential primary source reference material.

Howarth, S. (2006), *The Knights Templar: The Essential History*, London, Continuum

Lord, E. (2002), *The Knights Templar in Britain*, Harlow, Longman

Melville, M. (1974), *La Vie des Templiers*, Paris, Gallimard. The classic French work.

Morton, N. (2013), *The Medieval Military Orders, 1120 – 1314*, Harlow, Pearson. A good general overview of all the military orders.

Newman, S. (2007), *The Real History Behind the Templars*, New York, Berkley. A useful work containing a personal but well-balanced view of Templar activity without recourse to fantasy or pseudo-history.

Nicholson, H. (2001), *A Brief History of the Knights Templar*, Philadelphia PA, Robinson. Not all that brief, but an essential background read.

Parker, T. (1963), *The Knights Templar in England*, Tucson AZ, University of Arizona Press. Contains some little-known facts about the Templars in England.

Ralls, K. (2007), *Knights Templar Encyclopaedia: The Essential Guide to the People, Places, Events, and Symbols of the Order of the Temple*, Franklin Lakes, NJ, Career Press. A useful and accessible collection of material.

Runciman, S. (1954), *A History of the Crusades*, 3 vols, Cambridge, Cambridge University Press. Provides an unrivalled account of the crusades for essential background reading.

Tibble, S. (1989), *Monarchy and Lordships in the Latin Kingdom of Jerusalem 1099–1291*, Oxford, Clarendon Press. Much-cited analysis of the geography and development of crusader lordships.

Other Publications

Barber, M. (ed.) (1994), *The Military Orders: Fighting for the Faith and Caring for the Sick*, Aldershot, Routledge

Bird, J., Peters, E. and Powell, J. (eds) (2013), *Crusade and Christendom. Annotated Documents in Translation from Innocent III to the Fall of Acre (1187–1291)*, Philadelphia PA, University of Pennsylvania Press

Nicholson, H.J. (ed.) (1993), *Templars, Hospitallers, and Teutonic Knights: images of the military orders, 1128–1291*, Leicester, Leicester University Press

Nicholson, H.J. (1998), *The Military Orders, Vol 2. Welfare and Warfare*, Aldershot, Routledge

Nicholson, H.J. and Burgtorf, J. (eds) (2005), *International Mobility in the Military Orders (Twelfth to Fifteenth Centuries): Travelling on Christ's Business*, Cardiff, University of Wales Press

BY CHAPTER
ORIGINS
The Danger to Pilgrims

Babcock, E.A. and Krey, A.C. (trans) (1943), *William of Tyre, A History of Deeds Done Beyond the Sea*, New York, Columbia University Press. This primary source is of great importance for the whole period right up to the eve of Hattin.

Brooke, C.N.L., James, M.R. and Mynors, R.A.B. (eds and trans) (1983), *Walter Map. De Nugis Curialium*, Oxford, Oxford University Press

Brownlow, W.R.B. (1892), *Seawulf (1102. 1103 AD)*, London, Palestinian Pilgrims' Text Society

Wilson, C.W. (ed.) (1895), *The Pilgrimage of the Russian Abbot Daniel to the Holy Land, 1106–1107 AD*, London, Palestinian Pilgrims' Text Society

The Poor Knights of Christ

Barber, M. (1970), 'The Origins of the Order of the Temple', *Studia Monastica*, 12, 219–40. For a general introduction to the beginnings of the order.

Brooke, C.N.L., James, M.R. and Mynors, R.A.B. (eds and trans) (1983), *Walter Map. De Nugis Curialium*, Oxford, Oxford University Press. Not a great fan of the Templars, Map provides his own version of the foundation story.

Chabot, J.B. (ed. and trans.) (1905), *Chronique de Michel Le Syrien, Patriarche Jacobite d'Antioche (116–1199). Vol III*, repr. 1963, Bruxelles, Culture et Civilisation

Chibnall, M. (trans.) (1968–80), *The Ecclesiastical History of Orderic Vitalis*, 6 vols, Oxford, Oxford Medieval Texts

Constable, G. (2008), *Crusaders and Crusading in the Twelfth Century*, Aldershot, Ashgate, pp. 165–82. Examines the origins of the military orders and provides a good general background.

Forey, A.J. (1985), 'The Emergence of the Military Order in the Twelfth Century', *Journal of Ecclesiastical History*, 36, Cambridge, Cambridge University Press, 175–95. A good general background.

Luttrell, A. (1996), 'The Earliest Templars', in M. Balard (ed.), *Autour de la Première Croisade*, Paris, Publications de la Sorbonne, pp. 193–202

Morgan, M.R. (1974), *Chronicle of Ernoul and the Continuations of William of Tyre*, Oxford, Oxford University Press

Nicholson, H. (2001), *A Brief History of the Knights Templar*, Philadelphia PA, Robinson. See p. 26 for Nicholson's translation of Simon of Saint-Bertin, taken from O. Holder-Egger (ed.) (1881), *Simon de St. Bertin, 'Gesta abbatum Sancti Bertini Sithensium', in* Monumenta Germanica Historica Scriptores, Vol. 13, p. 649.

The Council of Troyes, 1129

Barber, M. (1994), *The New Knighthood*, Cambridge, Cambridge University Press, pp. 8–10 and 13–20. For a breakdown of the deliberations of the Council.

Nicholson, H.J. (2001), *A Brief History of the Knights Templar*, Philadelphia PA, Robinson, pp. 28–31

The Latin Rule

Barber, M. and Bate, K. (eds) (2002), *The Templars. Selected Sources translated and annotated by Malcolm Barber and Keith Bate*, Manchester, Manchester University Press, pp. 31–54. For a translation of the Latin Rule.

In Praise of the New Knighthood

Evans, G.R. (2000), *Bernard of Clairvaux*, Oxford, Oxford University Press

Barber, M. and Bate, K. (eds) (2002),*The Templars. Selected Sources translated and annotated by Malcolm Barber and Keith Bate*, Manchester, Manchester University Press, pp. 215–26. For a translation of 'In Praise of the new Knighthood'.

BATTLES and CAMPAIGNS
IN THE LATIN EAST
Damascus and the Early Campaigns, 1129–47

Barber, M. and Bate, K. (eds) (2002), *The Templars. Selected Sources translated and annotated by Malcolm Barber and Keith Bate*, Manchester, Manchester University Press, pp. 59–63 for the translation of *Omne datum optimium*, p. 64 for the translation of *Milites Templi* and pp. 65–6 for the translation of *Militia Dei*.

Chibnall, M. (trans.) (1978), *The Ecclesiastical History of Orderic Vitalis, Vol VI, Book XIII*, Oxford, Oxford Medieval Texts, pp. 496–7. For the description of the action around Montferrand.

Gibb, H.R.A. (ed.) (1932), *Ibn al-Qalanisi, Damascus Chronicle of the Crusades*, London, repr. 2002, Dover Publications

Runciman, S. (1954), *A History of the Crusades. Vol II. The Kingdom of Jerusalem*, Cambridge, Cambridge University Press, pp. 143–244. This comprises the whole of Book II. Good background reading for the period under consideration.

Swanton, M. (1996), *The Anglo-Saxon Chronicle*, London, J.M Dent, p. 259. For the entry for 1129 referring to Hugh of Payns.

The Second Crusade, 1147–8
Berry, V.G. (trans.) (1948), *Odo of Deuil,* De profectione Ludovici VII in Orientem, New York, W.W. Norton and Co. The classic translation includes the account of how the Templars re-organised the army of Louis VII, pp. 125–7.
Forey, A.J. (1984), 'The Failure of the Siege of Damascus in 1148', *Journal of Medieval Military History*, 10, Woodbridge, Boydell & Brewer, 13–23. For an assessment of the Christian debacle around the key city of Damascus.

The Siege of Ascalon, 1153
Babcock, E.A. and Krey, A.C. (trans) (1943), *William of Tyre, A History of Deeds Done Beyond the Sea*, New York, Columbia University Press, Book 17, Chapter XXVII. Covers the siege and the Templar involvement.
Gibb, H.R.A. (ed.) (1932), *Ibn al-Qalanisi, Damascus Chronicle of the Crusades*, London, repr. 2002, Dover Publications

The Struggle for Egypt, 1154–68
Barber, M. and Bate, K. (eds) (2002), *The Templars. Selected Sources translated and annotated by Malcolm Barber and Keith Bate*, Manchester, Manchester University Press, pp. 97–9. For the letter of Geoffrey Fulcher.
Pertz, G.H. et al. (eds) (1826–1934), *Lambert de Wattrelos, Annales Cameracenses. Monumentia Germaniae Historica Scriptores. 16*, 32 vols, Hanover, from p. 529. For Egyptian campaign and Templar and Hospitaller involvement.
Runciman, S. (1954), *A History of the Crusades. Vol II. The Kingdom of Jerusalem*, Cambridge, Cambridge University Press, Book IV, pp. 362–402. For the period under consideration.

The Assassins
Daftary, F. (1994), *The Ismailis: Their History and Doctrines*, Cambridge, Cambridge University Press
Nowell, C.E. (1947), 'The Old Man of the Mountain', *Speculum*, 22, 497–519

The Battle of Montgisard, 1177
Erlich, Michael (2013), 'Saint Catherine's Day Miracle – the Battle of Montgisard', in C.J. Rogers, K. Devries and J. France (eds), *Journal of Medieval Military History Volume XI*, Woodbridge, Boydell and Brewer, pp. 95–106. One of the better and more concise accounts of the Templars' finest hour.
Stubbs, W. (ed.) (1876), 'Ralph of Diss. "Ymagines Historiarum"', in *The Historical Works of Master Ralph of Diceto*, Rolls Series 68, 2 vols, London, Longman, Vol. 1, pp. 423–4. For Montgisard.

Marj Ayyun and the Siege of Chastellet, 1179
Abu Shama, *Le Livre Des Deux Jardins. Recueil Des Historiens des Criosades Historiens orientaux*, 5 vols (1872–1906), Paris, Imprimierie royale, Vol. 4, pp. 205–7. For description of Chastellet and the siege.

Mitchell, P.D., Nagar, Y. and Ellenblum, R. (2006), 'Weapon Injuries in the 12th Century Crusader Garrison of Vadum Iacob Castle, Galilee', *International Journal of Osteoarchaeology* 16, No. 2, 145–55

The Springs of Cresson and the Battle of the Horns of Hattin, 1187
Nicholson, H.J. (1997) (ed.), *The Chronicle of the Third Crusade. The* Itinerarium Peregrinorum et Gesta Regis Ricardi. *Crusade Texts in Translation III*, Aldershot, Ashgate, p. 25. For the Springs of Cresson.
Nicolle, D. (1993), *Hattin 1187. Saladin's Greatest Victory*, Osprey Campaign Series, 19, Oxford
Runciman, S. (1954), *A History of the Crusades. Vol II. The Kingdom of Jerusalem*, Cambridge, Cambridge University Press, pp. 436–74 and 486. For analysis of sources.
Smail, R.C. (1995), *Crusading Warfare 1097–1193*, 2nd edn, first pub. 1956, Cambridge, Cambridge University Press, pp. 189–97

The Third Crusade, 1189–92
Edbury, P.W. (1996), *The Conquest of Jerusalem and the Third Crusade. Sources in Translation*, Aldershot, Ashgate
Gillingham, J. (1999), *Richard I. Yale English Monarchs*, New Haven CT, Yale University Press
Nicholson, H.J. (ed.) (1997), *The Chronicle of the Third Crusade. The* Itinerarium Peregrinorum et Gesta Regis Ricardi. *Crusade Texts in Translation III*, Aldershot, Ashgate. Modern translation of a classic crusade text. Essential for how the Templars dealt with assisting a large crusader force.

Stalemate, 1192–1216
Runciman, S. (1954), *A History of the Crusades. Vol III. The Kingdom of Acre*, Cambridge, Cambridge University Press, pp. 76–107. For coverage of this era.

The Fifth Crusade, 1217–21
Peters, E. (ed.) (2017), *Christian Society and the Crusades, 1198–229. Sources in Translation, including 'The Capture of Damietta' by Oliver of Paderborn*, Philadelphia PA, University of Pennsylvania Press
Runciman, S. (1954), *A History of the Crusades. Vol III. The Kingdom of Acre*, Cambridge, Cambridge University Press, pp. 132–70

The Sixth Crusade of Frederick II of Germany, 1228–9
Runciman, S. (1954), *A History of the Crusades. Vol III. The Kingdom of Acre*, Cambridge, Cambridge University Press, pp. 171–204

The Barons' Crusade, 1239–41
Denholm-Young, N. (1947), *Richard of Cornwall*, Oxford, Blackwell

Lower, M. (2005), *The Barons' Crusade. A Call to Arms and its Consequences*, Philadelphia PA, University of Pennsylvania Press

La Forbie, 1244
Berkovich, I. (2011), 'The Battle of Forbie and the Second Frankish Kingdom of Jerusalem', *The Journal of Military History*, 75, 9–44. Examines the background to the disaster and the battle itself.
Lotan, S. (2012), 'The Battle of La Forbie (1244) and its Aftermath – Re-examination of the Military Orders' Involvement in the Latin Kingdom of Jerusalem in the Mid Thirteenth Century', in *Ordines Militares. Colloquia Torunensia Historica. Yearbook for the Study of the Military Orders Vol. XVII*, Torun, Nicolaus Copernicus University Press, pp. 53–67

The Seventh Crusade, 1248–54
Luard, H.R. (2012), *Matthaei Parisiensis [Matthew Paris] Chronica Majora*, 7 vols, firs pub. 1880, New York, Cambridge University Press. Contains much on the Templars including their role on the Seventh Crusade.
Wailly, N. (ed.) (1874), *Joinville, Jean (sire de) Histoire de Saint Louis*, trans. and pub. in English by J. Evans (1938), Oxford. Oxford University Press

Mongols and Mamelukes
Crawford, P. (trans.) (2003), *The 'Templar of Tyre': Part III of the Deeds of the Cypriots, Crusade Texts in Translation VI*, Aldershot, Ashgate. Essential for the final years of the crusader states and the relationship of the Temple with the rest of the leaders of Outremer.
Humphries, R.S. (1977), 'The Emergence of the Mamluk Army', *Studia Islamica*, 45, 74–6
Runciman, S. (1954), *A History of the Crusades. Vol III. The Kingdom of Acre*, Cambridge, Cambridge University Press, pp. 237–350. For the rise and dominance of the Mamelukes.

The Final Stand – Acre, 1291
Favreau-Lillie, M-L. (1993), 'The Military Orders and the Escape of the Christian Population from the Holy Land in 1291', *Journal of Medieval Military History*, 19, Woodbridge, Boydell & Brewer, 201–27
Nicolle, D. (2005), *Acre 1291*, Osprey Campaign Series, 154, Oxford

IN THE IBERIAN PENINSULA
A Brief Introduction to the Reconquista
Nicholson, H. (2001), *A Brief History of the Knights Templar*, Philadelphia PA, Robinson, pp. 97–124. For a concise background.
Morton, N. (2013), *The Medieval Military Orders 1120–1314*, Harlow, Pearson, pp. 36–49. For a brief overview.

Portugal

Barber, M. (1994), *The New Knighthood*, Cambridge, Cambridge University Press, pp. 31–4. For the Templar contribution in the twelfth century.

Forey, A.J. (1992), *The Military Orders From the Twelfth to the Early Fourteenth Centuries*, London, Macmillan, pp. 23–5 and 64–6

Lay, S. (2009), *The Reconquest Kings of Portugal: Political Cultural Reorientation on the Medieval Frontier*, Basingstoke, Palgrave Macmillan

Livermore, H.V. (1977), *A New History of Portugal*, Cambridge, Cambridge University Press. The classic history of Portugal covering in detail the military orders and their contribution to the wars against the Moors.

Spain

Barber, M. and Bate, K. (eds) (2002), *The Templars. Selected Sources translated and annotated by Malcolm Barber and Keith Bate*, Manchester, Manchester University Press, pp. 93–4. For the grant of multiple castles to the Templars by Raymond Berenguer IV.

Buffery, H. and Smith, D.J. (2003), *The Book of Deeds of James I of Aragon. A Translation of the Medieval Llibre dels Fets*, Aldershot, Ashgate

Forey, A.J. (1973), *The Templars in the Corona de Aragon*, London, Oxford University Press

Forey, A.J. (1984), 'The Military Orders and the Spanish Reconquest in the Twelfth and Thirteenth Centuries', *Traditio*, 40, Cambridge, Cambridge University Press, 197–234. The classic account of the Spanish experience.

Forey, A.J. (1992), *The Military Orders From the Twelfth to the Early Fourteenth Centuries*, London, Macmillan, pp. 55–7 and 64–7. For castles.

O'Callaghan, J.F. (2003), *Reconquest and Crusade in Medieval Spain*, Philadelphia PA, University of Pennsylvania Press

ON THE EASTERN FRONTIERS OF EUROPE
A Different Frontier

Morton, N. (2013), *The Medieval Military Orders 1120–1314*, Harlow, Pearson, pp. 72–85. For background to the situation in Eastern Europe and the Baltic.

Nicholson, H. (2001), *A Brief History of the Knights Templar*, Philadelphia PA, Robinson, pp. 112–24

Battles of Liegnitz (Legnica) and Mohi (Muhi), 1241

Jackson, P. (1991), 'The Crusade Against the Mongols (1241)', *Journal of Ecclesiastical History*, 42, 1–18

Nicholson, H. (2001), *A Brief History of the Knights Templar*, Philadelphia PA, Robinson, pp. 118–19. For a translation of Thomas of Split's account of the Templars in action and of Pons D'Aubon's letter to Louis IX.

MILITARY ORGANISATION

Recruitment and Reception

Barber, M. (1994), *The New Knighthood*, Cambridge, Cambridge University Press, pp. 183–4, 211–13 and 301–3. For reception procedures.

Forey, A.J. (1986), 'Novitiate and Instruction in the Military Orders During the Twelfth and Thirteenth Centuries', *Speculum*, Vol. 61, Part 1, 1–17. Concentrating on certain aspects across the orders.

Forey, A.J. (1986), 'Recruitment to Military Orders (Twelfth to Mid 14th Centuries)', *Viator*, 17, 148–53

The Hierarchical Statutes

Barber, M. and Bate, K. (eds) (2002), *The Templars. Selected Sources translated and annotated by Malcolm Barber and Keith Bate*, Manchester, Manchester University Press, pp. 67–72. For the sections on camping, marching, squadron formation and charging.

Upton-Ward, J.M. (trans.) (2002), *The French Text of the Rule of the Order of the Knights Templar*, Woodbridge, Boydell & Brewer. The Hierarchical Statutes are summarised, pp. 13–14 and translated, pp. 39–72. An essential modern translation.

Strategic Raiding, Camping and Marching

Bennet, M. (2001), 'The Crusaders' Fighting March Revisited', *War in History*, 8, repr. 2016, 1–18

Marshall, C. (1992), *Warfare in the Latin East 1192–1291*, Cambridge, Cambridge University Press, pp. 183–209. Takes up the reins from Smail (see below). An excellent section on how strategic raiding was carried out and what the reasons usually were for it.

Smail, R.C. (1995), *Crusading Warfare 1097–1193*, 2nd edn, first pub. 1956, Cambridge, Cambridge University Press. Classic account of how crusading armies were formed, how they marched and what types of battles were fought in the Holy Land.

Battlefield Tactics

Bennet, M. (1989), 'La Régle du Temple as a Military Manual or How to Deliver a Cavalry Charge', in C. Harper-Bill, C.J. Holdsworth and J.L. Nelson (eds), *Studies in Medieval History presented to R. Allen Brown*, Woodbridge, Boydell & Brewer, pp. 7–19. A good breakdown of the role and function of individual units within a Templar force and the position occupied by the Rule amongst other classical and medieval military training manuals.

France, J. (1999), *Western Warfare in the Age of the Crusades. 1000–1300*, London, UCL Press. Some good accounts of battle tactics as they were known in the West.

France, J. (2017), 'Templar Tactics: The Order on the Battlefield', in K. Borchardt, K. Döring, P. Josserand and H.J. Nicholson (eds), *The Templars and their Sources*, Abingdon, Routledge, pp. 156–67. An up-to-date reassessment of the evidence.

Heath, I. (1978), *Armies and Enemies of the Crusades. Organisation, Tactics, Dress and Weapons*, n.p., Wargames Research Group. Excellent illustrations based on original manuscript depictions of crusading warriors. Also discusses tactics.

Nicholson, H.J. (2004), *Knight Templar 1120–1312*, Oxford, Osprey Publishing. Well-illustrated short book with good descriptions of Templar armour and arms and their approach to battle.

Stewart, A. (1894), 'Anonymous Pilgrims, I–VII (11th and 12th Centuries), *Palestine Pilgrims' Text Society*, 6, London, 29–30. For description of the Templars.

Training

Bennet, M. (1989), 'La Régle du Temple as a Military Manual or How to Deliver a Cavalry Charge', in C. Harper-Bill, C.J. Holdsworth and J.L. Nelson (eds), *Studies in Medieval History presented to R. Allen Brown*, Woodbridge, Boydell & Brewer, pp. 7–19. The whole subject of the training of the Templars is poorly understood and the problems associated with the lack of evidence are touched upon in this paper.

Penances and Life in the Convent

Upton-Ward, J.M. (trans.) (2002), *The French Text of the Rule of the Order of the Knights Templar*, Woodbridge, Boydell & Brewer, pp. 73–82 and 142–67

Upton-Ward, J.M. (2003), *The Catalan Rule of the Templars*, Woodbridge, Boydell & Brewer. An essential modern translation which also covers some penances not mentioned in the French Rule.

Logistics, Supply and Shipping

Barber, M. (1992), 'Supplying the Crusader States: The Role of the Templars', in B.Z. Kedar (ed.), *The Horns of Hattin*, Jerusalem, Israel Exploration Society, pp. 314–26. One of the key studies of Templar logistics.

Webb, J. (1844), 'Notes of the Preceptory of the Templars at Garway in the County of Herefordshire', *Archaeologia*, XXI, 35

CASTLES and FORTIFICATIONS
The Role of the Templar Castles

Boas, A.J. (2006), *Archaeology of the Military Orders*, Abingdon, Routledge. Contains a good introduction and a detailed summary of all aspects of Crusader castles in the Latin East.

Edwards, R.W. (1987), *The Fortifications of Armenian Cilicia*, Washington DC, Dumbarton Oaks

Kennedy, H. (1994), *Crusader Castles*, Cambridge, Cambridge University Press

Pringle, D. (1993), *The Churches of the Crusader Kingdom of Jerusalem. Vol I.*, Cambridge, Cambridge University Press

Pringle, D. (1998), 'Templar Castles between Jaffa and Jerusalem', in H.J. Nicholson (1998), *The Military Orders, Vol 2. Welfare and Warfare*, Aldershot, Routledge, p. 89

Templar Fortifications in Outremer
Heath, I. (1980), *A Wargamers' Guide to the Crusades*, Cambridge, Patrick Stephens Ltd. An underrated contribution from a much-maligned hobbyist group, this volume includes a remarkable gazetteer of crusader castles and their potted histories. No references, however.

AFTER ACRE
Military Activity and the Plans for a New Crusade
Forey A.J. (1980), 'The Military Orders in the Crusading Proposals of the Late Thirteenth and Early-Fourteenth Centuries', *Traditio*, 36, 317–45. Looks at the continuing importance of the military orders in the wake of the loss of Acre.
Schein, S. (1989), 'The Templars: the Regular Army of the Holy Land and the spearhead of the army of its Reconquest', in G. Minnucci and F. Sardi (eds), *I Templari: Mito e Storia. Atti del Convegno Internationale di Studi alla Magione Templare di Poggibonsi-Siena, 29–31 Maggio 1987*, pp. 15–25. An essential paper on the importance of the military orders in any plans for a re-conquest of the Holy Land.

CONCLUSION
Gabrieli, F. (ed. and trans.) (1957), *The Arab Historians of the Crusades*, New York, Dorset. For a look at the Muslim recollection.
Hillenbrand, C. (1999), *The Crusades. Islamic Perspectives*, Edinburgh, Edinburgh University Press
Mallett, A. (2014), *Medieval Muslim Historians and the Franks in the Levant*, Leiden, Brill
Orr, J. (ed.) (1915), 'Guiot de Provins "La Bible"', in *Les Oevres de Guiot de Provins, poète lyrique et satirique*, Manchester, University of Manchester Press. The pious yet satirical poet, sometimes critical of the Templars, gives his respectful reasons for never joining.

Index

Page numbers in italic indicate illustrations. Written entries in italic indicate written works.